Mastering Google App Engine

Build robust and highly scalable web applications
with Google App Engine

Mohsin Shafique Hijazee

BIRMINGHAM - MUMBAI

Mastering Google App Engine

First published: September 2015

Production reference: 1011015

Published by Packt Publishing Ltd.
Livery Place
35 Livery Street
Birmingham B3 2PB, UK.

ISBN 978-1-78439-667-1

www.packtpub.com

Credits

Author

Mohsin Shafique Hijazee

Reviewers

Aristides Villarreal Bravo

Johann du Toit

Acquisition Editor

Nikhil Karkal

Content Development Editor

Athira Laji

Technical Editor

Naveenkumar Jain

Copy Editor

Ting Baker

Vedangi Narvekar

Project Coordinator

Harshal Ved

Proofreader

Safis Editing

Indexer

Priya Sane

Production Coordinator

Komal Ramchandani

Cover Work

Komal Ramchandani

About the Author

Mohsin Shafique Hijazee started his programming adventure by teaching himself C, and later C++, mostly with the Win 32 API and MFC. Later, he worked with Visual Basic to develop an invoicing application for local distributors. In the meantime, .NET came along and Mohsin happened to be working with C# and Windows Forms. All of this was around desktop applications, and all of this happened during his days at university.

Very few people have had a chance to work with fonts, and that's exactly what Mohsin happened to do as his first job—developing OpenType fonts for complex right to left calligraphic styles such as Nastaleeq. He developed two different fonts, one based on characters and joining rules, and the other one contained more than 18,000 ligatures both of which are in public domain.

His first serious interaction with web development started with Ruby on Rails. Shortly after that, he discovered Google App Engine and found it to be a very interesting platform despite its initial limitations back in 2008, with Python being the only available runtime environment. Mohsin kept experimenting with the platform and deployed many production applications and mobile backends that are hosted on Google App Engine to this day.

Currently, Mohsin is working as a backend software engineer with a large multinational Internet company that operates in the online classified space in dozens of countries across the globe.

Acknowledgments

This book and a lot more would not have been possible without my parent's constant support in my earlier years. My father, Mohammad Shafique, taught me how to read, and later write, in multiple languages by using novels, literature, and other means that are not a part of traditional education in schools. This book would not have been possible if my mother, Azra Khanam, hadn't trained me in counting, adding, and playing with numbers even before I joined school. It was of course my mother who, in later years, helped me apply for a course in computer science for further education. My younger sisters Sara and Rida have been constant support by probing status on the book and keeping me motivated. Thank you both of you!

This book would not have been possible if my dear wife, Dr. Farzana, did not help to work around the tough schedule and absorbed moments or absent mindedness this piece of writing that you hold in your hands, brought to my life. She would quickly place a cup of tea on my table whenever I'd feel exhausted. Thanks a lot, patient is doing well now after being done with the writing project.

I'm not sure about whether I'd like to thank or complain about the little, cute, and aggressive boy Alyan, in our house who was way too young and in the cradle when I started the book, and by the time I finished it, he had started plucking out my laptop keys. Alyan, I hope you'll not repeat our mistakes and you'll make your own.

Special thanks goes to my newly found friend and colleague Naveed ur Rehman, who basically turned out to be an inspiration for me to write such technical text. Thank you Naveed, I've utmost respect for you.

I would like to thank my editors, Nikhil, Ajinkya, and Naveenkumar, for going through the tons of mistakes that I made throughout the text in painstaking detail, being tolerant about it, and constantly providing suggestions on how to improve the content. I became aware of their hard work when I had the chance to read my own script carefully. Thank you, gentlemen!

About the Reviewers

Aristides Villarreal Bravo is a Java developer. He is the CEO of Javscaz Software Developers. He is also a member of the NetBeans Dream Team and he is part of Java User Groups leaders and members. He lives in Panamá. He has organized and participated in various national and international conferences and seminars related to Java, JavaEE, NetBeans, the NetBeans platform, free software, and mobile devices. He also writes tutorials and blogs related to Java and NetBeans and for web developers.

He has reviewed several books for Packt Publishing. He develops plugins for NetBeans and is a specialist in JSE, JEE, JPA, Agile, and Continuous Integration.

He shares his knowledge via his blog, which can be viewed by visiting `http://avbravo.blogspot.com`.

I would like to thank my family for the support throughout the book process.

Johann du Toit is an entrepreneur and a technical lead for various startups, ranging from national microchip databases to website verification systems.

He was appointed as the first Google Developer Expert in Africa for Cloud by Google.

He has experience that ranges from building large distributed systems that scale for millions of requests every day to embedded devices that serve Wi-Fi and medical information across Africa.

Visit `http://johanndutoit.net` for his latest details and whereabouts.

I would like to thank my family and especially my sister, Philanie du Toit, for her support through out the book process.

www.PacktPub.com

Support files, eBooks, discount offers, and more

For support files and downloads related to your book, please visit www.PacktPub.com.

Did you know that Packt offers eBook versions of every book published, with PDF and ePub files available? You can upgrade to the eBook version at www.PacktPub.com and as a print book customer, you are entitled to a discount on the eBook copy. Get in touch with us at service@packtpub.com for more details.

At www.PacktPub.com, you can also read a collection of free technical articles, sign up for a range of free newsletters and receive exclusive discounts and offers on Packt books and eBooks.

https://www2.packtpub.com/books/subscription/packtlib

Do you need instant solutions to your IT questions? PacktLib is Packt's online digital book library. Here, you can search, access, and read Packt's entire library of books.

Why subscribe?

- Fully searchable across every book published by Packt
- Copy and paste, print, and bookmark content
- On demand and accessible via a web browser

Free access for Packt account holders

If you have an account with Packt at www.PacktPub.com, you can use this to access PacktLib today and view 9 entirely free books. Simply use your login credentials for immediate access.

Table of Contents

Preface   **ix**

Chapter 1: Understanding the Runtime Environment   **1**

The overall architecture   **2**
    The challenge of scale   2
    How to scale with the scale?   2
    Scaling in practice   4
    Infrastructure as a Service   5
    Platform as a Service   5
        Containers   6
    How does App Engine scales?   7
Available runtimes   **9**
    Python   10
    The Java runtime environment   10
    Go   11
    PHP   11
The structure of an application   **11**
The available services   **12**
    Datastore   13
    Google Cloud SQL   13
    The Blobstore   13
    Memcache   14
    Scheduled Tasks   14
    Queues Tasks   14
    MapReduce   15
    Mail   15
    XMPP   15
    Channels   16

Users	16
OAuth	16
Writing and deploying a simple application	**16**
Installing an SDK on Linux	17
Installing an SDK on Mac	18
Installing an SDK on Windows	18
Writing a simple app	18
Deploying	24
Summary	**26**
Chapter 2: Handling Web Requests	**27**
Request handling	**27**
The CGI program	28
Streams and environment variables	29
CGI and Google App Engine	30
WSGI	31
Problems with CGI	31
Solutions	32
What WSGI looks like	32
WSGI – Multithreading considerations	34
WSGI in Google App Engine	35
Request handling in App Engine	**36**
Rendering templates	**39**
Serving static resources	**44**
Cache, headers, and mime types	45
Serving files	47
Using web frameworks	**48**
Built-in frameworks	48
Using external frameworks	50
Using Bottle	52
Summary	**54**
Chapter 3: Understanding the Datastore	**55**
The BigTable	**56**
The data model	57
How is data stored?	**59**
The physical storage	60
Some limitations	61
Random writes and deletion	62
Operations on BigTable	64
Reading	64
Writing	65
Deleting	65
Updating	65
Scanning a range	66

Selecting a key	67
BigTable – a hands-on approach	69
Scaling BigTable to BigData	**70**
The datastore thyself	**73**
Supporting queries	77
Data as stored in BigTable	77
The implementation details	78
Summary	**79**
Chapter 4: Modeling Your Data	**81**
The data modeling language	**81**
Keys and internal storage	85
The application ID	86
Namespaces	87
The Kind	88
The ID	88
The key	92
Modeling your data	**94**
The first approach – storing a reference as a property	94
The second approach – a category within a key	97
Properties	102
The required option	103
The default option	103
The repeated option	104
The choices options	104
The indexed option	105
The validator option	105
The available properties	106
Structured Properties	108
The computed properties	109
The model	**110**
The constructor	110
Class methods	110
The allocate_ids() method	111
The get_by_id() method	111
The get_or_insert() method	111
The query() method	111
The instance methods	111
The populate() method	112
The put() method	112
The to_dict() method	112
Asynchronous versions	112
Model hooks	113
Summary	**115**

Chapter 5: Queries, Indexes, and Transactions   **117**

Querying your data   **117**

Queries under the hood   **125**

Single-property queries   126

    Examples of single-property queries   128

Multiple property indexes   129

Working with indexes   132

The query API   **134**

The Query object   135

    App   136

    Namespace   136

    Kind   136

    The ancestor   136

    The projection   137

    Filters   137

    The orders   137

    Further query options   138

Filtering entities   141

    Filtering repeated properties   142

Filtering structured properties   143

    The AND and OR operations   144

Iterating over the results   146

    Conclusions   149

Transactions   **149**

Summary   **152**

Chapter 6: Integrating Search   **153**

Background   **153**

The underlying principle   **154**

Indexing your data   **155**

Sample data   156

Indexing thyself   160

Documents   162

Fields   162

    The text fields   163

Placing the document in an index   164

Getting a document   165

Updating documents   166

Deleting documents   166

Indexing the documents   167

Queries   **169**

Simple queries   169

Multiple value queries   170

Logical operations	170
Being specific with fields	171
Operators on NumberField	172
Operators on DateField	172
Operations on AtomField	173
Operations on TextField and HTMLField	173
Operations on GeoField	174
Putting it all together	175
Selecting fields and calculated fields	177
Sorting	**181**
Pagination	**185**
Offset-based pagination	186
Cursor-based pagination	187
Facets	**190**
Indexing facets	191
Fetching facets	194
Asking facets via automatic discovery	195
Asking specific facets	198
Asking facets with specific values	198
Asking facets in specific ranges	199
Filtering by facets	201
Summary	**202**
Chapter 7: Using Task Queues	**203**
The need to queue things	**204**
The queue	**205**
Defining queues	207
Adding to a queue	212
Processing tasks	216
Putting it all together	220
Using a deferred library	230
Pull queues	**234**
Summary	**236**
Chapter 8: Reaching out, Sending E-mails	**237**
About e-mails	**237**
Sending e-mails	**239**
The object-oriented API	242
E-mail on the development console	244
Headers	245
Receiving e-mails	**246**
Handling bounce notifications	250
Putting it all together	**252**
Summary	**262**

Chapter 9: Working with the Google App Engine Services   **265**

Memcache   **266**

  The Memcache operations   267

  Memcache in Google App Engine   269

  The Memcache client   269

    The object-oriented client   272

Multi-tenancy   **273**

  Automatically setting the namespace   275

  The API-specific notes   276

    The Datastore   276

    Memcache   276

    Task queues   276

    Search   277

    Blobstore   277

Blobs   **277**

  Uploads   278

    Getting BlobInfo   281

    More BlobInfo methods   283

  Serving   284

  Reading   287

Users   **287**

  Storing users in datastore   291

Images   **292**

Putting it all together   **294**

Summary   **303**

Chapter 10: Application Deployment   **305**

Deployment configurations   **305**

  Deployment revisited   306

  Versions   307

  The instance classes   308

    Instance addressability   309

Scaling types   **310**

  Manual scaling   310

  Basic scaling   312

  Automatic scaling   313

  Modules   315

    Accessing the modules   320

The dispatch.yaml file   **321**

Scheduled tasks   **322**

  The Scheduled tasks format   324

  Protecting cron handling URLs   327

Logs	328
The Remote API	332
AppStats	**333**
Summary	**335**
Index	**337**

Preface

Google App Engine is a Platform as a Service that builds and runs applications on Google's infrastructure. App Engine applications are easy to build, maintain, and scale.

Google App Engine allows you to develop highly scalable web applications or backends for mobile applications without worrying about the system administration's plumbing or hardware provisioning issues. You can just focus on writing your business logic, which is the meat of the application, and let Google's powerful infrastructure scale it to thousands of requests per second and millions of users without any effort on your part.

This book introduces you to cloud computing, managed Platform as a Service, the things that Google has to offer, and the advantages. It also introduces you to a sample app that will be built during the course of the book. It will be a small invoice management application where we have clients, products, categories, invoices, and payments as a sample SaaS application. The most complex part is that of reporting, as datastore has certain limitations on this.

What this book covers

Chapter 1, Understanding the Runtime Environment, explains the runtime environment, how requests are processed and handled, and how App Engine scales. This chapter also explores the limitations of runtime environments with respect to the request time and response size, among other factors.

Chapter 2, Handling Web Requests, introduces ways to handle web requests by using a built-in framework or Django and others. It also discusses how to serve static files and caching issues, render templates.

Chapter 3, Understanding the Datastore, covers the problem of storing huge amounts of data and processing it in bulk with the ability to randomly access it. This chapter explains the datastore in detail, which is built on top of Bigtable.

Chapter 4, Modeling Your Data, explains the new ndb Python library on top of Google datastore. It will also teach you how to model your data using its API.

Chapter 5, Queries, Indexes, and Transactions, focuses on how to query your data, the limitations, and ways to work around these limitations.

Chapter 6, Integrating Search, builds upon the datastore and shows how to make data searchable.

Chapter 7, Using Task Queues, introduces the reader to task queues, which enable the background repeated execution of tasks.

Chapter 8, Reaching out, Sending E-mails, talks about how the app can send and receive e-mails and how to handle bounce notifications.

Chapter 9, Working with the Google App Engine Services, introduces you to the other services that are provided by Google App Engine to make you aware of your available options.

Chapter 10, Application Deployment, talks in detail about deploying the GAE apps.

What you need for this book

In order to run the code demonstrated in this book, you need an interpreter that comes with the Python 2.7.x series and the latest Google App Engine SDK release of the 1.9.x series.

Additionally, to access the example application, once it runs on App Engine, you need a recent version of a web browser such as Google Chrome, Mozilla Firefox, Apple Safari, or Microsoft Internet Explorer.

Who this book is for

If you have been developing web applications in Python or any other dynamic language but have always been wondering how to write highly scalable web applications without getting into system administration and other areas that plumbing, this is the book for you. We will assume that you have no experience of writing scalable applications. We will help you build your skill set to a point where you can fully leverage the environment and services of Google App Engine, especially the highly distributed NoSQL datastore, to neatly knit and jot down a very robust and scalable solution for your users, be it a web application or a backend for your next killer mobile app.

Conventions

In this book, you will find a number of styles of text that distinguish between different kinds of information. Here are some examples of these styles, and an explanation of their meaning.

Code words in text, database table names, folder names, filenames, file extensions, pathnames, dummy URLs, user input, and Twitter handles are shown as follows: " We can include other contexts through the use of the `include` directive."

A block of code is set as follows:

```
class Person(ndb.Model):
    name = ndb.StringProperty()
    age = ndb.IntegerProperty()
```

Any command-line input or output is written as follows:

```
$ appcfg update /path/to/my/app/containing/app.yaml/
```

New terms and **important words** are shown in bold. Words that you see on the screen, in menus or dialog boxes for example, appear in the text like this: " Now, double-click on the **Launcher** icon that you just dragged to the `Applications` folder ".

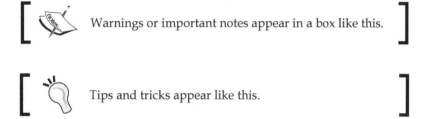

> Warnings or important notes appear in a box like this.

> Tips and tricks appear like this.

Reader feedback

Feedback from our readers is always welcome. Let us know what you think about this book—what you liked or may have disliked. Reader feedback is important for us to develop titles that you really get the most out of.

To send us general feedback, simply send an e-mail to `feedback@packtpub.com`, and mention the book title via the subject of your message.

If there is a topic that you have expertise in and you are interested in either writing or contributing to a book, see our author guide on `www.packtpub.com/authors`.

Customer support

Now that you are the proud owner of a Packt book, we have a number of things to help you to get the most from your purchase.

Downloading the example code

You can download the example code files for all Packt books you have purchased from your account at http://www.packtpub.com. If you purchased this book elsewhere, you can visit http://www.packtpub.com/support and register to have the files e-mailed directly to you.

Errata

Although we have taken every care to ensure the accuracy of our content, mistakes do happen. If you find a mistake in one of our books—maybe a mistake in the text or the code—we would be grateful if you would report this to us. By doing so, you can save other readers from frustration and help us improve subsequent versions of this book. If you find any errata, please report them by visiting http://www.packtpub.com/submit-errata, selecting your book, clicking on the **errata submission form** link, and entering the details of your errata. Once your errata are verified, your submission will be accepted and the errata will be uploaded on our website, or added to any list of existing errata, under the Errata section of that title. Any existing errata can be viewed by selecting your title from http://www.packtpub.com/support.

Piracy

Piracy of copyright material on the Internet is an ongoing problem across all media. At Packt, we take the protection of our copyright and licenses very seriously. If you come across any illegal copies of our works, in any form, on the Internet, please provide us with the location address or website name immediately so that we can pursue a remedy.

Please contact us at copyright@packtpub.com with a link to the suspected pirated material.

We appreciate your help in protecting our authors, and our ability to bring you valuable content.

Questions

You can contact us at questions@packtpub.com if you are having a problem with any aspect of the book, and we will do our best to address it.

1
Understanding the Runtime Environment

In this chapter, we will look at the runtime environment that is offered by Google App Engine. Overall, a few details of the runtime environment pertaining to the infrastructure remain the same no matter which runtime environment—Java, Python, Go, or PHP—you opt for.

From all the available runtimes, Python is the most mature one. Therefore, in order to master Google App Engine, we will focus on Python alone. Many of the details vary a bit, but in general, runtimes have a commonality. Having said that, the other runtimes are catching up as well and all of them (including Java, PHP, and Go) are out of their respective beta stages.

Understanding the runtime environment will help you have a better grasp of the environment in which your code executes and you might be able to tweak code in accordance and understand why things behave the way they behave.

In this chapter, we will cover the following topics:

- The overall architecture
- Runtime environments
- Anatomy of a Google App Engine application
- A quick overview of the available services
- Setting up the development tools and writing a basic application

The overall architecture

The scaling of a web application is a hard thing to do. Serving a single page to a single user is a simple matter. Serving thousands of pages to a single or a handful of users is a simple matter, too. However, delivering just a single page to tens of thousands of users is a complex task. To better understand how Google App Engine deals with the problem of scale, we will revisit the whole problem of scaling in next chapter's, how it has been solved till date and the technologies/techniques that are at work behind the scenes. Once armed with this understanding, we will talk about how Google App Engine actually works.

The challenge of scale

The whole problem of complexity arises from the fact that to serve a simple page, a certain amount of time is taken by the machine that hosts the page. This time usually falls in milliseconds, and eventually, there's a limit to the number of pages that can be rendered and served in a second. For instance, if it takes 10 milliseconds to render a page on a 1 GHz machine, this means that in one second, we can serve 100 pages, which means that at a time, roughly 100 users can be served in a second.

However, if there are 300 users per second, we're out of luck as we will only be able to serve the first 100 lucky users. The rest will get time-out errors, and they may perceive that our web page is not responding, as a rotating wait icon will appear on the browser, which will indicate that the page is loading.

Let's introduce a term here. Instead of pages per second, we will call it requests or queries per second, or simply **Queries Per Second (QPS)**, because users pointing the browser to our page is just a request for the page.

How to scale with the scale?

We have two options here. The first option is to bring the rendering time down from 10 milliseconds to 5 milliseconds, which will effectively help us serve double the number of users. This path is called **optimization**. It has many techniques, which involve minimizing disk reads, caching computations instead of doing on the fly, and all that varies from application to application. Once you've applied all possible optimizations and achieved a newer and better page rendering time, further reduction won't be possible, because there's always a limit to how much we can optimize things and there always will be some overhead. Nothing comes for free.

The other way of scaling things up will be to put more hardware. So, instead of a 1 GHz machine, we can put a 2 GHz machine. Thus, we effectively doubled the number of requests that are processed from 100 to 200 QPS. So now, we can serve 200 users in a second. This method of scaling is called **vertical scaling**. However, yet again, vertical scaling has its limits because you can put a 3 GHz processor, then a 3.5 GHz one, or maybe clock it to a 4.8 GHz one, but finally, the clock frequency has some physical limits that are imposed by how the universe is constructed, and we'll hit the wall sooner or later. The other way around is that instead of putting a single 1 GHz machine, we can put two such machines and a third one in front. Now, when a request comes to the third front-end machine, we can distribute it to either of the other two machines in an alternate fashion, or to the machine with the least load. This request distribution can have many strategies. It can be as simple as a random selection between the two machines, or **round-robin fashion** one after the other or delegating request to the least loaded machine or we may even factor in the past response times of the machines. The main idea and beauty of the whole scheme is that we are no more limited by the limitations of the hardware. If a 1 GHz machine serves 100 users, we can put 10 such machines to serve 1000 users. To serve an audience of 1 million users, we will need ten thousand machines. This is exactly how Google, Facebook, Twitter, and Amazon handle tens of millions of users. The image shows the process of load balancer:

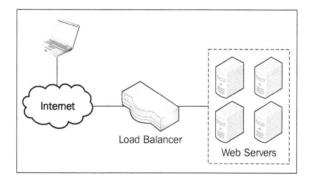

Load balancer splitting the load among machines.

A critical and enabling component here is the machine at front called **load balancer**. This machine runs the software that receives requests and delegates them to the other machines. Many web servers such as Ngnix and Apache come with load-balancing capabilities and require configurations for activating load balancing. The HAProxy is another open source load balancer that has many algorithms at its disposal, which are used to distribute load among the available servers.

A very important aspect of this scaling magic is that each machine, when added to the network, must respond in a manner that is consistent with the responses of the other machines of the cluster. Otherwise, users will have an inconsistent experience, that is, they might see something different when routed to one machine and something else when routed to another machine. For this to happen, even if the operating system differs (consider an instance where the first machine runs on Ubuntu with Cpython and the second one runs on CentOS with Jython), the output produced by each node should be exactly the same. In order to keep things simple, each machine usually has an exactly identical OS, set of libraries, and configurations.

Scaling in practice

Now that you have a load balancer and two servers and you're able to ramp up about 200 QPS (200 users per second), what happens when your user base grows to about 500 people? Well, it's simple. You have to repeat the following process:

1. Go to a store and purchase three more machines.
2. Put them on racks and plug in the network and power cables.
3. Install an OS on them.
4. Install the required languages/runtimes such as Ruby or Python.
5. Install libraries and frameworks, such as Rails or Django.
6. Install components such as web servers and databases.
7. Configure all of software.
8. Finally, add the address of the new machines to the load balancer configuration so that it can start delegating requests from users to machines as well.

You have to repeat the same process for all the three machines that you purchased from the store.

So, in this way, we scaled up our application, but how much time did it take us to do that all? The setting up of the server cables took about 10 minutes, the OS installation another 15 minutes, and the installation of the software components consumed about 40 minutes. So approximately, it took about 1 hour and 5 minutes to add a single node to the machine. Add the three nodes yourself, this amounts to about 4 hours and 15 minutes, that too if you're efficient enough and don't make a mistake along the way, which may make you go back and trace what went wrong and redo the things. Moreover, the sudden spike of users may be long gone by then, as they may feel frustrated by a slow or an unresponsive website. This may leave your newly installed machines idle.

Infrastructure as a Service

This clunky game of scaling was disrupted by another technology called virtualization, which lets us emulate a virtual machine on top of an operating system. Now that you have a virtual machine, you can install another operating system on this virtual machine. You can have more than one virtual machine on a single physical machine if your hardware is powerful enough, which usually is the case with server-grade machines. So now, instead of wiring a physical machine and installing the required OS, libraries, and so on, you can simply spin a virtual machine from a binary image that contains an OS and all the required libraries, tools, software components, and even your application code, if you want. Spinning such a machine requires few minutes (usually about 40 to 150 seconds). So, this is a great time-saving technique, as it cuts down the time requirement from one and a half hour to a few minutes.

Virtualization has created a multibillion-dollar industry. It is a whole new cool term that is related to Cloud computing for consultants of all sorts, and it is used to furnish their resumes. The idea is to put hundreds of servers on racks with virtualization enabled, let the users spin the virtual machines of their desired specs and charge them based on the usage. This is called **Infrastructure as a Service** (**IaaS**). Amazon, Racksapce, and Digital Ocean are the prime examples of such models.

Platform as a Service

Although Infrastructure as a Service gives a huge boost in building scalable applications, it still leaves a lot of room for improvements because you have to take care of the OS, required libraries, tools, security updates, the load balancing and provisioning of new machine instances, and almost everything in between. This limitation or problem leads to another solution called **Platform as a Service** (**Paas**), where right from the operating system to the required runtime, libraries and tools are preinstalled and configured for you. All that you have to do is push your code, and it will start serving right away. Google App Engine is such a platform where everything else is taken care of and all that you have to worry about is your code and what your app is supposed to do.

However, there's another major difference between IaaS and PaaS. Let's see what the difference is.

Containers

We talked about scaling by adding new machines to our hosting fleet that was done by putting up new machines on the rack, plugging in the wires, and installing the required software, which was tedious and very time-consuming and took up hours. We then spoke about how virtualization changed the game. You can instantiate a whole new (virtual) machine in a few minutes, possibly from an existing disk image, so that you don't have to install anything. This is indeed a real game changer.

However, the machine is slow at the Internet scale. You may have a sudden increase in the traffic and you might not be able to afford waiting for a few minutes to boot new instances. There's a faster way that comes from a few special features in the Linux kernel, where each executing process can have its own allocated and dedicated resources. What this abstract term means is that each process gets its own partition of the file systems, CPU, and memory share. This process is completely isolated from the other processes. Hence, it is executed in an isolated container. Then, for all practical purposes, this containment actually works as a virtual machine. An overhead of creating such an environment merely requires spinning a new process, which is not a matter of minutes but of a few seconds.

Google App Engine uses containment technology instead of virtualization to scale up the things. Hence, it is able to respond much faster than any IaaS solution, where they have to load a whole new virtual machine and then the whole separate operating system on top of an existing operating system along with the required libraries.

The containers use a totally different approach towards virtualization. Instead of emulating the whole hardware layer and then running an operating system on top of it, they actually are able to provide each running process a totally different view of the system in terms of file system, memory, network, and CPU. This is mainly enabled by **cgroups** (short for **control groups**). A kernel feature was developed by the engineers at Google in 2006 and later, it was merged into Linux kernel 2.6.24, which allows us to define an isolated environment and perform resource accounting for processes.

A container is just a separation of resources, such as file system, memory, and other resources. This is somewhat similar to chroot on Linux/Unix systems which changes the apparent root directory for the current running process and all of its parent-child. If you're familiar with it, you can change the system that you're working on, or simply put, you can replace the hard drive of your laptop with a hard drive from another laptop with identical hardware but a different operating system and set of programs. Hence, the mechanism helps to run totally different applications in each container. So, one container might be running **LAMP stack** and another might be running **node.js** on the same machine that runs at bare metal at native speed with no overhead.

This is called operating system virtualization and it's a vast subject in itself. Much more has been built on top of cgroups, such as **Linux Containers** (**LXC**) and Docker on top of LXC or using `libvirt`, but recently, docker has its own library called `libcontainer`, which sits directly on top of cgroups. However, the key idea is process containment, which results in a major reduction of time. Eventually, you will be able to spin a new *virtual machine* in a few seconds, as it is just about launching another ordinary Linux process, although contained in terms of what and how it sees the underlying system.

A comparison of virtual machines versus application containers (App Engine instances in our case) can be seen in the following diagram:

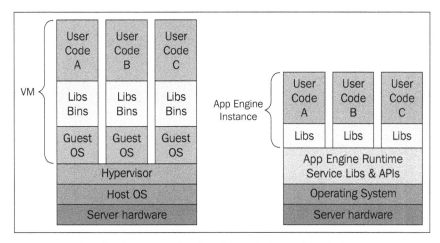

Virtualization vs container based App Engine machine instances.

How does App Engine scales?

Now that we understand many of the basic concepts behind how web applications can be scaled and the technologies that are at work, we can now examine how App Engine scales itself. When a user navigates to your app using their browser, the first thing that receives the users are the Google front end servers. These servers determine whether it is a request for App Engine (mainly by examining the HTTP Host header), and if it is, they are handed over to the **App Engine server**.

The App Engine server first determines whether this is a request for a static resource, and if that's the case, it is handed over to the static file servers, and the whole process ends here. Your application code never gets executed if a static resource is requested such as a JavaScript file or a CSS stylesheet. The following image shows the cycle of Google App Engine server request process:

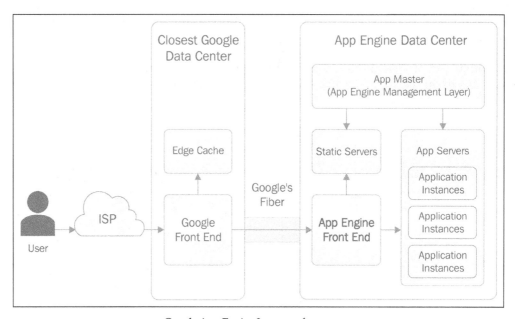

Google App Engine Journey of a request.

However, in case the request is dynamic, the App Engine server assigns it a unique identifier based on the time of receiving it. It is entered into a request queue, where it shall wait till an instance is available to serve it, as waiting might be cheaper then spinning a new instance altogether. As we talked about in the section on containers, these instances are actually containers and just isolated processes. So eventually, it is not as costly as launching a new virtual machine altogether. There are a few parameters here that you can tweak, which are accessible from the application performance settings once you've deployed. One is the minimum latency. It is the minimum amount of time a request should wait in the queue If you set this value to a higher number, you'll be able to serve more requests with fewer instances but at the cost of more latency, as perceived by the end user. App Engine will wait till the time that is specified as minimum latency and then, it will hand over the request to an existing instance. The other parameter is maximum latency, which specifies the maximum time for which a request can be held in the request queue, after which, App Engine will spin a new instance if none is available and pass the request to it. If this value is too low, App Engine will spin more instances, which will result in an increase in cost but much less latency, as experienced by the end user.

However by default, if you haven't tweaked the default settings. (we'll see how to do this in the *Chapter 10, Application Deployment*) Google App Engine will use heuristics to determine whether it should spin a new instance based on your past request history and patterns.

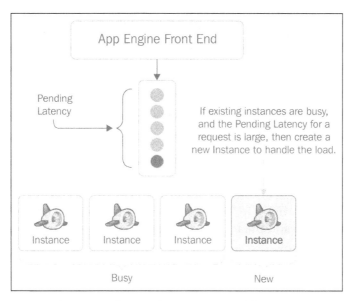

App Engine: Request, Request queues and Instances.

The last but a very important component in the whole scheme of things is the App Engine master. This is responsible for updates, deployments, and the versioning of the app. This is the component that pushes static resources to static servers and code to application instances when you deploy an application to App Engine.

Available runtimes

You can write web applications on top of Google App Engine in many programming languages, and your choices include Python, Java, Go, and PHP. For Python, two versions of runtimes are available, we will focus on the latest version.

Let's briefly look at each of the environments.

Python

The most basic and important principle of all runtime environments, including that of Python, is that you can talk to the outside world only by going through Google's own services. It is like a completely sealed and contained sandbox where you are not allowed to write to the disk or to connect to the network. However, no program will be very useful in that kind of isolation. Therefore, you can definitely talk to the outside world but only through the services provided by the App Engine. You can also ship your own code and libraries but they must all be in pure Python code and no C extensions are allowed. This is actually a limitation and tradeoff to ensure that the containers are always identical. Since no external libraries are allowed, it can be ensured that the minimal set of native required libraries is always present on the instance.

At the very beginning, App Engine started with the Python runtime environment, and version 2.5 was the one that was available for you. It had a few external libraries too, and it provided a CGI environment for your web app to talk to the world. That is, when a web request comes in, the environment variables are set from the request, the body goes to `stdin` and the Python interpreter invoked with given program. It is up to your program to then handle and respond to the request. This runtime environment is now deprecated.

Later, the Python 2.7 runtime environment came along, with new language features and updated shipped libraries. A major departure from the Python 2.5 runtime environment was not only the language version, but also a switch from CGI to WSGI. Because of this switch, it became possible for web apps to process requests concurrently. This boosted the overall throughput per instance. We will examine CGI and WSGI in detail in the next chapter.

The Java runtime environment

Java runtime environment presents a standard Servlet version 2.5 environment, and there are two language versions available—Java 5 and Java 6. The Java 6 runtime environment is deprecated and will be soon removed. The Java 6 runtime environment will be replaced and new applications users can only be able to use Java 7. The `app.xml` is a file that defines your application, and you have various standard Java APIs available to talk to Google services, such as JPA for persistence, Java Mail for mail, and so on.

This runtime environment is also capable of handling concurrent requests.

Go

This runtime environment uses the new Go programming language from Google. It is a CGI environment too, and it's not possible to handle concurrent requests, the applications are written in Go version 1.4.

PHP

This is a preview platform, and the PHP interpreter is modified to fit in the scalable environment with the libraries patched, removed, or the individual functions disabled. You get to develop applications just as you would do for any normal PHP web application, but there are many limitations. Many of the standard library modules are either not available, or are partially functional, the applications are written in PHP version 5.5.

The structure of an application

When you are developing a web application that has to be hosted on Google App Engine, it has to have a certain structure so that the platform can deploy it. A minimal App Engine application is composed of an application manifest file called app.yaml and at least one script / code file that handles and responds to requests. The app.yaml file defines the application ID, version of the application, required runtime environment and libraries, static resources, if any, and the set of URLs along with their mappings to the actual code files that are responsible for their processing.

So eventually, if you look at the minimum application structure, it will comprise only the following two files:

- app.yaml
- main.py

Here, app.yaml describes the application and set of URLs to the actual code files mappings. We will examine app.yaml in greater detail in a later section. The app.yaml is not the only file that makes up your application. There are a few other optional configuration files as well. In case you are using datastore, there may be another file called index.yaml, which lists the kind of indexes that your app will require. Although you can edit this file, it is automatically generated for you, as your application runs queries locally.

You then might have a `crons.yaml` file as well, that describes various repeated tasks. The `queus.yaml` file descries your queue configurations so that you can queue in long running tasks for later processing. The `dos.yaml` is the file that your application might define to prevent DoS attacks.

However, most importantly, your application can have one or more logical modules, where each module will run on a separate instance and might have different scaling characteristics. So, you can have a module defined by `api.yaml` that handles your API calls, and its scaling type is set to **automatic** so that it responds to requests according to the number of consumers. Another named `backend.yaml` handles various long running tasks, and its scaling type is set to **manual** with 5 instances on standby, which will keep running all the time to handle whatever the long running tasks handled to them.

We will take a look at modules later in this book when discussing deployment options in *Chapter 10, Application Deployment*.

The available services

By now, you probably understand the overall architecture and atmosphere in which our app executes, but it won't be of much use without more services available at our disposal. Otherwise, with the limitation of pure Python code, we might have to bring everything that is required along with us to build the next killer web app.

To this end, Google App Engine provides many useful scalable services that you can utilize to build app. Some services address storage needs, others address the processing needs of an app, and yet, the other group caters to the communication needs. In a nutshell, the following services are at your disposal:

- **Storage**: Datastore, Blobstore, Cloud SQL, and Memcache
- **Processing**: Images, Crons, Tasks, and MapReduce
- **Communication**: Mail, XMPP, and Channels
- **Identity and security**: Users, OAuth, and App Identity
- **Others**: such as various capabilities, image processing and full text search

If the list seems short, Google constantly keeps adding new services all the time. Now, let's look at each of the previously listed services in detail.

Datastore

Datastore is a NoSQL, distributed, and highly scalable column based on a storage solution that can scale to petabytes of data so that you don't have to worry about scaling at all. App Engine provides a data modeling library that you can use to model your data, just as you would with any **Object Relational Mapping (ORM)**, such as the Django models or SQL Alchemy. The syntax is quite similar, but there are differences.

Each object that you save gets a unique key, which is a long string of bytes. Its generation is another topic that we will discuss later. Since it's a NoSQL solution, there are certain limitations on what you can query, which makes it unfit for everyday use, but we can work around those limitations, as we will explore in the coming chapters.

By default, apps get 1 GB of free space in datastore. So, you can start experimenting with it right away.

Google Cloud SQL

If you prefer using a relational database, you can have that too. It is a standard MySQL database, and you have to boot up instances and connect with it via whatever interface is available to your runtime environment, such as JDBC in case of Java and MySQLdb in case of Python. Datastore comes with a free quota of about 1 GB of data, but for Cloud SQL, you have to pay from the start.

Because dealing with MySQL is a topic that has been explored in much detail from blog posts to articles and entire books have been written on the subject, this book skips the details on this, it focuses more on Google Datastore.

The Blobstore

Your application might want to store larger chunks of data such as images, audio, and video files. The Blobstore just does that for you. You are given a URL, which has to be used as the target of the upload form. Uploads are handled for you, while a key of the uploaded file is returned to a specified callback URL, which can be stored for later reference. For letting users download a file, you can simply set the key that you got from the upload as a specific header on your response, which is taken as an indication by the App Engine to send the file contents to the user.

Memcache

Hitting datastore for every request costs time and computational resources. The same goes for the rendering of templates with a given set of values. Time is money. Time really is money when it comes to cloud, as you pay in terms of the time your code spends in satisfying user requests. This can be reduced by caching certain content or queries that occur over and over for the same set of data. Google App Engine provides you with memcache to play with so that you can supercharge your app response.

When using App Engine's Python library to model data and query, the caching of the data that is fetched from datastore is automatically done for you, which was not the case in the previous versions of the library.

Scheduled Tasks

You might want to perform some certain tasks at certain intervals. That's where the scheduled tasks fit in. Conceptually, they are similar to the Linux/UNIX Cron jobs. However, instead of specifying commands or programs, you indicate URLs, which receive the HTTP GET requests from App Engine on the specified intervals. You're required to process your stuff in under 10 minutes. However, if you want to run longer tasks, you have that option too by tweaking the scaling options, which will be examined in the last chapter when we examine deployment.

Queues Tasks

Besides the scheduled tasks, you might be interested in the background processing of tasks. For this, Google App Engine allows you to create tasks queues and enqueue tasks in them specifying a target URL with payload, where they are dispatched on a specified and configurable rate. Hence, it is possible to asynchronously perform various computations and other pieces of work that otherwise cannot be accommodated in request handlers.

App Engine provides two types of queues—push queues and pull queues. In push queues, the tasks are delivered to your code via the URL dispatch mechanism, and the only limitation is that you must execute them within the App Engine environment. On the other hand, you can have pull requests where it's your responsibility to pull tasks and delete them once you are done. To that end, pull tasks can be accessed and processed from outside Google App Engine. Each task is retried with backoffs if it fails, and you can configure the rate at which the tasks get processed and configure this for each of the task queues or even at the individual task level itself. The task retries are only available for push queues and for pull queues, you will have to manage repeated attempts of failed tasks on your own.

Each app has a default task queue, and it lets you create additional queues, which are defined in the `queues.yaml` file. Just like the scheduled tasks, each task is supposed to finish its processing within 10 minutes. However, if it takes longer then this, we'll learn how to accommodate such a situation when we examine application deployment in the last chapter.

MapReduce

MapReduce is a distributed computing paradigm that is widely used at Google to crunch exotic amounts of data, and now, many open source implementations of such a model exist, such as Hadoop. App Engine provides the MapReduce functionality as well, but at the time of writing this book, Google has moved the development and support of MapReduce libraries for Python and Java to Open source community and they are hosted on Github. Eventually, these features are bound to change a lot. Therefore, we'll not cover MapReduce in this book but if you want to explore this topic further, check `https://github.com/GoogleCloudPlatform/appengine-mapreduce/wiki` for further details.

Mail

Google is in the mail business. So, your applications can send mails. You can not only send e-mails, but also receive them as well. If you plan to write your app in Java, you will use JavaMail as the API to send emails. You can of course use third-party solutions as well to send email, such as SendGrid, which integrates nicely with Google App Engine. If you're interested in this kind of solution, visit `https://cloud.google.com/appengine/docs/python/mail/sendgrid`.

XMPP

It's all about instant messaging. You may want to build chat features in your app or use in other innovative ways, such as notifying users about a purchase as an instant message or anything else whereas for that matter. XMPP services are at your disposal. You can send a message to a user, whereas your app will receive messages from users in the form of HTTP POST requests of a specific URL. You can respond to them in whatever way you see fit.

Channels

You might want to build something that does not work with the communication model of XMPP, and for this, you have channels at your disposal. This allows you to create a persistent connection from one client to the other clients via Google App Engine. You can supply a client ID to App Engine, and a channel is opened for you. Any client can listen on this channel, and when you send a message to this channel, it gets pushed to all the clients. This can be useful, for instance, if you wish to inform about the real-time activity of other users, which is similar to you notice on Google Docs when editing a spreadsheet or document together.

Users

Authentication is an important part of any web application. App Engine allows you to generate URLs that redirect users to enter their Google account credentials (yourname@gmail.com) and manage sessions for you. You also have the option of restricting the sign-in functionality for a specific domain (such as yourname@yourcompany.com) in case your company uses Google Apps for business and you intend to build some internal solutions. You can limit access to the users on your domain alone.

OAuth

Did you ever come across a button labeled **Sign in with Facebook, Twitter, Google,** and **LinkedIn** on various websites? Your app can have similar capabilities as well, where you let users not only use the credentials that they registered with on your website, but also sign in to others. In technical jargon, Google Engine can be an OAuth provider.

Writing and deploying a simple application

Now that you understand how App Engine works and the composition of an App Engine app, it's time to get our hands on some real code and play with it. We will use Python to develop applications, and we've got a few reasons to do so. For one, Python is a very simple and an easy-to-grasp language. No matter what your background is, you will be up and running it quickly. Further, Python is the most mature and accessible runtime environment because it is available since the introduction of App Engine, Further almost all new experimental and cutting-edge services are first introduced for Python runtime environment before they make their way to other runtimes.

Enough justification. Now, to develop an application, you will need an SDK for the runtime environment that you are targeting, which happens to be Python in our case. To obtain the Python SDK, visit `https://developers.google.com/appengine/downloads`. From the download page, select and download the SDK version for your platform. Now let's examine installation process for each platform in detail.

Installing an SDK on Linux

The installation of the Linux SDK is quite simple. It is just a matter of downloading and unzipping the SDK. Besides this, you have to ensure that you have Python 2.7.x installed, which usually is the case with most Linux distributions these days.

To check whether you have Python, open a terminal and type the following command:

```
$ python --version
Python 2.7.6
```

If you get a response that states that the command was not found or your version number shows something other than 2.7.x (the least significant digit isn't important here), then you'll have to install Python. For Ubuntu and Debian systems, it will be simple:

```
$ sudo apt-get install python2.7
```

Once you're done with the preceding process, you just have to unzip the SDK contents into a directory such as `/home/mohsin/sdks`.

The best way to work with SDK is to add it to system's PATH environment variable. This way, all the command line tools would be available from everywhere. To do that, you can modify the PATH like this:

```
$ export PATH=$PATH:/path/to/sdk
```

This change would stay as long as the shell is active to better you add the above like in your `.bashrc` which is located at `~/.bashrc`.

So as you can see, the installation on Linux is pretty simple and involves simply uncompressing the SDK contents and optionally adjusting the system path.

Installing an SDK on Mac

The requirements for Python presence on the system remain the same, and Mac OS X comes with Python. So, this is already satisfied and we're done with it. So now, drag the `.dmg` file to **Applications** as you'd install any normal app for Mac and perform the following steps:

1. In **Finder**, browse **Go | Applications**. This shall open the `Applications` folder.

2. Double-click on the `.dmg` file that you just downloaded and drag the `GoogleAppEngineLauncher` icon to the `Applications` folder.

3. Now, double-click on the **Launcher** icon that you just dragged to the `Applications` folder.

4. When you're prompted for to make the `symlinks` command, click on **OK** because Launcher alone is just a useful utility that is used to run the App Engine apps locally, but its GUI lacks many of the features and commands that are otherwise available in the SDK. So, making `symlinks` will let you access them on a terminal from anywhere.

5. Your SDK contents will be at `/usr/local/google_appengine`.

Now, you're done with the installation.

Installing an SDK on Windows

A little unwarranted rant—Windows is usually not a very good platform for development if you want to use open source tool chains, because from Ruby to Python and node.js, everything is developed, tested, and usually targeted for the `*nix` systems. This is why they might not work out of the box on Windows. On this note, the Python SDK for App Engine is available for Windows, and it requires a Python installation too, which can be downloaded from `http://www.python.org`.

Download the `.msi` installer for Python 2.7.x (where x is whatever latest minor version which right now is 10) and follow the instructions. You will have everything right there required to run Python programs. Next, download the Google App Engine SDK for Windows and install that too and you are done.

Writing a simple app

Now that we have a good overview of how App Engine scales, available runtimes, and the services that are at our disposal, it's time to do something real and write our first app.

We will write a simple app that will print all the environment variables. Before you write any code, you'll need to create the app on Google App Engine. If you don't do this, you can still test and run the applications locally, but to deploy, you have to create an app on Google App Engine. To do this, navigate to `http://appengine.google.com`. Here, you'll be asked to log in using your Gmail credentials. Once you've logged in, you will have to click on Create a Project… from the drop down menu as shown below:

Creating a new project from Google Developer Console.

Once you click this, you'll be presented with this dialog:

Popup to enter information for your new project

In its most basic form, the pop-up would only contain the name of the project, but we have expanded all the options to demonstrate. The first thing is the **Project name** and this can be anything you like it to be. The second thing is the **Project ID**. This is the ID that you will use in your `app.yaml` file. This ID must be unique across all the App Engine applications and it is automatically generated for you, but you can specify your own as well. If you specify your own, you will be warned if it is not unique and you won't be able to proceed.

The next advanced option is about the location that your app would be served from. By default, all the applications would be hosted from the data centers located in USA, but you can select the European ones. You should select the European data center if most of the user base is close to or is in Europe. For example, if we're building an app for which we expect most of the traffic from Asia, Middle-east, or Europe, then probably it would make more sense to go for European data center.

Once done, left-click on **Compute | App Engine | Dashboard**. When presented with the dialog box, select **Try App Engine**:

You'll be greeted with this dialog on selecting Google App Engine.

And finally, you'll see the following screen:

The welcome page shows steps to deploy a sample application.

This welcome page appears because you have no application deployed as yet. Once deployed, you'll see a dashboard, which we'll see in a while.

You can follow the above instructions from the welcome page, if you want to deploy a sample application as shown in the preceding screenshot, but for our purpose, we will deploy our own application. To deploy our own app, all we need is the project ID for which you can click on **Home** on the left side, which will show the following page:

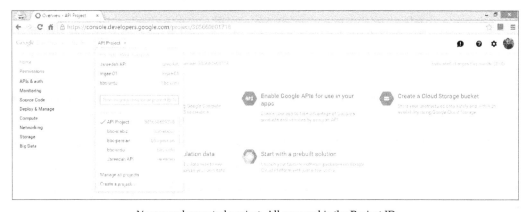

Your newly created project. All we need is the Project ID

We only need the **Project ID** from the first box on the top-left, which we will enter in app.yaml for application directive and then we're all good. For example, in this chapter, we used mgae-01 as the **Project ID** and that's what we are using. Because application IDs must be unique across all the App Engine applications, therefore, you cannot use this ID while deploying your own application and you will have to select something else.

Once you have deployed the app, your dashboard (accessible from **Compute | App Engine | Dashboard**) will look like this, instead of the welcome page that we saw earlier:

The application dashboard of a deployed application

Now that we are done with the basic setup, we will write the code and run and test it locally.

Create a directory somewhere. Create a file named app.yaml and enter the following into it:

```
application: mgae-01
version: 1
runtime: python27
api_version: 1
threadsafe: false

handlers:
- url: /.*
  script: main.py
```

This `app.yaml` file is what defines your application. Application is the unique ID that we discussed. The `version` is your version of the app. You can have multiple versions of the same app. As you change this string, it will be considered a new version and would be deployed as a new version, whereas the previous version will be retained on the App Engine servers. You can switch to a previous version from the dashboard whenever you like. Besides this, you can also split the traffic between the various versions of an application.

The next attribute is the `runtime`. We have many choices here, such as `go` if we want to have our app in the Go programming language. Previously for Python, we had choice of either Python 2.7 or Python 2.5. However, support for the Python 2.5 runtime environment is deprecated, and new apps cannot be created with Python 2.5 since January 2014.

Next comes the `api_version`. This indicates the version of the system services that you'd like to use. There is only one version of all the available system APIs (the ones that we discussed under runtime services), but in case Google does release any incompatible changes to the services, this API version number will be incremented. Thus, you will still be able to maintain the apps that you developed earlier, and you can opt for a newer version of APIs if you want to use them in newer applications or upgrade your existing applications to use newer versions.

Next comes the thread safe thing. Here, you indicate whether your application is thread-safe or not. As a rule of thumb, if your code does not write to any global variables or compute them on the fly to populate their values for later reference, your app is thread-safe. Hence, multiple requests can be handed over to your App Engine instance. Otherwise, you'll be handed over a single request at a time, which you'll have to finish processing before you can get the next request to be processed.

Multithreading was not available for the Python 2.5 environment because it worked via CGI, but Python 2.7 supports WSGI, which allows concurrent requests. However, this particular app uses the 2.7 runtime environment, but it is not a WSGI app. All of this might seem Greek to you for now, but we shall discuss CGI, WSGI, and concurrent requests in detail in the next chapter.

Next comes the `handlers` section. Here, we list URLs as regular expressions and state what has to be done with them. They might be handled by a script or mapped to a static directory. We'll discuss the latter case in the next chapter, which will let us serve static application resources, such as images, styles, and scripts. An important thing that you should note is that the URLs in the list are always checked in the order in which they are defined, and as soon as the first match is found, the listed action is taken. Here, are mentioning tell that whatever URL we get, simply execute the Python script. This is the CGI way of doing things. WSGI will be slightly different, and we'll examine this in detail later.

So, this was the explanation of the `app.yaml`, which describes the contents and details of your app. Next comes the actual script, which will generate the output for the web page. Create a `main.py` file in the same directory as that of `app.yaml` and enter the following code:

```
import os
print 'Content-Type: text/plain'
print ''

print "ENVIRONMENT VARIABLES"
print "======================\n"

for key in os.environ:
print key, ": ", os.environ[key]
```

Now, let's examine this. This is actually a CGI script. First, we imported a standard Python module. Next, we wrote to the standard output (`stdout`), and the first statement actually is writing an HTTP header, which indicated that we are generating plain text.

Next, the `print` statement printed a blank line because the HTTP headers are supposed to be separated by a blank line from the HTTP body.

Next, we actually iterated over all the environment variables and printed them to `stdout`, which in turn will be sent to the browser. With that, we're done with our example application.

Now that we understand how it works, let's run it locally by executing the following command:

```
$ ~/sdks/google_appengine/dev_appserver.py ~/Projects/mgae/ch01/hello/
```

Here, `~/Project/mgae/ch01/hello` is the directory that contains all the previously mentioned application files. Now, when you point your browser to `http://localhost:8080`, you'll find a list of environment variables printed. Hit it with any URL, such as `http://localhost:8080/hello`, and you'll find the same output except for a few environment variables, which might have a different value.

Deploying

Let's deploy the application to the cloud, as follows:

```
$ ~/sdks/google_appengine/appcfg.py update ~/Projects/mgae/ch01/hello/
--oauth2
10:26 PM Application: mgae-01; version: 1
10:26 PM Host: appengine.google.com
```

```
10:26 PM
Starting update of app: mgae-01, version: 1
10:26 PM Getting current resource limits.
Email: mohsinhijazee@gmail.com
Password for mohsinhijazee@gmail.com:
10:26 PM Scanning files on local disk.
10:26 PM Cloning 2 application files.
10:27 PM Uploading 2 files and blobs.
10:27 PM Uploaded 2 files and blobs
10:27 PM Compilation starting.
10:27 PM Compilation completed.
10:27 PM Starting deployment.
10:27 PM Checking if deployment succeeded.
10:27 PM Deployment successful.
10:27 PM Checking if updated app version is serving.
10:27 PM Completed update of app: mgae-01, version: 1
```

This that indicates that our app is deployed and ready to sever. Navigate your browser to http://yourappid.appspot.com and you will see something like this:

```
REQUEST_ID_HASH :   FCD253ED
HTTP_X_APPENGINE_COUNTRY :   AE
SERVER_SOFTWARE :   Google App Engine/1.9.11
SCRIPT_NAME :
HTTP_X_APPENGINE_CITYLATLONG :   0.000000,0.000000
DEFAULT_VERSION_HOSTNAME :   mgae-01.appspot.com
APPENGINE_RUNTIME :   python27
INSTANCE_ID :   00c61b117c09cf94de8a5822633c28f2f0e85efe
PATH_TRANSLATED :   /base/data/home/apps/s~mgae-01/1.378918986084593129/
main.pyc
REQUEST_LOG_ID :
54230d4200ff0b7779fcd253ed0001737e6d6761652d3031000131000100
HTTP_X_APPENGINE_REGION :   ?
USER_IS_ADMIN :   0
CURRENT_MODULE_ID :   default
CURRENT_VERSION_ID :   1.378918986084593129
USER_ORGANIZATION :
APPLICATION_ID :   s~mgae-01
USER_EMAIL :
DATACENTER :   us2
USER_ID :
HTTP_X_APPENGINE_CITY :   ?
AUTH_DOMAIN :   gmail.com
USER_NICKNAME :
```

The --oauth2 option will open the browser, where you will have to enter your Google account credentials. You can do without   oauth2. In this case, you will be asked for your email and password on the command shell, but you'll also get a notice that states that this mode of authentication is deprecated.

Let's examine a few interesting environment variables that are set by Google App Engine. REQUEST_ID_HASH and REQUEST_LOG_ID are set by App Engine to uniquely identify this request. That's the request ID that we talked about in the section about how scaling works. The APPENGINE_RUNTIME indicates the runtime environment that this app is running on. There is a **DATACENTER** header that is set to us2, which indicates that our app is being executed in the US data centers. Then, we have INSTANCE_ID, which is the unique ID that is assigned to the instance handling this request.

Then, some user-specific headers such has USER_IS_ADMIN, USER_EMAIL, USER_ID, USER_NICKNAME, and AUTH_DOMAIN are set by the User service that we discussed in the services section. If a user had logged in, these headers will have their email, ID, and nickname as values.

These headers are added by Google App Engine, and a feature of the environment in which your code executes. So that's all, folks!

Summary

This chapter described how the App Engine works in terms of scaling and the anatomy of a typical App Engine application. We then turned our attention towards the services that are at the disposal of an App Engine application. We had a brief overview of each one of these services. Next, we moved towards writing a simple web app that would print all the environment variables. Next, we ran it locally and deployed it on the cloud to examine its output and noted a few interesting headers that are added by App Engine.

This understanding of the environment is essential towards mastering Google App Engine. By now, you have a pretty good understanding of the environment under which your code executes. In the next chapter, we are going to examine request handling in detail and check out the options that we have while serving requests.

2
Handling Web Requests

Now that you understand the runtime environment of Google App Engine quite well, how it deals with an incoming web requests, and how they are handed over to your application, it's time to divert our attention to the most important aspect of web application development—handling and responding to web requests. In this chapter, we will have a look at how to handle web requests from an application that is deployed on Google App Engine. We will study the two main modes of web request handling and then focus on how to render templates, serve static files, and finally, how to use web frameworks.

In this chapter, we will cover the following topics:

- The CGI and WSGI way of request handling
- Rendering templates
- Serving static files
- Working with web frameworks

Request handling

Instead of jumping straight into the alphabet soup of HTTP, **CGI (Common Gateway Interface)**, **WSGI (Web Server Gateway Interface)**, and so on, we will examine the entire problem of request handling from where all it started. The basic design goal of the Web was sharing information in the form of documents. So, all in all, it was a document-sharing system, where each document had a unique URL like a unique path for each file (ignoring links and shortcuts for the sake of discussion) on a file system. Each document could be linked to other documents. This was the simple HTTP Web.

The initial Web was simple and consisted of two pair of programs. One piece of program, which was called the client (nowadays, it is mostly in the form of a modern desktop or a mobile browser), would request a document by opening a socket for a given server and on a specific port using a very specific request format like this as textual data:

```
Host: www.mit.edu
GET /publications/quantum/computing/future.html
```

The preceding text would be sent to `www.mit.edu` (actually, to whatever IP this address corresponds to after the DNS resolution, which is yet another detailed area and not within the scope of our discussion), where a program called server would be listening on port 80. The program that would parse this request would see that `/publications/quantum/computing/future.html` is the document that it needs to return from its directory of documents (which of course would be specified somewhere in the configuration), and the connection would be closed. This is exactly the thing that happens when you visit any dummy URL:`http://www.mit.edu/publications/quantum/computing/future.html` in your browser.

The text that the client program sent is actually an HTTP protocol, and the server program that we talked about is called HTTP server because it understands and responds to the HTTP protocol. It is called HTTP server because there are many other types of servers such as FTP servers, SMTP servers, DNS servers, and so on. An HTTP server traditionally listens on port 80, and it was probably the 1980s when all of this started. Actually 1989 is the year when the idea of linked documents and HTTP protocol also known as World Wide Web was proposed. Probably that is why they used port 80 because in the decade of 80s, just a wild guess. Eventually, and most probably, this tradition continued and is still with us today; this is just a guess.

The CGI program

The preceding system, although very simple, elegant, and yet powerful, has one drawback. If you request the same document, you will always get the same content, unless you modify the document yourself on the server using some text editor. To get different content, you have to request a different document altogether. You will never come across a case where you request the same document but get different results.

This kind of requirement might sound absurd, but it is at the heart of the modern Web. That's how the same HTML page lists a different set of emails depending on who logs in and what they opt for. So, this leads us to dynamic content generation. In other words, you can generate pages on the fly, which don't yet exist on the disk, except maybe in the form of a template, where the actual content is yet to be filled in on the fly. From compilers and assemblers to almost any other imaginable program, it is always about input, processing, and producing output, and that's exactly what we need here. So eventually, as a part of the evolution, the HTTP servers were configured to execute a program and return its output as a response to the requester instead of a static document. This is how the wave of dynamic web was born. The question is, how does one pass information about an HTTP request to a program and collect the output? There's a convention that emerged for this that we will examine, and it is called CGI.

Streams and environment variables

Before we discuss how CGI works, there are few ingredients that are worth examining for ease of understanding. An important thing that emerged from the UNIX world and eventually has support in virtually all operating systems is the environment variables. So, the idea is that the operating system itself or any program can create variables that are managed by the operating system, but anyone on the system can read from or write these variables.

The other important concept is that of I/O streams. In POSIX-compliant operating systems (which borrowed this convention yet again from the UNIX world).

A program has three special files available at all times to read and write. One file is used to read the input. So, the input from the keyboard is made available via this file, which is called **standard input** or **stdin**. A smart trick that can be played by some other program is to write its output on the input stream (stdin) of another program, which in turn would see as if its input is coming from the keyboard. The main concept here is that the input stream is what is read by a program and which might be populated by another program or input devices.

The other two files, which are as follows, are used to write the output of the program:

- The first one is called **standard output** or stdout for short, and that's where all your print statements in Python and Ruby leave their mark, and that's where printf and cout will write their output in a C/C++ program

- The second output file is called **standard error** or stderr and is used to writing error messages for anything that is not an output of the program but output about the output or whatever happens during that output's generation

Now, back to the CGI program. The plain HTTP text, as shown in the preceding example, is received by the HTTP server. Then, the HTTP server will execute a program. The headers (represented by colons separated by key value pairs) and query string parameters (such as http://www.example.com?sample_query_param=1) will be placed in the environment variables before the program is invoked. A request body (usually with a HTTP POST) is made available via the standard input or (stdin). Now, when the program is executed, it will read the environment variables (that contains the HTTP headers) and stdin (the request body, if any exists) and write its output on stdout, which will be collected by the server once the program is done. This program output finally will be sent back to the client, which is usually a web browser.

CGI and Google App Engine

The Python 2.5 runtime environment, which is now deprecated, uses CGI as its request handling mechanism. The request would be received by the frontend Google servers, placed in a queue, as we learned in the previous chapter, and then finally handed over to an instance where a Python interpreter process reads in all the environment variables and stdin of the process will be set from the incoming request as well. The output of the program on stdout will be collected and sent to the client. The currently available mainstream and Python 2.7 runtime environment, the CGI is still available. When you indicate a script name with .py (or a compiled Python byte code file with .pyc) extension, the request is handed over to it in the CGI fashion.

The program that we wrote in the first chapter, though targeting the Python 2.7 runtime environment, was a CGI program. Now that you have a better understanding of CGI, it's time to implement it. To save you a lot of trouble, copy the directory from the first chapter, rename it to cwsgi, and make the following changes:

- Rename main.py to cgimain.py

- Edit app.yaml and replace main.py with cgimain.py

- Change url: /.* to url: /cgi

Now, start the app with the following command:

```
python ~/sdks/google_appengine/dev_appserver.py ~/Projects/mgae/ch02/
cwsgi/
```

After doing this, open your browser and visit `http://localhost:8080/cgi`. You'll see that all the environment variables are listed just as in the original version of the program from the previous chapter.

WSGI

Nothing makes sense until you really understand the rationale behind it and therefore, yet again, instead of jumping straight into what WSGI is and how it fits into the overall picture, we will examine the problems with CGI first.

Problems with CGI

The CGI approach is surely a big step forward, but it has a very serious drawback. It creates a process for every incoming request, and creating a process is expensive in terms of computing time as it involves the allocation of memory and initialization of many internal data structures. More often than not, the actual computational time that is required to render a page is barely a fraction (sometimes one-fifth to one-tenth) of the process creation time. This means that about 80 percent of the request time, as perceived by the end user, is actually spent in spawning a new process. This mechanism is repeated over and over for every single incoming request.

For a concrete example, assume that creating a process takes 1.5 seconds, which equals 1500 milliseconds. However, responding to an actual request barely takes 0.3 seconds, or 300 milliseconds. This means that the time taken to create a process alone is five times the actual time that is required to serve a request. The mechanism of request handling actually has a name. It is called a **process-per-request model** because a new process is spawned for every incoming request.

Besides the extra lag experienced by the end user, the main issue is that of sheer inefficient resource utilization. While framing the scalability problem in the previous chapter, we observed that the number of requests processed per second is an important metric and this process-per-request model is quite inefficient because of the overheads involved as we just examined.

Solutions

Many solutions were devised to eliminate this process creation overhead, but all of them are actually based on either of the two approaches. The first approach revolves around a simple observation that the creation of a process creates a bottleneck. Hence, instead of creating a process for every request, it will be created only once. For every incoming request, a separate thread should be created instead of a whole new process. This is called **thread-per-request model**. As thread creation is lightweight in comparison to process creation, this yields much more throughput, but on the downside, it has a side effect as well. This is the case with every multithreaded program, and we will examine it in a while. WSGI from Python, Rack from Ruby, and Servlet Specifications from the Java world are all examples of this thread-per-request model.

A slight improvement for the above solution that sprung up over time is that instead of creating a thread for every incoming request, a fixed (configurable) number of threads are created at the time of creating the process. Now, whenever a new request comes in, it is assigned a thread from this collection (called the thread pool). Once the request is served, the thread sits idle again in the set of threads that were created during the startup of the process. This is called thread pooling.

The other model is a more recent one and relies on the recent innovation in Linux kernels. Instead of listening on and blocking a port for a request, kernel invokes your program whenever there is some activity on the port that you specify. All such solutions are built on top of `libevent`, a C library that sits on top of the functionality provided by the Linux kernel. Further discussion and description of this model is beyond the scope of this book. An example of this approach includes `node.js` and `gevent` in Python, but this is also beyond this book's scope.

For those of you who are interested in the above mentioned request handling techniques shall check out the following links:

* `http://libevent.org/`
* `http://www.kegel.com/c10k.html`

What WSGI looks like

WSGI is a Python standard (PEP 3333) that defines how Python programs are supposed to interact with web servers. The specifications are quite detailed, and they are as dry as the committee could make them. So, let's not look at them. Instead, let's try to dismantle the concept in the simplest possible terms. The idea of **Web Server Gateway Interface (WSGI)** is very simple. You define a function that accepts a number of arguments of certain types, and the function returns a specific type of data to you.

The function and arguments can have any name whatever you want to, but the type, the number of arguments passed, and the values that are returned back must adhere to the standard. The arguments are passed to the function from the web server and the return value of the function is received by the web server and passed back to the client. The web server is supposed to call this function whenever it receives a request. All request headers and the other data will be passed to this function as arguments.

This is how a WSGI script with the function that we talked about look like:

```
def application(environ, start_response):
    start_response('200 OK', [('Content-Type', 'text/plain')])
    return "Hello from WSGI!"
```

Now, let's take a detailed look at the arguments that are supplied to the function from the web server. The first argument is a Python dictionary. All the HTTP request headers are placed in this dictionary as key-value pairs. All other environment variables are also included in the same dictionary. The second argument is a function that the application must call to indicate that it has started generating a response. This function must be called with the help of two arguments. The first argument is a string, and the other is a list. The string is returned to the web server as the HTTP status code (for instance, HTTP 404, 301, 302, or the famous HTTP 500). The second argument which is a list comprises tuples, where each tuple represents a response header name and its value. So, in the preceding example, we returned HTTP 200 (because of the first argument to `start_response`). `Content-Type` is set to `text/plain` because of the second list that is being passed to `start_response`. If more response headers were sent, they would end up in this list as two member tuples in the form of key value pairs.

The return value of the function must be an iterator. A list or a tuple where each element is a response line or you might use the yield keyword thus forming a Python generator and the response to be returned can be generated such as fetched from a database, a large file, or some other network resource. You can also return just a string because a string can be iterated as well. However, it will be inefficient, as we shall explain shortly. In the preceding example, we returned a string so that the server software that would receive this would iterate over this string, which means iterating character by character because it is a string, which is bit inefficient. Therefore, we are better off yielding individual lines or a list of response lines and return it, which in turn will be sent back to the client. So, that's how the last line is supposed to be:

```
return ["Hello from better and proper way of returning WSGI response"]
```

That's all about WSGI that you need to know. Now that the whole of your web application is merely just a function, it can be executed on separate threads. Hence, new threads can be created when new requests come along, which is far more efficient than spawning a whole new process on every incoming request. Remember that thread pooling can dramatically eliminate the time required for thread creation as well which will be even more efficient.

WSGI – Multithreading considerations

Now, there's one caveat that we should discuss about WSGI model. In the CGI paradigm, a new process is created for each incoming request, which means that global variables are totally isolated from any other Python process that is created at the same time (or an overlapping time slot) to serve another request. Hence, any code that is writing and reading too and from the global variables is totally constrained to be process spawning request alone.

However, in the case of a WSGI model, which goes for a one-thread-per-request paradigm, local variables are of course within the scope of the function, but the global variables are visible to two incoming requests, that are being executed on the same or an overlapping time frame. Now, when one request is writing to the global variables and another is reading them at the same time, it might so happen that the variables are in an inconsistent state (for instance, the whole value is not yet written while it is being accessed and read by another request as it is), which might result in a strange, unpredictable, and very hard-to-debug behavior that shows up only under very specific conditions.

In other words, CGI versus WSGI exhibits the same problems as that of the **Process** versus **Threads** paradigms of multiprocessing. When you perform multiprocessing using processes as the atomic blocks of concurrency, each process has its own separate state, which of course includes the global variables only visible to the process itself. Thus, this reduces complexity. However, this is inefficient because process creation is a heavyweight process. On the other hand, multiprocessing with threads is much lightweight. But multi-threading brings up the problem of conflicting state due to shared global data structures.

To cater to this, all you can do is to ensure that you don't read and write to the global variables without some thread synchronization mechanism, such as locks or may be don't write at all.

WSGI in Google App Engine

WSGI was not supported in the now deprecated Python 2.5 environment, but with Python 2.7, it is the preferred way although CGI apps are possible as well. However, some of the Python 2.7 features might not work if your application is not a WSGI app. To indicate that you are using WSGI instead of CGI, you simply have to indicate your script name and the name of the WSGI application function in `app.yaml` instead of the script name alone.

So, instead of this code:

```
- url: /about
  script: main.py
```

We will follow this code:

```
- url: /about
  script: main.application
```

This way, the Google App Engine runtime environment will treat your application as a WSGI app instead of a CGI app. We already discussed about the consequences of the thread-per-request model in the previous paragraphs. In light of the same, you have to indicate to Google App Engine whether your application is thread-safe or not. That is, are you reading and writing to the global variables, data structures or lists? If you are, you should set the thread safety to `false` in `app.yaml`. With multi-threading safety flag turned off only one request will be handed over to your application instance at a time. Once you have returned a response to current request, only then will the next request be handed over to you. This way, your app will be stable, but the number of requests that are being processed in a given time frame will be reduced because only one request would be processed at a time. If you set `threadsafe` to `true`, multiple requests will be handed over concurrently to your application, which will increase the throughput. However, it is your responsibility to ensure that you are not reading or writing to the global variables, as discussed in the previous section.

If you only need to pick two things out of this whole discussion, the first one is to always use WSGI. The second is to ensure that your applications are thread-safe. And if they are not set the `threadsafe` flag to `false`.

Now, it's time to put all the theory into practice. Let's write a WSGI program that runs on Google App Engine. We will extend the program from the previous section to add the WSGI handler into it. To accomplish this, perform the following steps:

1. Copy the `cgi` application and create a new file named `wsgimain.py`. Enter the following code into it:

```
def application(environ, start_response):
    response_body = ""
    for key in environ:
       response_body += "%s: %s\n" % (key, environ[key])
    status = "200 OK"
    response_headers = [
       ('Content-Type', 'text/plain')
    ]

    start_response(status, response_headers)

    return [response_body]
```

Now, edit `app.yaml` and add the following handler to it:

```
- url: /wsgi
  script: wsgimain.application
```

2. Note that besides the name of the Python file without its extension, we have the name of the application function separated by a dot.

3. Run this application and navigate to `http://localhost:8080/cgi`. Open another window and browse `http://localhost:8080/wsgi`. Then, compare the headers that are being printed.

You can see the differences between the CGI and WSGI environments on Google App Engine.

Request handling in App Engine

Now that we know about the two modes of request handling in Google App Engine, how they work, and their respective pros and cons, it's time to divert our attention to request handlingfrom another aspect. As we discussed in the previous chapter, `app.yaml` is a manifest of your application, and it defines what your application really is. One of the major things that it defines is how your application processes URLs. There are three things that `app.yaml` defines:

*   Which URLs or URL patterns are processed?

- In what order are the URLs or URL patterns processed?
- How exactly are the URLs or URL patterns processed?

To define which URLs are processed, you can define absolute URLs that start with the / character. Alternatively, if you want some flexibility, you can use regular expressions. Regular expressions might contain regular expression groups, which can later be used in a handler description to specify the URL patterns. We will see this in an example shortly.

The next thing is, in what order will the listed URLs be processed? The answer is simple. They will be processed in the order in which they are defined. As soon as the first match is made, further matching is not performed and this process stops here. This makes it important for you to list your specific URLs (mostly, those without regular expressions are absolute ones) first and the generic ones later. Otherwise, the generic ones will match with even the specific URLs as well, and the handlers dealing with the specific URLs will never get executed. We'll examine this as well shortly.

The third thing is, what exactly responds to the listed URLs? One of the options is that the script (a Python program actually) shall respond to it

You may indicate a directory within your application and the corresponding files from that directory will be returned from there

The latter option is what we call static file serving, and we will examine it in a later section. Coming back to the first option, we again have two sub options here. Either enlist the script name with the `.py` (or `.pyc`) extension. In this case, it will be treated as a CGI program, and the request will be handed over to it in that fashion. The second option is enlisting the name of the script and the WSGI application function name that handles the requests. This way, it will be treated as a WSGI application. We have already discussed CGI, WSGI, their respective pros and cons, and how they fit into Google App Engine's request processing. So, we won't repeat ourselves here again.

So coming back to request handling, all the handlers are listed under the `handlers` section in `app.yaml`. Here's an example:

```
- handlers:
  - url: /api/.*
     - script: api.application
  - url: /(audio|video)/archive
     -script: \1_archive.application
   - url· /.*
- script: main.application
```

The first pattern will match the URLs that start with `api`. Requests matching this pattern will be handed over to the `api.py` file, where a function named `application` will be called. Just a reminder. The name of the function can be anything and does not need to be application.

Next, the URL pattern will process any URL that starts with `audio` or `video` preceded by `archive`. An important thing to note is the presence of the parenthesis around the `audio | video` portion, which forms a regular expression group . This group is being referred to as `\1` because it is the first group in the regular expression. If there were more groups , they would be addressed by their position within the regular expression. Now, this URL will be handled by `audio_archive.py` or `video_archive.py`, depending upon the matched URL. So, this is just a clever way of using regular expression groups to execute different scripts for a single URL pattern.

The next one starts with a `"."`which means any character, and is preceded by `*`, which means any number of times. This effectively means that anything and everything matches this URL pattern, which in turn calls `main.py`. This is a kind of catch-all pattern.

Now, the thing worth considering is the order of these URLs. This has some important consequences. If the last URL pattern in our example is moved to the top and made the first pattern, then the entire incoming request URLs will be checked against this pattern first. Now, because this is a catch-all pattern, it will match everything, and the search will stop right there. Eventually, the `/api` and `audio |` `video` patterns will never be matched. Thus, no one would be able to access our API because the `/api/.*` pattern will never be matched and the `audio | video` archives for the same reason.

The key take away is that the URL patterns are processed in the order they appear in `app.yaml`, and the search stops as soon as the first match is made.

Now that we understand URL processing in sufficient detail, let's create an application to put all of this together:

1. Create a directory named `handlers`, and create a Python file named `main.py` with the following contents:

```
def application(environ, start_response):
    status = "200 OK"
    response_headers = [('Content-Type', 'text/plain')]
    start_response(status, response_headers)
    return ["Everything else from %s" % __file__]
```

This response handler will handle everything else, as we will see when we put and bind all of this together with `app.yaml`. Now, simply copy the `main.py` as `api.py` and replace the last line with the following:

```
return ["%s Shall handle all API requests!" % __file__]
```

2. Next, create `audio_archive.py` and `video_archive.py`. Replace the last line of both the files with the following:

```
return ["This URL handled from %s" % __file__]
```

3. Now create `app.yaml` and enter following into that:

```
application: request-handlers
version: 1
runtime: python27
api_version: 1
threadsafe: true

handlers:
- url: /api/?.*
  script: api.application
- url: /(audio|video)/archive/?
  script: \1_archive.application
- url: .*
  script: main.application
```

This probably needs almost no explanation as we discussed about this before, but still, let's have a brief recap. All the `/api` URLs are handled by one file, `/audio/archive` and `video/archive` by two separate files, but they are listed as a single handler entry in `app.yaml`. Everything else goes to `main.py`. Because of the order in which these handlers are listed, when nothing matches from the first two handlers, it does match the third one, which acts as a catch-all pattern.

Rendering templates

We have been returning plain strings so far, and that's been handy for a while. However, things get pretty complicated if you have to return more information with a more detailed and structured page to the user. This is where this string approach gets very complicated and hard to manage.

That's where templates come into play. Just to recap, the idea of a template is to have some placeholder within the content, where the actual values will be rendered so that you can pass to them. There are many templating libraries (each have their different syntax as well at times), but one of the most widely used one is the templating language, which is used by Django, the popular web framework. It is quit intuitive and easy to understand. There's another third-party library named `jinja2` that adopts the Django template language in the form of a separate library. Google App Engine has both the Django templates and `jinja2` available. If you want to use some other templating library, you can do that too.

For the purpose of this book, we will opt `jinja2` for its simplicity, widespread usage, and the fact that it is available on Google App Engine and it does not tie us to `Django` as our dependency, which would be the case if we used the `Django` templates. If you want to use some other `templating` library, you can do that too. However, to do this, we will examine how to use external libraries in Django.

As we just mentioned, jinja2 is available on Google App Engine as a library, but if you try to import it, you will encounter an import error. To use any libraries that are shipped with Google App Engine, you have to mention them along with the required version in your `app.yaml` under the `libraries` node, which will look like this:

```
libraries:
    -name: jinja2
    -version: latest
```

From this point onwards, you will be able to use this library. One thing that is worth pointing out is that we indicated that we want to use the latest version of the library. For each library, there are a limited number of versions available to choose from, and `latest` means that we want to use the latest one. The available libraries and their versions can be seen at `https://cloud.google.com/appengine/docs/python/tools/libraries27`.

As we have indicated that we want to use the latest version, that's fine for an example. However, for something production-worthy, you are better off specifying the exact library version so that in case any breaking changes are introduced in the later version of the libraries, your code will still work.

Let's convert our environment variable-printing WSGI application to use templates. So, the first thing that you should have is an `app.yaml`, which looks like this:application: templates:

```
version: 1
runtime: python27
api_version: 1
```

```
threadsafe: true

handlers:
- url: /wsgi
  script: wsgimain.application

libraries:
  - name: jinja2
    version: latest
```

Everything is business as usual except for the fact that we indicated that we want to use the `jinja2` library's latest version. This will allow us to import `jinja2` in our code and render templates.

The next thing that you should have is HTML templates. We'll create a directory called `templates`. All of our HTML templates will be stored in it. Then, we will create a file called `index.html` inside the `templates` directory, which looks like this:

```html
<!doctype>
<html>
  <head>
    <title>GAE WSGI Headers</title>
    <style>
      body {
        font-family: Arial;
      }

    </style>
  </head>
    <body>
    <h2>Google App Engine WSGI Headers</h2>
    <p>
      Google App Engine supports WSGI for Python 2.7 runtime and
        following are the headers
      that are passed to your application from the front end web
        servers:
    </p>
    <ul>
      {% for header in wsgi_headers %}
      <li><code>{{ header }}</code>{{ wsgi_headers[header] }}</li>
      {% endfor  %}
    </ul>
    </body>
</html>
```

The important and main workhorse of the template file is highlighted. It contains a loop-like structure, which actually is a template loop. This loop actually iterates over the `wsgi_headers` variable (which will be passed to it when we will render it, as we'll see shortly), which is a dictionary. So effectively, we iterate over all the keys of the `wsgi_headers` dictionary.

Now, for each key in the dictionary, we generate a `<li>` list item with the key (using the header variable from the loop) and the corresponding value in the `wsgi_headers` dictionary. Pretty simple.

Now comes the actual code that responds to the requests and renders this template, which goes in `wsgimain.py`:

```python
import os
import jinja2

TEMPLATES_DIRECTORY =  os.path.dirname(__file__) + "/templates"
fs_loader = jinja2.FileSystemLoader(TEMPLATES_DIRECTORY)

JINJA_ENV = jinja2.Environment( loader=fs_loader)

def application(environ, start_response):

template_values = {'wsgi_headers': environ}
  template = JINJA_ENV.get_template("index.html")
  response_body = template.render(template_values)
  status = "200 OK"
  response_headers = [
      ('Content-Type', 'text/html')
  ]

  start_response(status, response_headers)

  return [response_body.encode("utf-8")]
```

Okay. There are a lot of new things here, as highlighted in the preceding code. We imported the `os` package, which is from the standard Python library. Besides this, we imported the `jinja2` library that we just configured in our `app.yaml`.

We want to calculate the full path to our `templates` directory. How are we going to do this? We will start with the full path of the current file (the `wsgmain.py`), which is defined by the `__file__` magic constant. Then, we will obtain the directory in which this file resides by calling the `os.path.dirname()` method. Once we have this, we simply append `/templates` to it, and the whole thing is assigned to the `TEMPLATES_DIRECTORY` variable. So, when everything is combined, it will look like this:

```python
TEMPLATES_DIRECTORY =  os.path.dirname(__file__) + "/templates"
```

Now, the templates can be loaded from various sources, including the filesystem or even from Python packages. However, we are only interested in reading the template files from the filesystem. So, we will create the `FileSystemLoader` instance and assign it to the `fs_loader` variable. The constructor takes one required argument, which is the directory that contains the `templates` files:

```
fs_loader = jinja2.FileSystemLoader(TEMPLATES_DIRECTORY)
```

You can read about the other types of loaders that are documented within the `jinja2` source itself by visiting https://github.com/mitsuhiko/jinja2/blob/master/jinja2/loaders.py.

Finally, we will create a `jinja2` environment. An environment is actually a collection of settings that determine things such as the location to load the templates, whether the generated content should be `autoescaped`, and many other options. So, we will create an environment that loads the templates using the `FileSystemLoader` that we created earlier:

```
JINJA_ENV = jinja2.Environment( loader=fs_loader)
```

Now, the environment is ready and we are good to go. When it comes to rendering templates, there are two steps. First, we need to get the template that we want to render. We can do this by calling the `get_template()` method of the environment instance:

```
template = JINJA_ENV.get_template("index.html")
```

Once we have the template, we can render it, which is as simple as calling the `render()` method on the `template` instance. This will return a string, and we can return this string as our response:

```
response_body = template.render()
```

However, what's the point of templates when there are no pluggable values to make them dynamic? Therefore, we can actually pass a dictionary that contains the values. Each key in the dictionary is available as a variable within `template` with the corresponding value. So, the whole thing looks like this:

```
template_values = {'wsgi_headers': environ}
template = JINJA_ENV.get_template("index.html")
response_body = template.render(template_values)
```

What we did here was pass the `environ` dictionary (which is passed to our WSGI application from the Google App Engine runtime environment) to the `index.html` template as a `wsgi_headers` variable.

Lastly, we need to return the response to the user, as follows:

```
return [response_body.encode("utf-8")]
```

Why do we have to call the `encode()` method? We have to call it because the string returned by the `render()` method is always a `unicode` string, whereas the Google App Engine runtime (actually the WSGI standard) doesn't support Unicode directly, because HTTP itself doesn't. You can read more about this issue in the WSGI specifications by visiting `https://www.python.org/dev/peps/pep-0333/#unicode-issues`.

The bottom line is that you cannot pass the Unicode strings, and only the `str` strings are accepted. So, we encoded our Unicode output into Python byte strings, or simply put, ASCII, which is also known as ISO-8859-1 encoding, where the value of each character is in the range of 0 to 255.

Run this example on your local machine like this:

```
$ /path/to/gae/sdk/dev_appserver.py /path/to/app/
```

Point your browser to `http://localhost:8080/wsgi`. It should give you the same output, but this time, in a bit more elegant appearance.

Templating is not a very vast subject. There are a handful control structures, which are semantically the same as those available in Python. Besides this, you can define blank holes within your templates that other template files can fill in, thus making composition and reusability of partial templates easy. You can read more about Jinja2 by having a look at the online documentation while we will cover the features of `Jinja2 templating` as we need them. In case you want to learn more about `jinja2`, visit `http://jinja.pocoo.org/docs/dev/`.

Serving static resources

We are making progress. From strings to templates, but still no cosmetics. Just plain HTML is what we are serving. However, to add some beautification to the pages, we will have to style it. To style the pages better, we will need style sheets, and style sheets might need images to beautify our pages This means that we have to serve static files as well.

Serving static files is pretty simple. You just need to add a handler in your `app.yaml` file as usual, but instead of the script node, you need to add a `static_dir` node, which indicates the directory in which the files that you want to serve are present. Let's modify our earlier app to serve some static files such as style sheets and images:

```
- handlers:
  - url:/assets/.*
    static_dir: assets
```

You may have already guessed that any URL that starts with `/assets` will be handled by this handler. However, instead of invoking a script, it maps itself to a directory called `assets`, which is located at the root of your application directory. You certainly can nest this directory deep below your application, but in that case, you will have to give the full relative path, such as `files/public/assets`. You definitely can name the URL anything you want. The same goes for the directory name as well.

Now, if `/assets/img.png` is the incoming URL, App Engine will look and return `assets/img.png`. If the incoming request is `/assets/css/main.css` then it will return `assets/css/main.css`. Got an idea about how it works? There are a few more things about serving static files that we must mention.

Cache, headers, and mime types

One of the things as regards serving static files is about the mime type of the returned files, as set in the HTTP headers. App Engine automatically detects the mime type of the file being returned and sets it in the HTTP headers as a `Content-Type` header. However, there might be situations where you'd like to set up the mime type yourself. In this case, your handler definition will look like this:

```
- handlers:
  - url:/assets/.*
    static_dir: assets
    mime_type: text/plain
```

Now, everything that is matched by this URL will have `text/plain` as its mime type outgoing response. However, you might want to do something more than this. The mime type is sent as the `Content-Type` header, and you might want to add further headers to the outgoing response as well. This is the job of the `http_headers` node. So, let's return some HTTP headers with our static files::

```
- handlers:
  - url:/assets/.*
    static_dir: assets
    mime_type: text/plain
    http_headers:
        X-MyHeader: header value
        X-AndFooter: HTTP has no footers
```

That's it! However, there is yet another minor thing left about caching. Your static files will be cached by intermediate servers, but you might want to indicate how long the time period is after which your files should be considered expired and a fresh copy should be obtained. That's where the expiration directive comes in. You can specify the expiration as a string that indicates various units (d for days, h for hours, m for minutes, and s for seconds), which are separated by spaces. Let's say that you have something like this:

```
- handlers:
  - url:/assets/.*
    static_dir: assets
    expiration: 10d 20h 10m 5s
```

This sets the expiration of the files returned by this static directory handler to 10 days, 20 hours, 10 minutes, and 5 seconds. So, this means that this file will be cached and a new copy of the file will only be requested after this time, which is 10 days, 20 hours roughly.

There are two important points about expiration. One is that you might want to set the expiration for every file and every response from all the handler to some specific interval. That is to say, you can set the expiration time for the whole application. To do this, use the `default_expiration` directive at the top level in `app.yaml`, as follows:

```
application: mypp
version: beta
runtime: python27
api_version: 1
default_expiration: 1d 25h
```

The other point about expiration is that if you set the expiration value to something large, such as 5 days, any intermediate servers that may exist will cache this file. This file will be returned for the next five days after it is first accessed. Now, if you change the file in your application, your users will continue receiving the old file even if they clear their browser caches because they will receive the same copy from the intermediate caching servers, and there's no way to clear those cache. Therefore, if you expect some file to be changed, set the expiration time to something such as 1 hour. If you don't specify any expiration, the default expiration time on Google App Engine is ten minutes.

There is one last point that you should note. The directory containing the static files that you indicate in your `app.yaml` URL handlers is not readable by the application code. These directories are actually bundled and served by the Google CDNs, which is more efficient because of the fact that your application code is never invoked. Hence, no CPU cycles are wasted and there is no CPU billing for serving that static content except for the bandwidth that is utilized to serve these static files. However, a situation might arise where you want to both serve these files from this directory and be able to read these files as well. That's simple. Just set `application_readable` to `true` in the handler definition, and these files will be readable from within your application code. However, still you can't write to them. If you want to know more about various configuration options, you can explore the documentation by visiting `https://cloud.google.com/appengine/docs/python/config/appconfig`.

Serving files

Previously, we just mapped a URL pattern to a whole directory, but you might want to serve only individual files instead. That's possible too. The process of serving individual files works in three parts:

- The first is the URL pattern just as we saw in the previous section
- Second, instead of using `static_dir`, we use the `static_files` node, which defines the files that need to be served by using a regular expression
- The third one is of course the files that you want to be served

Consider a situation where all your images, style sheets, and JavaScript files are in the same directory. Let's look at an example:

```
handlers:
  -url: /images/(.*\.(gif|png|jpg))$
   static_files: static/\1
   upload: static/.*\.(gif|png|jpg)$
```

Now, this will match any URL starting with /images and an image file name. Next, we tell App Engine that the static files are to be served using static_files directive. Because we used a regular expression group to match the file name, we refer to the same matched file name with \1. So, if the incoming request was /images/banner.png, the static file will be static/banner.png. This alone is not enough, because App Engine doesn't know which files need to be uploaded from the static directory. So, with the upload node, we tell that any files that match the image file pattern should be uploaded. That's it! All the other options such as expiration, http headers, and the mime type are applicable to static_files as well.

Using web frameworks

Until now, we have been writing either plain CGI programs, or WSGI handlers that we map in our application manifest file by using regular expressions. This approach of course works, but it is not scalable for even small projects with few pages to be served. This is where we need to grow beyond this and use web frameworks. We have a lot of variety in Python web frameworks, and everyone has their own favorite list of frameworks. App Engine has built-in frameworks that are a part of the App Engine libraries that are available within the runtime environment. However, these might not be the frameworks that you prefer to work with. You might want to use your own favorite web frameworks. Fortunately, that's possible and easy too. We shall review both using built-in frameworks or rolling in your own favorite in the following sections.

Built-in frameworks

There are a couple of web frameworks that come with Google App Engine. The first one is Django, and the second one is webapp2. We will demonstrate how use the webapp2 and explore it further as and when required. To use webapp2, you have to list it under the libraries section of your app.yaml.

The name webapp2 might suggest that there may be something called webapp1 as well. Well, there's no such thing as webapp1. However, there's something called webapp that used to exist since the introduction of the Python 2.5 runtime. The webapp2 is just webapp rewritten with the same API to a point where if you just replace the import statement of webapp with that of webapp2, everything will work just fine.

The webapp2 (or its earlier version) is inspired by the `web.py` micro framework, which has a very simple, elegant way of dealing with requests. Every URL that needs to be handled is defined as a regular expression and mapped to a simple plain Python class (not inherited from anywhere except the object itself). For each HTTP method that needs to be handled (such as GET, PUT, POST, and DELETE), a method of the same name of the HTTP method is defined.

Let's revise our `hello world` example with `webapp2`:

1. Create a directory named `hellowebapp` with `app.yaml` with the following contents in it:

```
application: hellowebapp
version: 1
runtime: python27
api_version: 1
threadsafe: true

handlers:
- url: .*
  script: main.application
libraries:
    -name: webapp2
     version: latest
```

2. Next, create another file that will actually handle requests. Create a file named `main.py` with the following contents:

```
import webapp2
class MainPage(webapp2.RequestHandler):

    def get(self):
       self.response.headers['Content-Type'] = 'text/plain'
       self.response.write('Hello from webapp2!')
application = webapp2.WSGIApplication([
    ('/', MainPage),
], debug=True)
```

Now, that's a lot of new code all of sudden. It's quite different from what we have been doing in the CGI/WSGI stuff. Let's explore it bit by bit. If we look at it, there are three main parts. The first one imports the webapp2 framework, the second is a class definition, and the third one that is next to it is a function call with some arguments, whose return value is being assigned to a variable named `application`.

Let's start with the last piece, which is a function call. The main purpose of this function is to return a WSGI function that is similar to the one that we have been writing in all of our examples. We assigned it to a variable named `application`, whereas this variable used to be a function in our pure WSGI examples. The input to the `webapp2.WSGIApplication` function is a list of mappings from the URL patterns to the classes that handle them. So here, we passed a list of tuples, where each tuple's first member is a regular expression (representing a URL pattern), and the second member is a class that will handle the incoming requests for that particular URL pattern.

We are done with understanding two parts of the code including the simple import. Now, let's focus on the class definition. The responsibility of this class is to handle all requests for the URL pattern that it is mapped to, and this includes responding to all the HTTP methods that you want to respond to. We only wanted to respond to HTTP GET. So, we defined a method named `get` (the same name as that of the HTTP method that we wanted to handle). Now, this class, when instantiated by `webapp2`, comes with request and response objects. So, we can access them and make use of them. The response method comes with a dictionary called **headers**, which are just key value pairs and represents the response headers that you want to send to the client. We just want to tell them (the clients) that the content is plain text. So, that's what we have done there. The other thing that we want to do is of course write something to the clients. So, we called the `write` method on the `response` object to do just that.

So, that's all that you need to know about webapp2 right now. A more detailed elaboration will turn this discussion into a `webapp2` tutorial, which is something that we don't want here, as our main subject and quest here is to master Google App Engine. We will explore more features of this framework along the way as and when the need arises.

Using external frameworks

You are not restricted to the aforementioned frameworks; you can choose one of your own favorite ones. Using an external framework is quite simple. If it is a single-file framework such as Bottle or present within a single package such as `web.py`, you can simply copy the file or directory at the root of your application. Because the root of your application is on PYTHONPATH (the list of paths on which the Python interpreter will look for modules whenever it encounters an import statement), importing your framework will work flawlessly.

However, this is a poor man's approach towards the problem and might break down soon, mostly when the framework itself depends on many other external Python libraries that are not available on Google App Engine. Just a gentle reminder; your framework must be in pure Python code, and if it has any external dependencies, then they must be pure Python. In case they are not, they must be available on Google App Engine. Fortunately, most web frameworks are in pure Python, and most of the times, their external dependencies are also pure Python, besides the Python standard library.

Coming back to the task of using an external framework of your choice, let's visit the theory first. Because your framework might have other dependences as well, it may get very tedious and error-prone to collect and place all of them in your application. A better way would be to use something that can do this for you automatically. Fortunately, you have Python's package manger at your disposal also known as pip. You can put the required Python packages in a text file and hand over this text file to pip. It will ensure that every enlisted package and its dependencies are installed.

However, here's the catch—all the installed packages and libraries will go to your system's Python directory. When you upload your application, they won't be deployed with it, because they are not a part of your application directory. In order to fix this, we can create a directory within our app (named lib, for instance) and tell pip to install everything within this directory. Thus, when you deploy your application, all the required libraries and packages will be deployed too.

Now, one last bit to this problem. All our desired libraries and packages are surely in the directory (lib, in our case) that we opted for, but yet, although the App Engine runtime's Python interpreter takes our application's root directory on the Python path, the lib directory is not there. Eventually, any imports that you perform in your code and which are supposed to come from the lib directory will fail. To fix this, we will create a file named app_config.py in our application's root directory. This file will import our modules, and from that point onwards, they will be made available to us. That's it!

Using Bottle

We will show how to use the Bottle framework with Google App Engine. The instructions here are generic enough and will work for any other Python framework or library as long as it, along with its dependencies, all are pure Python. In case the dependencies require native extensions, they are available on Google App Engine. Usually, almost all the major web frameworks will work fine. Now, let's get started:

1. Create a directory named `bframework`. Now, first things first, we need to install the Bottle framework.

2. Create a directory named `libs`. This will contain all of our libraries.

3. Create a file named `requirments.txt` with the following contents:

    ```
    bottle=0.11.6
    ```

4. Now, install Bottle with the help of the following command:

    ```
    $ pip install -r requirements.txt -t lib/
    ```

5. This will install the Bottle framework and all of its dependencies in the `lib` folder. Now, let's create `app.yaml` and `main.py`, which will be the only Python handlers that handle everything. Here's your `app.yaml`:

    ```
    application: bframework
    version: 1
    runtime: python27
    api_version: 1
    threadsafe: yes


    - url: .*  # This regex directs all routes to main.bottle
      script: main.bottle
    ```

6. Now that we have installed Bottle and have `app.yaml` in place, the next thing that we need is the actual file containing code that will handle the incoming requests. For this, create a file named `main.py` with the following contents:

    ```
    from bottle import Bottle
    # Create the Bottle WSGI application.
    bottle = Bottle()
    # Note: We don't need to call run() since our application is embedded within
    # the App Engine WSGI application server.
    ```

```
# Define an handler for the root URL of our application.
@bottle.route('/')
def hello():
    """Returns a simple response."""
    return 'Hello App Engine from Bottle!'

# Define an handler for 404 errors.
@bottle.error(404)
def error_404(error):
    """Return a custom 404 error."""
    return 'Sorry, Wrong number!'
```

7. Now, all the pieces are in place except for the fact that Google App Engine does not know yet that lib contains libraries that we want to use. We will amend sys.path to do this. To amend sys.path, create another file named appengine_config.py, which has the following contents:

```
import sys
import os
libraries = os.path.join(os.path.dirname(__file__),
'lib')sys.path.append(libraries).
```

Alternatively, you can use the following code instead of manipulating sys.path yourself:

```
from google.appengine.ext import vendor
# Add the lib directory to import path
vendor.add('lib')
```

8. The appengine_config.py is executed at the start, and the initialization of your instance prior to any request handler code gets executed. Here, we are actually taking advantage of this fact and adding the lib directory to sys.path so that the imports, if any do exist, work properly. We have already discussed this in detail. Now, run the application:

```
~/sdks/google_appengine/dev_appserver ./bframework
```

9. Now, navigate to http:localhost:8080. You should be able to see a greeting message.

Although we demonstrated Bottle, the same instructions are what you should use to deploy any other Python web framework on Google App Engine.

Summary

In this chapter, we examined the problem of web pages with dynamic content and its solution. We took an in-depth look at the CGI standard. We examined how web servers pass information through `stdin` and environment variables to an external program and how the output from a program on `stdout` is collected and sent back to clients. We also learned that CGI is available in Google App Engine. Then, we examined the problems with CGI, with the biggest problem being that it spawns a process for every request, which is quite expensive in terms of time. We looked at the possible solutions and WSGI in particular, which is Python's standard way of interfacing with web servers. We examined how concurrent requests can be processed in WSGI and the implications that it has on our code.

Next, we turned our attention to Google App Engine's URL handling and examined how we can direct different URL patterns to different scripts. We looked at how we can render templates by filling in values so that we don't have to hard-code the strings within our code. We also looked at how we can serve static files and resources without actually executing any Python code on our behalf. After this, we looked at how to write maintainable and readable programs by using the built-in webapp2 framework.

Finally, we wrapped up the chapter by examining how we can use external web frameworks. We used Bottle to write a hello world program. This concluded our tour of the web layer of Google App Engine and the problems associated with it.

Now, it's time to shift our attention to storing something. We will examine Google's NoSQL solution called **datastore** in the next few chapters.

3

Understanding the Datastore

Learning is hard, but unlearning something is even harder. The main reason why learning something hard is not because it is hard in and of itself, but for the fact that most of the time, you have to unlearn a lot in order to learn a little. This is quite true for the datastore. Basically, it is built to scale to the so-called **Google scale**. That's why, in order to be proficient with it, you will have to unlearn some of the things that you know. Your learning as a computer science student or a programmer has been deeply enriched by the relational model so much that it is natural to you. Anything else may seem quite hard to grasp, and this is the reason why learning Google datastore is quite hard.

However, if this were the only glitch in all that, things would have been way simpler because you could ask yourself to forget the relational world and consider the new paradigm afresh. Things have been complicated due to Google's own official documentation where it presents the datastore in such a manner that it seems closer to something like Django's ORM, Rails ActiveRecord or SQLAlchemy. And then all of a sudden, the official documentation starts to enlist limitations of the Google datastore with a very brief mention or at times, no mention at all of why the limitations exist.

Since the official documentation tells you only about the limitations but not why the limitations are there in the first place, a lack of this explanation results in you being unable to work around those limitations or mold the problem space into the new solution space, which is Google datastore.

We will try to fix it in this chapter. The following are the learning objectives for us in this chapter:

- To understand the underlying BigTable and its data model on which datastore is built.

- To have a look at the physical data storage in BigTable and the operations that are available.

- To understand how BigTable scales.
- To understand datastore and the way it models data on top of BigTable.

So there's lot to explore. Let's get started.

The BigTable

If you decided to download every web page hosted on the planet, store a copy of it and later process every page to extract data from it, you'll find that your own laptop or desktop is not up to the task. It has barely enough storage to store every page. Usually, laptops these days come with 1 TB hard disk drives, and this seems to be quite enough for someone not much into video content such as movies.

Assuming that there are 2 billion websites, each with an average of 50 pages and each page around 250 KB in size, it sums up to around 23,000+ TB (or roughly 22 petabytes) which would need 23,000 such laptops to store all the web pages with a 1 TB hard drive in each.

Assuming the same statistics, if you are able to download at a whopping speed of 100 MBps, it would take you about 7 years to download the whole content to one such gigantic hard drive if you had one in your laptop.

Let's suppose that you somehow downloaded all the content in whatever time it took to do so and stored it as well. Now you need to analyze and process it too. If processing takes about 50 milliseconds per page, it would take about two months to process the entire data that you downloaded. The world would have changed a lot by then already, leaving your data and processed results obsolete, not to mention that many of those downloaded pages would already have been updated at their respective websites.

This is the kind of scale for which BigTable is built. Every Google product that you see – Search, Analytics, Finance, Gmail, Docs, Drive and Google Maps – is built on top of BigTable. If you want to read more about BigTable, you can go through the academic paper from Google Research, which is available at `http://static. googleusercontent.com/media/research.google.com/en//archive/bigtable-osdi06.pdf`.

The data model

Let's examine the data model of BigTable at a logical level. BigTable is basically a key-value store. So, everything that you store falls under a unique key, just like PHP's arrays, Ruby's hash, or Python's `dict`:

```
# PHP
$person['name'] = 'Mohsin';
# Ruby or Python
person['name'] = 'Mohsin'
```

However, this is a partial picture. We will learn the details gradually in a while, but you can just think of this as a key-value data structure, as shown in the code snippet. So let's understand this step by step.

Just like you can have multiple dictionaries in Python, a BigTable installation can have multiple tables. No matter how many dictionaries you have in Python, all store key-value pairs. You can group the relevant key-value pairs in separate dictionaries like the following two dictionaries:

```
heights = {'peter': 5.8, 'david': 6.1}
marks = {'peter': 18, 'david': 70}
```

As you can see, `heights` and `marks` are two different dictionaries. That's exactly what BigTable tables are—Big dictionaries. They are independent of each other.

If you would still like to get some analogy from the RDBMS world, this is just like MySQL database, which can have multiple tables. The difference here is that a MySQL installation might have multiple databases, which in turn might have multiple tables. However, in case of BigTable, the first major storage unit is a table.

Each BigTable table can have hundreds of columns, which can be divided into groups called column families. You can define column families at the time of creating a table. They cannot be altered later, but each column family might have hundreds of columns that you can define even after the creation of the table. The notation that is used to address a column and its column families is like `job:title`, where `job` is a column family and `title` is the column. So here, you have a `job` column family that stores all the information about the job of the user, and `title` is supposed to store the job title. However, one of the important facts about these columns is that there's no concept of datatypes in BigTable as you'd encounter in other relational database systems. Everything is just an uninterpreted sequence of bytes, which means nothing to BigTable. What they really mean is just up to you. It might be a very long integer, a string or JSON-encoded data.

To summarize what we know about BigTable so far:

- You can have many separate tables.
- Each table can have column families that can be defined at the time of creating the table.
- Each column family can have hundreds of columns that can be removed or added later on.
- The contents of the column are an uninterpreted string of bytes. So, there's no concept of datatypes.

Now, let's turn our attention to the rows. There are two major characteristics of the rows that we are concerned about. First, each row has a key, which must be unique. The contents of the key again consist of an uninterpreted string of bytes that is up to 64 KB in size. A key can be anything that you want it to be. All that's required is that it must be unique within the table and in case it is not, you will be actually replacing the contents of the existing row with the same key.

Which key should you use for a row in your table? That's the question that requires some consideration. To answer this, you need to understand how the data is actually stored. Till then, you can assume that each key has to be a unique string of bytes within the scope of a table and should be up to 64 KB in length.

Now that we know about tables, column families, columns, rows, and row keys, let's look at an example of BigTable that stores 'employees' information. Let's pretend that we are creating something similar to LinkedIn here. So here's the table:

	Personal		**Professional**	
Key (name)	`personal:lastname`	`personal:age`	`professional:company`	`professional:designation`
Mohsin	Hijazee	29	Sony	Senior Designer
Peter	Smith	34	Panasonic	General Manager
Kim	Yong	32	Sony	Director
Ricky	Martin	45	Panasonic	CTO
Paul	Jefferson	39	LG	Sales Head

So that is a sample BigTable. The first column is the name, and we have chosen it as a key. It is of course not a good key, because the first name might not necessarily be unique, even in small groups, let alone in millions of records. However, for the sake of this example, we will assume that the name is unique. Another reason behind assuming the name's uniqueness is that we want to increase our understanding gradually. The key point here is that we have picked the first name as the row's key for now, but we will improve on this as we learn more.

Next, we have two column groups. The `personal` column group holds all the personal attributes of the employees, and the other column family named `professional` has all the other attributes pertaining to the professional aspects. When referring to a column within a family, the notation is `family:column`. So `personal:age` contains the age of the employees.

If you look at `professional:designation` and `personal:age`, it seems that the first one's contents are strings, while the second one stores integers. That's false. No column stores anything but just plain bytes without any distinction of what they mean. The meaning and interpretation of these bytes is up to the user of the data. From BigTable's point of view, each column just contains plain old bytes. Another thing that is drastically different from RDBMS' such as MySQL, is that each row need not have the same number of columns. Each row can adopt whatever layout it seems fit. So, the second row's `personal` column family can have two more columns that store gender and nationality.

For this particular example, the data is in no particular order, and I wrote it down as it came to my mind. Hence, there's no order of any sort in the data at all. The order of the rows is a very critical and a rather defining element of BigTable, and we'll examine it later.

To summarize, BigTable is a key-value store where keys should be unique and have a length that is less than or equal to 64 KB. The columns are divided into column families, which can be created at the time of defining the table, but each column family might have hundreds of columns created as and when needed. Also, content has no data type and comprises of just plain old bytes.

There's one minor detail left which is not important to us but for the sake of completeness, we will mention it here. Each value of the column is stored with a timestamp that is accurate to microseconds and in this way, multiple versions of a column value are available. The number of last versions that should be kept is something that is configurable at the table level, but since we are not going to deal with BigTable directly, this detail is not important to us.

How is data stored?

Now that we know about row keys, column families and columns, we will gradually move towards examining this data model in more detail and understand how the data is actually stored. We will examine the logical storage and then dive into the actual structure, as it ends up on the disk.

The data that we presented in the earlier table had no order and was listed as it came to my mind. However, while storing, the data is always sorted by the row key. So now, the data will actually be stored like this:

	Personal		professional	
Key(name)	personal:lastname	personal:age	professional:company	professional:designation
Kim	Yong	32	Sony	Director
Mohsin	Hijazee	29	Sony	Senior Designer
Paul	Jefferson	39	LG	Sales Head
Peter	Smith	34	Panasonic	General Manager
Ricky	Martin	45	Panasonic	CTO

OK, so what happened here? The name column indicates the key of the table and now, the whole table is sorted by the key. That's exactly how it is stored on the disk as well. An important thing about sorting: it is lexicographic sorting and not semantic sorting. By lexicographic, we mean that they are sorted by the byte value and not by textness or semantics. This matters because even within the Latin character set, different languages have different sort orders for letters, such as letters in English versus German and French. So in this lexicographic sort, all of this and the Unicode collation order isn't valid and it is just sorted by the byte values. In our instance, since K has a smaller byte value (because K has a lower ASCII/Unicode value) than letter M, it comes first. Now, suppose that some European language considers and sorts M before K. That's not how the data would be laid out here, because it is a plain, blind, and simple sort by byte value. So, the moral of the story is that the data is sorted by the byte value, with no consideration to the semantic value. In fact, for BigTable, this is not even text. It's just a plain string of bytes.

Just a hint. This order of keys is something that we will exploit when modeling data. How? We'll see later.

The physical storage

Now that we understand the logical data model and how it is organized, it is time to take a closer look at how this data is actually stored on the disk. On a physical disk, the stored data is also sorted by the key. So, first key in order is followed by its respective value, next key in order is followed by its respective value, and so on. At the end of the file, there's a sorted list of just the keys and their offset in the file from the start, which is something like the block to the left in the diagram:

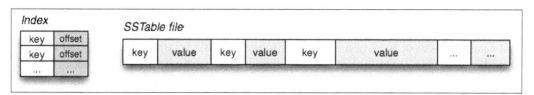

Key values: physical storage on disk

Ignore the block on your left that is labeled Index. We will come back to it in a while. This particular format actually has a name **SSTable (Sorted String Table)** because it has strings (the keys) and they are sorted. It is of course tabular data and hence the name.

Whenever your data is sorted, you have certain advantages. The first and foremost advantage is that when you look up an item or a range of items, your dataset is already sorted by the key. We will discuss this in detail later in this chapter. Now, if we start from the beginning of the file and read sequentially, noting down every key and its offset in a format `key:offset`, we have effectively created an index of the whole file in a single scan. That's where the first block to your left in the preceding diagram comes from. So, rephrasing it, since the keys are sorted in the file, we simply read it sequentially till the end of the file, effectively creating an index of the data. Furthermore, since this index only contains keys and their offsets in the file, it is much smaller in terms of the space it occupies.

Now, assuming that SSTable has a table that is, say, 500 MB in size, we only need to load the index from the end of the file and not the whole table into the memory, and whenever we are asked for a key or a range of keys, we just search within the memory index, not touching the disk at all. If we find the data, only then do we seek the disk at the given offset because we know the offset of that particular key from the index that we already loaded in the memory.

Some limitations

Pretty smart, neat, and elegant, you would say! Yes it is. However, there's a catch. If you want to create a new row, key must come in a sorted order. This means that even if you are sure about where exactly this key should be placed in the file to avoid the need to sort the data, you still need to rewrite the whole file in a new, sorted order along with the index. Hence, large amount of I/O is required for just a single row insertion.

The same goes for deleting a row because now, the file should be sorted and rewritten again. Updates are OK as long as the key itself is not altered because, in that case, it is sort of having a new key altogether. This is because a modified key would have a different place in the sorted order depending on what the modified key actually is. Hence, the whole file would be rewritten. Just as an example, say you have a row with the key **all-boys**, and then you change the key of that row to **x-rays-of-zebra**. Now, you will see that after the new modification, the row will end up at nearly the end of the file, whereas previously, it was probably at the beginning of the file because **all-boys** comes before **x-rays-of-zebra** when sorted.

This seems pretty limiting, and it looks like inserting or removing a key is quite expensive. However, this is not the case, as we will see later.

Random writes and deletion

So, how does writing or deleting a row work given our description of the problem in the previous section? We need to understand this before we examine the operations that are available on a BigTable. We would like to examine how random writes and the deletion of rows are handled because that seems quite expensive, as we just discussed in the previous section.

The idea is very simple. All the read, writes, and removals don't go straight to the disk. Instead, the whole index section of the on-disk SSTable is loaded into the memory. This means that now, if we have to look up a row, we don't have to seek the disk. The whole information of what row is located at what offset in the file is in the memory. So, we can quickly look up the desired information, as we will see shortly.

An empty in-memory SSTable is created, which is blank, along with its in memory index, which is also blank. We will call this in-memory SSTable as *MemTable* to emphasize the fact that it is an in-memory SSTable. Do not get confused with the nomenclature; MemTable is just another ordinary SSTable with an index except for the fact that both the table and index are in the memory.

Now this is how the read, write, delete, and update operations work:

- To read a row, we first check the index of the MemTable and return the row if it is found there. If the row is not found in MemTable, we check the in-memory index that we loaded earlier to check the offset of the desired row in the file on disk, read that row, and return it. Besides returning the row, this row is also placed in MemTable along with its index.

- To write a row, we simply write it to MemTable, and its entry is placed along with its key and offset in the in-memory index of the MemTable. But all the rows should be in the sorted order. So, what about that? The newly created row is inserted in MemTable and sorted only within the scope of MemTable and not the bigger portion of the on-disk SSTable. This might seem odd, as the newly created row might need to go to the end of the SSTable based on the sort order, and we're only placing it within MemTable's sort scope. We'll see how this is fixed.

- In case of an update, if the row is in MemTable, it will be changed. Otherwise, it will be loaded from the on-disk SSTable and changed after being placed in MemTable. Next time, when asked for this row, the newly updated entry will be found in the MemTable and returned even though the on-disk SSTable will contain the older version of the row.

- To delete a row, the row is simply marked as deleted in the MemTable. If it is not in MemTable, it is loaded from the on-disk SSTable file and placed in MemTable along with being marked for deletion. Now, the next time we are asked to read the deleted row, we'll know that it is deleted from the MemTable index even though it is still in the on-disk SSTable.

Now, when , the size of the MemTable grows up to a certain size, and it is written to the disk as a new SSTable. Since the time consumed by this write operation only depends on the size of the MemTable and of course happens much infrequently, it is much faster. Each time the MemTable grows beyond a configured size, it is flushed to the disk as a new SSTable. However, the index of each newly flushed SSTable is still kept in the memory so that we can quickly check the incoming read requests and locate it in any table without touching the disk.

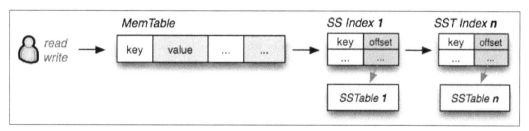

MemTable being written on disk as SSTable after it grows beyond a certain time.

Finally, when the number of on-disk SSTables reaches a certain count, the SSTables are merged and collapsed into a single SSTable. Since each SSTable is just an already sorted set of keys, a merge sort is applied. This merging process is quite fast, and this is the point where the sort order problem that we mentioned while talking about new row writes gets fixed, as now, the sort happens on the whole set of data and not just in the context of MemTable.

If you have got an intuitive idea of how the data is sorted by row keys, the index of the whole file is at the end of the file, the read, write operations happen only on the in-memory data, the in-memory set is flushed to disk, and the chunks of flushed in-memory data are merged together, then congratulations! You've just learned the most atomic storage unit in BigData solutions such as BigTable, Hbase, Hypertable, Cassandara, and LevelDB. That's how they actually store and process the data.

Now that we know how a big table is actually stored on the disk and how the read and writes are handled, it's time to take a closer look at the available operations.

Operations on BigTable

Until this point, we know that a BigTable table is a collection of rows that have unique keys up to 64 KB in length and the data is stored according to the lexicographic sort order of the keys. We also examined how it is laid out on the disk and how read, writes, and removals are handled. Now, the question is, what operations are available on this data? So the answer is that following are the operations that are available to us:

- Fetching a row by using its key
- Inserting a new key
- Deleting a row
- Updating a row
- Reading a range of rows from the starting row key to the ending row key

Reading

Now, the first operation is pretty simple. You have a key, and you want the associated row. Since the whole data set is sorted by the key, all we need to do is perform a binary search on it, and you'll be able to locate your desired row within a few lookups, even within a set of a million rows. In practice, the index at the end of the SSTable is loaded in the memory, and the binary search is actually performed on it. If we take a closer look at this operation in light of what we know from the previous section, the index is already in the memory of the MemTable that we saw in the previous section. In case there are multiple SSTables because MemTable was flushed many times to the disk as it grew too large, all the indexes of all the SSTables are present in the memory, and a quick binary search is performed on them.

Writing

The second operation that is available to us is the ability to insert a new row. So, we have a key and the values that we want to insert in the table. According to our new knowledge about physical storage and SSTables, we can understand this very well. The write directly takes place on the in-memory MemTable and its index is updated, which is also in the memory. Since no disk access is required to write the row as we are writing in memory, the whole file doesn't have to be rewritten on disk, because yet again, all of it is in the memory. This operation is very fast and almost instantaneous. However, if the MemTable grows in size, it will be flushed to the disk as a new SSTable along with the index while retaining a copy of its index in the memory. Finally, we also saw that when the number of SSTables reaches a certain number, they are merged and collapsed to form a new, bigger table.

Deleting

It seems that since all the keys are in sorted order on the disk and deleting a key would mean disrupting the sort order, a rewrite of the whole file would be a big I/O overhead. However, it is not, as it can be handled smartly. Since all the indexes, including the MemTable and the tables that were the result of flushing a larger MemTable to the disk, are already in the memory, deleting a row only requires us to find the required key in the in-memory indexes and mark it as deleted.

Now, whenever someone tries to read the row, the in-memory indexes will be checked, and although an entry will be there, it will be marked as deleted and won't be returned. When MemTable is being flushed to the disk or multiple tables are being collapsed, this key and the associated row will be excluded in the write process. And after that, they are totally gone from the storage.

Updating

Updating a row is no different but it has two cases. The first case is in which not only the values, but also the key is modified. In this case, it is like removing the row with an old key and inserting a row with a new key. We already have seen both of these cases in detail. So, the operation should be obvious.

However, the case where only the values are modified is even simpler. We only have to locate the row from the indexes, load it in the memory if it is not already there, and modify. That's all. Next time, when MemTable is flushed to the disk and other SSTables are merged, it will end up on the disk as well.

Scanning a range

This last operation is quite interesting. You can scan a range of keys from a starting key to an ending key. For instance, you can return all the rows that have a key greater than or equal to `key1` and less than or equal to `key2`, effectively forming a range. Since the look up of a single key is a fast operation, we only have to locate the first key of the range. Then, we start reading the consecutive keys one after the other till we encounter a key that is greater than `key2`, at which point, we will stop scanning and the keys that we scanned so far are our query's result. This is how it looks:

Name	Department	Company
Chris Harris	Research & Development	Google
Christopher Graham	Research & Development	LG
Debra Lee	Accounting	Sony
Ernest Morrison	Accounting	Apple
Fred Black	Research & Development	Sony
Janice Young	Research & Development	Google
Jennifer Sims	Research & Development	Panasonic
Joyce Garrett	Human Resources	Apple
Joyce Robinson	Research & Development	Apple
Judy Bishop	Human Resources	Google
Kathryn Crawford	Human Resources	Google
Kelly Bailey	Research & Development	LG
Lori Tucker	Human Resources	Sony
Nancy Campbell	Accounting	Sony
Nicole Martinez	Research & Development	LG
Norma Miller	Human Resources	Sony
Patrick Ward	Research & Development	Sony
Paula Harvey	Research & Development	LG
Stephanie Chavez	Accounting	Sony
Stephanie Mccoy	Human Resources	Panasonic

A BigTable example: Employees, departments and company.

In the preceding table, we start with the range where starting key will be greater than or equal to `Ernest` and the ending key will be less than or equal to `Kathryn`. So, we locate the first key that is greater than or equal to `Ernest`, which happens to be `Ernest Morrison`. Then, we start scanning further, picking and returning each key as long as it is less than or equal to `Kathryn`. When we reach `Judy`, it is less than or equal to `Kathryn`, but `Kathryn` isn't. So, this row is not returned. However, the rows before this are returned. So, that is the scan operation available to us on BigTable. Pretty simple! Let's move on to further discuss what the keys should be so that we can have an advantage while scanning our data.

Selecting a key

Now that we have examined the data model and the storage layout, we are in a better position to talk about the key selection for a table. As we know that the stored data is sorted by the key, it does not impact the writing, deleting, and updating to fetch a single row. However, the operation that is impacted by the key is that of scanning a range.

The rule of thumb for key selection is that you should select such a row key that puts your data closer when sorted so that the scan operations are possible to iterate over large batches of your data.

Let's think about the previous table again and assume that this table is a part of some system that processes payrolls for companies and the companies pay us for the task of processing their payroll. Now, let's suppose that Sony asks us to process their data and generate a payroll for them. Right now, we cannot do anything of this kind. We can just make our program scan the whole table, and hence all the records (which might be in millions), and only pick the records where `job:company` has the value of **Sony**. This would be inefficient.

Instead, what we can do is put this sorted nature of row keys to our use. Select the company name as the key and concatenate the designation and name along with it. So, the new table with the new key will look like this:

Key	Name	Department	Company
Apple-Accounting-Ernest Morrison	Ernest Morrison	Accounting	Apple
Apple-Human Resources-Joyce Garrett	Joyce Garrett	Human Resources	Apple
Apple-Research & Development-Joyce Robinson	Joyce Robinson	Research & Development	Apple
Google-Human Resources-Judy Bishop	Chris Harris	Research & Development	Google
Google-Human Resources-Kathryn Crawford	Janice Young	Research & Development	Google
Google-Research & Development-Chris Harris	Judy Bishop	Human Resources	Google
Google-Research & Development-Janice Young	Kathryn Crawford	Human Resources	Google
LG-Research & Development-Christopher Graham	Christopher Graham	Research & Development	LG
LG-Research & Development-Kelly Bailey	Kelly Bailey	Research & Development	LG
LG-Research & Development-Nicole Martinez	Nicole Martinez	Research & Development	LG
LG-Research & Development-Paula Harvey	Paula Harvey	Research & Development	LG
Panasonic-Human Resources-Stephanie Mccoy	Jennifer Sims	Research & Development	Panasonic
Panasonic-Research & Development-Jennifer Sims	Stephanie Mccoy	Human Resources	Panasonic
Sony-Accounting-Debra Lee	Debra Lee	Accounting	Sony
Sony-Accounting-Nancy Campbell	Fred Black	Research & Development	Sony
Sony-Accounting-Stephanie Chavez	Lori Tucker	Human Resources	Sony
Sony-Human Resources-Lori Tucker	Nancy Campbell	Accounting	Sony
Sony-Human Resources-Norma Miller	Norma Miller	Human Resources	Sony

Key	Name	Department	Company
Sony-Research & Development-Fred Black	Patrick Ward	Research & Development	Sony
Sony-Research & Development-Patrick Ward	Stephanie Chavez	Accounting	Sony

All else is the same; it is just that we have a new format for the row key. We just welded the `company`, `department`, and `name` as the key and as the table will always be sorted by the key, that's what it looks like, as shown in the preceding table. Now, suppose that we receive a request from Google to process their data. All we have to do is perform a scan, starting from the key greater than or equal to `Google` and less then `L` because that's the next letter. This scan is highlighted in the previous table.

Now, the next request is more specific. Sony asks us to process their data, but only for their accounting department. How do we do that? Quite simple! In this case, our starting key will be greater than or equal to `Sony-Accounting`, and the ending key can be `Sony-Accountinga`, where **a** is appended to indicate the end key in the range. The scanned range and the returned rows are highlighted in the previous table.

BigTable – a hands-on approach

Okay, enough of the theory. It is now time to take a break and perform some hands-on experimentation. By now, we know 80 percent of what BigTable is and the other remaining 20 percent is all about scaling it to more than one machine. Our current discussion only assumed and focused on a single machine environment, and we assumed that the BigTable table is on our laptop and that's all to it.

You might really want to experiment with what you learned. Fortunately, that's very easy as all these ideas are available as a standalone C++ library called LevelDB that has many bindings, including Ruby and Python.

You can find the source for LevelDB at `https://github.com/google/leveldb` and one of the useful Python bindings at `https://plyvel.readthedocs.org/en/latest/user.html`. Install this on your local system and you can experiment with a key-value store with sorted keys based on exactly the same ideas that we explored in the previous sections.

We'll not show you how to install LevelDB and its Python binding and how to play with its API, as that's not our main focus. We will leave this exercise for the curious souls out there to experiment with on their own.

We will next examine how BigTable can be scaled to store petabytes of data and serve millions of users.

Scaling BigTable to BigData

By now, you have probably understood the data model of BigTable, how it is laid out on the disk, and the advantages it offers. To recap once again, the BigTable installation may have many tables, each table may have many column families that are defined at the time of creating the table, and each column family may have many columns, as required. Rows are identified by keys, which have a maximum length of 64 KB, and the stored data is sorted by the key. We can receive, update, and delete a single row. We can also scan a range of rows from a starting key to an ending key.

So now the question arises: how does this scale? We will provide a very high-level overview, neglecting the micro details to keep things simple and build a mental model that is useful to us as the consumers of BigTable because we're not supposed to clone BigTable's implementation after all.

As we saw earlier, the basic storage unit in BigTable is a file format called **SSTable** that stores key-value pairs, which are sorted by the key, and has an index at its end. We also examined how the read, write, and delete work on an in-memory copy of the table and merged periodically with the table that is present on the disk. Lastly, we also mentioned that when the in-memory is flushed as SSTables on the disk reach a certain configurable count, they are merged into a bigger table.

The view so far presents the data model, its physical layout, and how operations work on it in cases where the data resides on a single machine, such as a situation where your laptop has a telephone directory of the whole of Europe.

However, how does that work at larger scales? Neglecting the minor implementation details and complexities that arise in distributed systems, the overall architecture and working principles are simple. In case of a single machine, there's only one SSTable (or a few in case they are not merged into one) file that has to be taken care of and all the operations are to be performed on it. However, in case this file does not fit on a single machine, we will of course have to add another machine, and half of the SSTable will reside on one machine, while the other half will be on another machine.

This split would of course mean that each machine would have a range of keys. For instance, if we have 1 million keys (that look like key1, key2, key3, and so on), then the keys from key1 to key500000 might be on one machine, while the keys from key500001 to key1000000 will be on the second machine. So, we can say that each machine has a different key range for the same table. Now, although the data resides on two different machines, it is of course a single table that sprawls over two machines. These partitions or separate parts are called **tablets**. Let's see the key allocation on two machines:

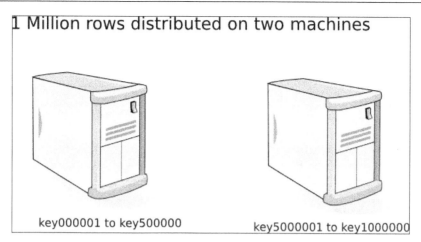

Large dataset divided between two machines

We will keep this system to only two machines and 1 million rows for the sake of discussion, but there may be cases where there are about 20 billion keys sprawling over some 12,000 machines with each machine having a different range of keys. But for now, let's continue with this small cluster consisting of only two nodes or machines.

Now, the problem is that as an external user who has no knowledge of which machine has which portion of the SSTable (and eventually, the key ranges on each machine), how can a key, say, `key489087` be located?

For this, we will have to add something like a telephone directory, where we look up the table name and our desired key and we get to know the machine that we should contact to get the data associated with the key. So we are going to add another node which will be called the *master*. This master will again contain a simple, plain SSTable which is familiar to us. However, the key-value pair would be a very interesting one. Since this table would contain data about the other BigTable tables, let's call it the **METADATA** table. In the METADATA table, we will adopt the following format for the keys: `tablename_ending-row-key`

Since we have only two machines and each machine has two tablets, the METADATA table will look like this:

Key	Value
employees_key500000	192.168.0.2
employees_key1000000	192.168.0.3

So as you can see, master machine stores the location of each tablet server with the row key that is combination of the table name and the ending row of the tablet.. The master assigns tablets to different machines when required so it ensures that METADATA table is up to date with latest locations. In practice, each tablet is about 100 MB to 200 MB in size. So, if we want to fetch a row, all we need to know is the following:

- Location of the master server.

- Table we are interested in.

- And of course, the key itself.

So to begin with, we will concatenate the table name with the key and perform a scan on the METADATA table on the master node. Let's suppose that we are looking for key600000 in the employees table. So, we would first be actually looking for the employees_key600000 key in the METADATA table on the master machine. As you are familiar with the scan operation on SSTable (and METADATA is just an SSTable), we are looking for a key that is greater than or equal to employees_key600000, which happens to be employees_key1000000. From this lookup, the key that we get is employees_key1000000 against which, IP address 192.168.0.3 is listed. This means that this is the machine that we should connect to, to fetch our data. Remember that the scan operation might return one more key. How's that useful? Let's look at an example where our desired data set is scattered between two machines.

Let's suppose that we want to process rows with keys starting from key400000 to key800000. Now, if you look at the distribution of data across the machine, you'll see that half of the required range is on one machine, while the other half is on the other. Now in this case, when we consult the METADATA table, two rows will be returned to us because key400000 is less then key500000 (which is the ending row key for data on the first machine) and key800000 is less then key1000000, which is the ending row for the data on the second machine. So, with these two rows returned, we have two locations to fetch our data from.

This leads to an interesting side-effect. As the data resides on two different machines, this can be read or processed in parallel, which leads to much improved system performance. This is one reason why even with larger datasets, the performance of BigTable won't deteriorate as it would have if it were a single, large machine with all the data on it.

All the details above are very high level conception overview of how BigTable works and are sufficient enough for us to examine our next subject: datastore.

The datastore thyself

So until now, everything that we talked about is about BigTable and we did not mention datastore at all. Now is the time to look at datastore in detail because we understand its underlying foundation BigTable quite well now. Datastore is an effective solution that is built on top of BigTable as a persistent NoSQL layer for Google App Engine.

As we know that BigTable might have different tables, data for all the applications is stored in six separate BigTable tables, where each table stores a different aspect or information about the data. We will explore datastore in detail in the next chapter from the usage standpoint, but for now, we will just go through some terminology related to it. Don't worry about memorizing things regarding data modeling and how to use it for now, as this is something that we are going to look in greater detail later.

The fundamental unit of storage in datastore is called a **property**. You can think of a property as a column. So, a property has a name and type. You can group multiple properties into a **Kind**, which effectively is a Python class and analogous to a table in the RDBMS world. Here's a pseudo code sample:

```
# 1. Define our Kind and how it looks like.
class Person(object):
    name = StringProperty()
    age = IntegerProperty()

# 2. Create an entity of kind person
ali = Person(name='Ali', age='24)
bob = Person(name='Bob', age='34)
david = Person(name='David', age='44)
zain = Person(name='Zain', age='54)

# 3. Save it
ali.put()
bob.put()
david.put()
zain.put()
```

This looks a lot like an ORM such as Django's ORM, SQLAlchemy or Rails ActiveRecord. So, `Person` class is called a **Kind** in App Engine's terminology. The `StringProperty` and `IntegerProperty` property classes are used to indicate the type of data that is supposed to be stored. We created an instance of the `Person` class as `ali`. This instance is called an **entity** in App Engine's terminology. Each entity, when stored, has a key that is not only unique throughout your application, but also combined with your application ID (refer to *Chapter 1, Understanding the Runtime Environment* to know more about the application ID). It becomes unique throughout all the applications that are hosted on Google App Engine.

All entities of all kinds, for all apps, are stored in a single BigTable, and are stored in a way where all the property values are serialized and stored in a single BigTable column. Hence, no separate BigTable columns are defined for each property.

This is interesting as well as necessary because if we are Google App Engine's architects, we do not know the kind of data that people are going to store or the number and types of properties that they would define so it makes sense to serialize the whole thing as one and store them in a single column.

So, this is how it looks:

Key	Kind	Data
agtkZXZ-bWdhZS0wMXIQTXIGUGVyc29uIgNBbGkM	Person	{name: 'Ali', age: 24}
agtkZXZ-bWdhZS0wMXIPCxNTVVyc29uIgNBbGsM	Person	{name: 'Bob', age: 34}
agtkZXZ-bWdhZS0wMXIPCxIGUGVyc29uIgNBbBQM	Person	{name: 'David', age: 44}
agtkZXZ-bWdhZS0wMXIPCxIGUGVyc29uIRJ3bGkM	Person	{name: 'Zain', age: 54}

The key appears to be random, but it is not. We will examine how the key is formed in more detail in the next chapter, but briefly, a key is formed by concatenating your application ID, your kind name (`Person` here), and either a unique identifier that is auto generated by Google App Engine, or a string that is supplied by you.

The key seems cryptic, but it is not safe to pass it around in public, as someone might decode it and take advantage of it. Basically, it is just base 64 encoded and can easily be decoded to know the entity's Kind name and ID. A better way would be to encrypt it using a secret key and then pass it around in public. On the other hand, to receive it, you will have to decrypt it using the same key. A gist of this is available on GitHub that can serve the purpose. To view this, visit `https://gist.github.com/mohsinhijazee/07cdfc2826a565b50a68`. However, for it to work, you need to edit your `app.yaml` file so that it includes the following:

```
libraries:
  - name: pycrypto
    version: latest
```

Then, you can call the `encrypt()` method on the key while passing around and decrypt it back using the `decrypt()` method, as follows:

```
person = Person(name='peter', age=10)
key = person.put()
url_safe_key = key.urlsafe()
safe_to_pass_around = encrypt(SECRET_KEY, url_safe_key)
```

Now, when you have a key from the outside, you should first decrypt it and then use it, as follows:

```
key_from_outside = request.params.get('key')
url_safe_key = decrypt(SECRET_KEY, key_from_outside)
key = ndb.Key(urlsafe=url_safe_key)
person = key.get()
```

The key object is now good to use. To summarize, just get the URL safe key by calling the `ndb.Key.urlsafe()` method and encrypt it so that it can be passed around. On return, just do the reverse.

If you really want to see how the encrypt and decrypt operations are implemented, they are reproduced as follows without any documentation/comments, as cryptography is not our main subject:

```
import os
import base64
from Crypto.Cipher import AES


BLOCK_SIZE = 32
PADDING='#'


def _pad(data, pad_with=PADDING):
    return data + (BLOCK_SIZE - len(data) % BLOCK_SIZE)
* PADDING


def encrypt(secret_key, data):
    cipher = AES.new(_pad(secret_key, '@')[:32])
    return base64.b64encode(cipher.encrypt(_pad(data)))


def decrypt(secret_key, encrypted_data):
    cipher = AES.new(_pad(secret_key, '@')[:32])
    return cipher.decrypt(base64.b64decode
        (encrypted_data)).rstrip(PADDING)


KEY='your-key-super-duper-secret-key-here-only-first-
32-characters-are-used'
decrypted =  encrypt(KEY, 'Hello, world!')
print decrypted
print decrypt(KEY, decrypted)
```

More explanation on how this works is given at https://gist. github.com/mohsinhijazee/07cdfc2826a565b50a68.

Now, let's come back to our main subject, datastore. As you can see, all the data is stored in a single column and if we want to query something, for instance, people who are older than 25, we have no way to do this. So, how will this work? Let's examine this next.

Supporting queries

Now, what if we want to get information pertaining to all the people who are older than, say, 30? In the current scheme of things, this does not seem to be something that is doable because the data is serialized and dumped in a single column, as shown in the previous table. Datastore solves this problem by putting the sorted values to be queried as keys. So here, we want to query by age. Datastore will create a record in another table called the **Index** table. This index table is nothing but just a plain BigTable, where the row keys are actually the property value that you want to query. Hence, a scan and a quick lookup is possible. Here's how it would look:

Key	Entity key
Myapp-person-age-24	agtkZXZ-bWdhZS0wMXIQTXIGUGVyc29uIgNBbGkM
Myapp-person-age-34	agtkZXZ-bWdhZS0wMXIPCxNTVVyc29uIgNBbGkM
Myapp-person-age-44	agtkZXZ-bWdhZS0wMXIPCxIGUGVyc29uIgNBbBQM
Myapp-person-age-54	agtkZXZ-bWdhZS0wMXIPCxIGUGVyc29uIRJ3bGkM

Data as stored in BigTable

Now as you can see, the key of this table is composed by joining the application ID, the Kind name, property name, and finally, the value. Against each key is listed the key of the entity from the entities table that we previously examined. So now, when you look for people with age greater than 30, all you have to do is scan from the `Myapp-person-page-30` key range onwards till you've read all the rows. Each row has the key to the original entity row that can be read and returned.

This was just for the `age` property. If you want to query by name, you will need to have a similar sort of data in the table. The preceding table stores the single property indexes for all the applications that were built on Google App Engine. There's another version of the same table, but the properties in it are in descending order (the reverse of the order is shown in this table).

The implementation details

All in all, datastore actually builds a NoSQL solution on top of BigTable by using the following six tables:

1. A table to store entities

2. A table to store entities by kind

3. A table to store indexes for the property values in the ascending order

4. A table to store indexes for the property values in the descending order

5. A table to store indexes for multiple properties together

6. A table to keep a track of the next unique ID for Kind

Let us look at each table in turn. The first table is used to store entities for all the applications. We have examined this in an example.

The second table just stores the Kind names. Nothing fancy here. It's just some metadata that datastore maintains for itself. Think of this—you want to get all the entities that are of the `Person` Kind. How will you do this? If you look at the entities table alone and the operations that are available to us on a BigTable table, you will know that there's no way for us to fetch all the entities of a certain Kind. This table does exactly this. It looks like this:

Key	Entity key
Myapp-Person-agtkZXZ-bWdhZS0wMXIQTXIGUGVyc29uIgNBbGkM	AgtkZXZ-bWdhZS0wMXIQTXIGUGVyc29uIgNBbGkM
Myapp-Person-agtkZXZ-bWdhZS0wMXIQTXIGUGVyc29uIgNBb854	agtkZXZ-bWdhZS0wMXIQTXIGUGVyc29uIgNBb854
Myapp-Person-agtkZXZ-bWdhZS0wMXIQTXIGUGVy748IgNBbGkM	agtkZXZ-agtkZXZ-bWdhZS0wMXIQTXIGUGVy748IgNBbGkM

As you can see, this is just a simple BigTable table where the keys are of the `[app ID]-[Kind name]-[entity key]` pattern.

The tables 3, 4, and 5 from the six tables that were mentioned in the preceding list are similar to the table that we examined in the *Supporting queries* section labeled *Data as stored in BigTable*.

This leaves us with the last table. As you know, while storing entities, it is important to have a unique key for each row. Since all the entities from all the apps are stored in a single table, they should be unique across the whole table. When datastore generates a key for an entity that has to be stored, it combines your application ID and the Kind name of the entity. Now, this part of the key only makes it unique across all the other entities in the table, but not within the set of your own entities. To do this, you need a number that should be appended to it. This is exactly similar to how AUTO INCREMENT works in the RDBMS world where the value of a column is automatically incremented to ensure that it is unique. So, that's exactly what the last table is for. It keeps a track of the last ID that was used by each Kind of each application, and it looks like this:

Key	Next ID
Myapp-Person	65

So, in this table, the key is of the [application ID]-[Kind name] format, and the value is the next value, which is 65 in this particular case. When a new entity of kind Person is created, it will be assigned 65 as the ID, and the row will have a new value of 66. Our application has only one Kind defined, which is Person. Therefore, there's only one row in this table because we are only keeping track of the next ID for this Kind. If we had another Kind, say, Group, it will have its own row in this table.

So, that's all about the datastore in brief. We have looked at how it uses six BigTables to store everything, from data to indexes and the next unique IDs. We will refer to and revisit these details in the next chapter as well when talking about datastore itself in detail when modeling our data in the next chapter.

Summary

We started this chapter with the problem of storing huge amounts of data, processing it in bulk, and randomly accessing it. This arose from the fact that we were ambitiously wanting to store every single web page on earth and process it to extract some results from it. We introduced a solution called BigTable and examined its data model. We saw that in BigTable, we can define multiple tables, with each table having multiple column families, which are defined at the time of creating the table. We learned that column families are logical groupings of columns, and new columns can be defined in a column family, as needed. We also learned that the datastore in BigTable has no meaning on its own, and it stores them just as plain bytes; its interpretation and meanings depend on the user of the data. We also learned that each row in BigTable has a unique row key, which has a length of 64 KB.

Once done with the logical model of BigTable, we turned our attention to how data is actually stored on the disk. We got to learn that data is always stored on the disk sorted by the lexicographic value of the row keys which actually is a clever file format called Sorted String table or SSTable. Next, we learned that when data is sorted this way, random, single-row reads are possible, and most importantly, it is possible, with the help of the in-memory MemTable, to write data instantaneously, flush it later on disk, and periodically merge these flushed MemTables with other already on-disk flushed SSTables. We also looked at how updates and deletes work in this model and turned our attention to the operations that are available to us, such as fetching, deleting, updating a row, and scanning a range of rows from a starting key to an ending key.

Once done with the data model of BigTable and its storage intricacies, we turned our attention towards how BigTable scales to multiple machines in order to serve enormous amounts of data. We learned that keys are distributed across the machines, and a single machine has a SSTable that stores the ending ranges of each table along with its IP. We also learned that since key ranges are distributed across the machines, this works to our advantage when a dataset grows because each machine can process the requests to its range of keys in parallel.

Lastly, we turned our attention to datastore, a NoSQL storage solution built on top of BigTable for Google App Engine. We briefly mentioned some datastore terminology such as properties (columns), entities (rows), and kinds (tables). We learned that all data is stored across six different BigTable tables each capturing a different aspect of data. Most importantly, we learned that all the entities of all the apps hosted on Google App Engine are stored in a single BigTable and all properties go to a single BigTable column. We also learned how querying is supported by additional tables that are keyed by the property values that list the corresponding row keys.

This concludes our discussion on Google App Engine's datastore and its underlying technology, workings, and related concepts. Next, we will learn how to model our data on top of datastore. What we learned in this chapter will help us enormously in understanding how to better model our data to take full advantage of the underlying mechanisms.

4
Modeling Your Data

This is an age of information and one of the major problems that you will face is managing information so that you can make sense out of it. And to make sense out of it, you have to first manage and organize your information. This organization of information is a "two-ended" problem. One end is about the kind of data that you have, and the other end is the storage medium or the solution in which you have to actually store the information. This process of information management and organization, keeping in mind both the ends, is called **data modeling**. This exactly is the process that we focus in this chapter.

In this chapter, we will cover the following topics:

- The basics of datastore's modeling language.
- The internal storage of data.
- Modeling your data around the datastore internals.
- Reviewing the available types of data storage in datastore.

So, these are our goals in this chapter. Let's get started with data modeling.

The data modeling language

The need for data storage has always been there since the existence of **VisiCalc**, the historic and killer spreadsheet program. Then came along databases with their relational models. Various vendors for the same popped up, and, right now, RDBMS is the most widely used paradigm for data storage. Many solutions exist, ranging from the lightest, SQLite, to the heaviest, Oracle, with SQLServer, MySQL, and Postgres in between.

To query and process data, a language called **Structured Query Language (SQL)** has also evolved. We currently have many dialects of this language that vary from vendor to vendor, although many standard bodies and standards exist for SQL.

Initially, each database software had its own low-level protocol. SQL and the results of the executed SQL would be communicated over this protocol. So, you required a special piece of software that could talk to your database, and this software was called a **database driver**. Then, the story of Connectivity Standards pops in such as ODBC and JDBC, which are standards from software vendors. Your database solution was supposed to expose its functionality to these standards, if you're a vendor. Finally, people started to feel the need for yet another layer of abstraction, where the data started to appear a part of the program itself. For example, you just have a class representing a table and its instance means a row. Calling a method on this instance would create, update, or delete the corresponding row in the underlying table. This is what we know as **Object Relational Mapping (ORM)**.

There are many libraries that solve this object to relational mapping in almost all languages but the most notable ones are Hibernate for Java, SQLAlchemy, and Django ORM for Python. However, the real trendsetter came with Ruby on Rails. Called **ActiveRecord** which inspired many other frameworks. No matter how well-designed ORM is, it is often said that the ORM problem is the Vietnam of computer science; that is, it isn't completely solved. There will be times when you find a gap between the underlying relational model and the objects that you have. Eventually, you will have no choice but to write a raw SQL query to get things done. You can read an interesting description of this at `http://blog.codinghorror.com/object-relational-mapping-is-the-vietnam-of-computer-science/`.

This is quite a long preamble for the datastore, mainly because of the fact that the overall look and feel of the datastore seems much like that of an ORM. However, this is not the case. Let's look at an example first, then we'll discuss things further.

For the examples in this chapter, most of the work can be done in the interactive console that is provided by the Python SDK. We'll mostly use the interactive console, unless there's an example where we are required to examine things beyond the datastore. Working with the interactive console will help us keep the examples short and to the point, and we will be able to interactively play with them.

To get started, run any example application by using the following command:

```
$ ~/sdks/google_appengine./dev_appserver.py ~/Projects/mgae/ch01/hello/
```

Then point your browser to `http://localhost:8000`. Now, click on the **Interactive Console**, which will look like this:

Interactive console for code execution

Here we can execute whatever code we'd like, and the code will be executed with the results shown next to it. Let's pretend that we are going to develop a classified portal where people can post their listings. Our initial model will be very simple. Type the following (which is available as listing.py in the code examples) into the text area:

```python
from google.appengine.ext import ndb

# Our simple listing model. No images, categories, dates.
class Listing(ndb.Model):
  title = ndb.StringProperty()
  price = ndb.IntegerProperty()

# Create three listings.
car = Listing(title="Honda Accord 2008 for Sale", price=25000)
job = Listing(title="Web developer required", price=6000)
apt = Listing(title="Apartment for rent", price=2500)

# Save them and get keys
k1 = car.put()
k2 = job.put()
k3 = apt.put()

print k1
print k2
print k3
```

Here's the output in this case; yours might be slightly different in that you will see different numbers:

```
Key('Listing', 5629499534213120)
Key('Listing', 5066549580791808)
Key('Listing', 6192449487634432)
```

Now, what happened here? Let's just examine it. First, we imported a Python module named `ndb` from `google.appengine.ext`. That's pretty obvious. Note that in this module, n stands for "new" and `db`, as you know, stands for "database". This is a new datastore library that was written by the creator of Python, Guido van Rossum, himself. The previous version of the API was simply `db`. The newer version is very intuitive to work with. It is a very elegant, straightforward API as compared to `db`. Furthermore, when you read data from datastore using the `db` library, you might want to cache it using the `memcache` services that are available on Google App Engine. However, in the case of `ndb`, this is done automatically for you. So, you do not need to write any cache management code yourself.

Now let's move to the next piece of the code. We defined a class that is inherited from `ndb.Model`. To keep things simple, the class has only one attribute of string type named `title`, which is actually an instance of `ndb.StringProperty`. The other attribute is `price`, which is an instance of `ndb.IntegerProperty`. That's the way you define a model for your data. If you have ever used or gone through the code that uses Django's ORM or SQLAlchemy, this will sound pretty familiar. The `ndb.Model` parent class has all the functionalities of writing and reading from datastore, whereas with `ndb.StringProperty`, we indicated that the title is of the string type and with `ndb.IntegerProperty`, we indicated that `price` will hold an integer.

 There certainly are many data types. We'll learn about them when we talk about data modeling in a later section.

We looked in detail at BigTable and datastore in the previous chapter, and we observed that BigTable has no concept of datatypes. Everything is stored as raw bytes. Here, we declared that `title` is actually a string and `price` is an integer. How does this work, then? The answer is that type checking and matters related to this are dealt with at the library level. The underlying BigTable has no knowledge or concern about data types or type checking. So, if you try to assign a string to `price`, an exception will be raised by the `ndb` library. Hence, that's effectively at the Python layer, and it has nothing to do with the underlying datastore (which is an arrangement to store data using six tables, as we mentioned in the previous chapter) or BigTable. We'll examine this further as we talk about how this is actually stored.

So, coming back to our code example, we next want to create three instances of three separate listings. The attribute values for the newly created instances are set right in the constructor using keyword arguments, but we can assign attribute values directly over the model instances as well. So, here's how it looks like from the preceding code:

```
# Create three listings.
car = Listing(title="Honda Accord 2008 for Sale", price=25000)
job = Listing(title="Web developer required", price=6000)
apt = Listing(title="Apartment for rent", price=2500)
```

Finally, the most interesting part. We call the `.put()` method on each instance that returns the key of this particular instance after storing it in datastore, which actually is an instance of the `ndb.Key` class. We will examine the key in detail later, but for now, this is how it looks:

```
# Save them and get keys
k1 = car.put()
k2 = job.put()
k3 = apt.put()
```

Now we will cover some terminology that is specific to datastore and Google App Engine. The `Listing` class is what we call a *kind*. So, effectively, we are going to define a kind. The class name is the name of the Kind, but we can have a class name that is different from the kind name. For this, we will have to define a `_get_kind()` method, and this value will be considered the name of the Kind instead of the name of the class. This can be useful. It has implications, which will be examined in a while. The instances of the kind are called **entities**. Hence, `job`, `apt`, and `car` are entities in the preceding code.

Keys and internal storage

Now let's examine the returned keys in detail. The key is supposed to be a sequence of bytes that is used to identify rows which are entities as one entity gets represented as a row. The key is a combination of a string, which is the Kind name, and a unique identifier, which is an integer in our case. So the key of the output in the previous example is actually an `str()` function on the `ndb.Key` object, which returns something that looks like `Key('Listing', 5629499534213120)`. As you can see, the first argument is the Kind name. The second is an integer. You may recall that we mentioned in the previous chapter that there's a BigTable table maintained by datastore that is used to generate the next unique ID for each Kind. This is exactly where this integer comes from.

We mentioned in the last chapter that datastore uses a single BigTable table to store all the entities of all the applications. Now, here, we have a key that includes a Kind name and an integer. It might happen that another developer is developing an application somewhere else in the datastore that has the same Kind name, which will eventually lead to a clash. Therefore, to make the entities unique across all the entities, two more pieces of information are welded together to make it unique across the entire datastore. One is your application ID, and the other is the namespace. We will talk about namespaces in detail later in this chapter. For now, you can think of a namespace as a logical division of the data. So for instance, if you are making an invoicing application, you can create namespaces for each organization you sell your subscription to, which will make everyone's data partitioned separately.

You may recall from the previous chapter that each BigTable row has a unique key limited to 64 KB. Also, we learned that BigTable stores data that is sorted by the key. The key that we got from the `.put()` method is exactly the same row key. Also, you may recall that datastore puts all the properties in a single column by serializing them. So, in light of this, this is how the stored data will look:

Key	Data
AppID-default-Listing-5066549580791808	{title: "Web dev...", price: 2500}
AppID-default-Listing-5629499534213120	{title: "Honda...", price: 6000}
AppID-default-Listing-6192449487634432	{title: "Apart...", price: 2500}

As you can see, the data is ordered according to the key, and each key has the following pattern:

```
[application ID]-[namespace]-[Kind]-[ID]
```

So, this is the blueprint or recipe of how datastore forms a key. Let's examine each ingredient in turn.

The application ID

The first ingredient is the application ID, which is something that you're well aware of, as we discussed it in the first chapter. You can choose an application ID when you are creating an App Engine application using the online form and you can mention the same application ID in `app.yaml`. This is the first component that datastore uses to form a key.

Namespaces

The next ingredient of the key is the namespace. If you have ever used namespaces in C# or C++, then namespaces in datastore are similar to namespaces in C++ or C#, as far as their purpose goes: they just scope your data similar to namespaces in programming languages that scope your identifiers such as classes, functions, and so on. So for example, you can have a namespace named clients that contains all the entities about clients, and the other namespace can be named suppliers that will contain all the data pertaining to the suppliers. The queries and code execution in each namespace is totally isolated from the other namespaces.

Let's make our understanding more concrete by having a look at an example. Suppose that you are building a simple invoicing solution and you want to store just three things—products, orders, and customers. So, our orders will indicate what products were sold to which customers and that's whole point of your system. You might want to sell this solution to multiple businesses. Each business will have a different list of customers, products, and orders. How do we keep the products, orders, and customers of each business apart? One way would be to include the business name in every product, customer and order. That way, if a business named *Wicked Solutions* has logged in, we filter the products, customers, and orders by that business' name. While placing new orders, or creating new customers and products, we include the business name as well.

That's good, but, there's a better solution called **namespaces**. When the user logs in, you can set the business name as a namespace. Now, from this point onwards, you do not need to mention anything. Every entity that you read or write will be scoped to or contained in this namespace. That's exactly what a namespace is in the key that we just examined in the previous section. Let's assume that you have set up a namespace like this:

```
from google.appengine.api import namespace_manager
# Now everything is in context of dumb-solutions
namespace_manager.set_namespace('dumb-solutions')
# Now from this point on wards, everything is in context of eagle-
traders
namespace_manager.set_namespace('eagle-traders')
```

From this point onwards, all the entities that you write or query for will have this namespace included in their keys. This scoping with namespaces is available for datastore, Memcache, task queues, and search services. For more details, see https://cloud.google.com/appengine/docs/python/multitenancy/multitenancy.

In summary, it is just a containment instrument where you can partition your data into isolated namespace containers.

The Kind

The next element is the Kind, which as you know, is actually a class that represents the structure of your data. So in our case, we have a class called `Listing`. Hence, the string `Listing` object will be used here. It might be the case that you want to have a Kind name that is different from the class name. That's possible too. Just provide a `_get_kind()` method that will return a string, which will be considered as the Kind name.

This can be useful in case your class name is long, such as `ArchivedSectionWiseCategoryListings`, and you're expecting to store millions of rows, which means that there will be millions of keys, and having a long Kind name will consume more space. This is the case where you can define the `_get_kind()` method to return a shorter name, such as `ASWCL`, which is short for `ArchivedSectionWiseCategoryListings`.

If you have an `ndb.Key` instance, you can get the Kind name of the entity to which it belongs like that:

```
kind = key.kind()
```

The ID

The last ingredient of a key is the unique ID. We talked about the unique ID in the last chapter and mentioned that there's a table that keeps a record of the next available unique ID. Now we'll examine the problem with the ID in more detail.

An ID is just a unique identifier that can be either a string or an integer. However, by default, if you don't specify an ID yourself, it is set as an integer, as we can see from the returned instances of the `Key` class from our interactive session earlier. This unique integer (technically, an integer of the long type) is generated by the datastore itself, and you do not need to worry about it. However, this does not have to be an integer, as we just mentioned, it can be either a string or an integer. You can also set a string as a unique identifier for an instance, but you cannot have both. You can have either numeric IDs or string IDs. Actually, we have few choices in generating the ID for our entities:

- Preallocating a list of unique IDs
- Setting something of your own that will be a string

Let's examine each of the preceding choices in order.

Pre-allocating numeric IDs

Let's examine the first possibility. Imagine a situation where you want to create 100 entities of the Listing Kind and want their IDs to be in sequence. Now, let's assume that your application is very popular. While you are creating these entities, millions of other users are also doing the same thing. So, as a result, the following might happen:

1. You create the first listing with the ID as 1.
2. You create a second listing with the ID as 2.
3. Next, someone else creates a listing in your app, which gets the ID of 3.
4. Another user creates a listing that gets an ID of 4.
5. Now, you create a listing that gets an ID of 5.
6. And so on and so forth.

Now, as you can see, by the time your code finishes executing, your listings won't get the ID numbers in sequence. Even for the five steps that were shown in the preceding example, your listings would get IDs of 1, 2, and 5, whereas 3 and 4 would be allocated to someone else who's creating entities within your application.

So how do you go about this? There is actually a way for you to allocate a range of IDs for yourself, and any entities created after this request will get IDs after the range allocated to you. This is how you can accomplish this:

```
from google.appengine.ext import ndb

# Our simple listing model. No images, categories, dates.
class Listing(ndb.Model):
  title = ndb.StringProperty()
  price = ndb.IntegerProperty()

# Allocate hundred IDs for me
# This returns a tuple containing start and end of a range with end
included
start, end = Listing.allocate_ids(size=100)

# Now iterate over it:
for listing_id in xrange(start, end + 1):
    listing = Listing(title='My dummy listing to be modified later
      %s' % listing_id , id=listing_id)
    listing.put()
```

We simply call the `allocate_ids()` method on the `Listing` class, which returns us the start and end of the allocated range. Next, we are just iterating over the range and setting the numeric ID on our own using the `id` keyword argument. Pretty simple.

Now, let's look at the next possibility, which is, setting a custom key of your own while creating an entity.

The string ID

As mentioned previously, you can also use strings as an identifier for the entities that you create. In Google App Engine's terminology, a string-based ID is called a key name. When using a string as an identifier, it is your responsibility to ensure that you generate unique strings. Otherwise, you would be overwriting the existing entities with the same string identifiers.

Let's look at an interactive example. Suppose that you have 10 job listings that you'd like to create, and would like to use key names such as `listing-1`, `listing-2`, `listing-3`, and so on. How can this be done? This is how we will do it:

```
from google.appengine.ext import ndb

# Our simple listing model. No images, categories, dates.
class Listing(ndb.Model):
    title = ndb.StringProperty()
    price = ndb.IntegerProperty()

# Total jobs
start = 1
end = 10
# Create each job listing
for i in xrange(start, end + 1):
    # That's new, we create a key instance here.
    key = ndb.Key(Listing, 'listing-%s' % i)
    listing = Listing(title='Dummy Listing', key=key)
    listing.put()
```

Before we look at what we did here, let's see how the entities look in **Datastore Viewer** of both the types that we just created:

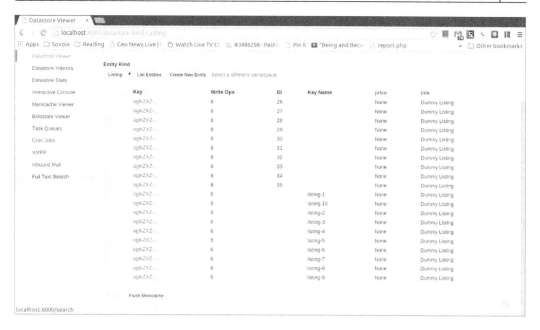

The first few entities are the ones that we created by using the allocated IDs and they are in sequence. You can see that the **Key Name** column is empty for those entities. Next are the ones that we just created using the key name. The **ID** column is empty, whereas **Key Name** has a value. This is because you cannot have both at the same time. You can use either a numeric ID, or a key name.

Now, it's time to explain the preceding code. Nothing new here. We just iterated and created entities. However, we also created custom keys by creating instances of the ndb.Key class. The first argument to the constructor is the Kind name, and the second one is the unique identifier. If this second argument was an integer, this would be a numeric ID, and if it was a string, this would be taken as a key name.

If you have an ndb.Key instance, you can get the ID part of the key with the following code:

```
id = key.integer_id()
```

This will return the integer ID if the key has it. Otherwise, it will return None. If the key has a string ID, we can get it like this:

```
id = key.string_id()
```

This will return the string ID, but if the key has an integer ID instead, this method will return None. But the following method will return a string or an integer, whatever type of ID the key has:

```
id = key.id()
```

Let's examine the key and corresponding key class in more detail.

The key

We have been talking about the key since the last chapter where we learned that each BigTable has a key that can be 64 KB long. In this chapter, we learned that because datastore stores all the entities in a single BigTable, the key is formed by joining the application ID, namespace, the Kind name, and an ID. We also learned that an ID can be an integer (which is autogenerated by datastore, and you can allocate a range as well) or a string that you can supply on your own.

However, how is the key actually presented in the Datastore API? We haven't looked at this in detail. Let's do this now. In the ndb library, the ndb.Key class represents a key. The basic way that is used to construct a key is as follows:

```
# Note, first argument is a class, second is a string.
key1 = ndb.Key(Listing, 'my-listing')
# Note that first argument is not class but name of the class as
string.
# It is same as key1
key2 = ndb.Key('Listing', 'my-listing')
# Note that first is class second is an integer
key3 = ndb.Key(Listing, 4)
```

So, basically, we can construct a key by supplying the Kind (either as a Python class object or a string) and an identifier (either a string or an integer), and we have the key instead read to be used. The application ID and the current namespace are combined to form the full key by the ndb.Key class constructor. The namespace and app ID are automatically filled in for you, but if you want to change that too, that's possible too, like this:

```
key = ndb.Key(Listing, 50, app='my-app-id', namespace='jungle')
```

Here, we are just creating a ndb.Key instance and also specifying the app and namespace using the respective keyword arguments.

If you have a key instance, you can call the .get() method to retrieve the corresponding entity and the .delete() method to delete the entity. In our first example, we created some entities and called the .put() method on them, which returned us the keys. If we want to get the listings back, we can use the following code:

```
# Construct a key instance. The ID is the one that was
# generated by datastore.
key = ndb.Key(Listing, 5629499534213120L)
# Now get the associated listing.
job = key.get()
print job.title
# we can also delete the entity
key.delete()
```

As you can see, we created a key instance by supplying the constructor a kind and an identifier for an entity that exists in datastore. We call the get() method and print the title property. Finally, we called the .delete() method on the key instance to delete it. That's simple.

There's one more thing about keys. We have studied Bigtable in detail and we know that the key of a BigTable table's row can have a maximum length of 64KB. That's a lot of space. One trick that is used is joining one or more keys. We will see the advantages that this has, but first let's see how the ndb.Key class supports this. Let's imagine that we have another class called Category that stores the category that the listings are in. Now, let's construct a key for Listing, but combined with a key of Category:

```
# A key for a category entity
# Internally in datastore, it would be: Category-used-cars
key1 = ndb.Key('Category', 'used-cars')
# Key for listing entity
# Internally in datastore, it would be Listing-343
key2 = ndb.Key('Listing', 343)
# Key for listing entity but whose 'parent' is key1
# Internally in datastore, it would be Category-used-cars-Listing-343
key3 = ndb.Key('Listing', 343, parent=key1)
# Same as above, just different syntax.
# Internally in datastore, it would be Category-used-cars-Listing-343
key4 = ndb.Key('Category', 'used-car', 'Listing', 343)
```

Let's look at what we did here. The first two things will be familiar to you. We just created two different key instances for different kinds—one that uses a string ID and the other that uses an integer ID. Pretty simple. Next, we created a key instance for the `Listing` Kind, but we declared the key for the `Category` Kind as its parent. "Parent" is the terminology in datastore's parlance where a key (or by extension, the entity of the key) is the parent of the key if it is welded before it. We have shown in the preceding code that, internally, the two keys will be welded and the BigTable row will have the key as `Category-used-cars-Listing-343`, which is just the second key appended to the first one.

Next we did the same thing again, but with a different syntax. The constructor for the `key` class accepts as many Kind-identifier pairs as you can give. The last pair is considered the pair for the key, and the rest are considered as parents.

What's the use of appending keys together like that? We will look at this next.

Modeling your data

Now let's model something that will explain how keys work. We have a Kind named `Listing`, which will be used to create listings. However, there is no way for us to put various listings in different categories as yet. How do we do that? There are two approaches.

The first approach – storing a reference as a property

The first approach is pretty simple and is known to us from the RDBMS world. We can create categories separately, and each category will have a reference in each listing. It is similar to how foreign keys work in databases. So, we will have a new property for the `Listing` entities, which will contain a reference to the category to which it belongs. The `category` attribute will actually contain the key of an entity of the `Category` Kind. Let's take a look at the code to better understand it:

```
from google.appengine.ext import ndb

# Represents a category
class Category(ndb.Model):
  name = ndb.StringProperty()

# Our simple listing model
class Listing(ndb.Model):
    title = ndb.StringProperty()
    price = ndb.IntegerProperty()
```

```
    # Will store a category key.
    category = ndb.KeyProperty(kind=Category)

# Create categories. Using custom string slugs/identifiers.
used_cars = Category(name="Used Cars", key=ndb.Key(Category, 'used-
cars'))
honda = Category(name="Honda", key=ndb.Key(Category, 'honda'))
toyota = Category(name="Toyota", key=ndb.Key(Category, 'toyota'))
jobs = Category(name="Jobs", key=ndb.Key(Category, 'jobs'))

used_cars.put()
honda.put()
toyota.put()
jobs.put()

print used_cars.key
print honda.key
print toyota.key
print jobs.key

accord = Listing(title="Honda Accord 2004", price=4000,
category=honda.key)
civic = Listing(title="Civic 1995 mint condition", price=4000,
category=honda.key)
crolla = Listing(title="Crolla 2000", price=4000, category=toyota.key)
kia = Listing(title="Kia Sportage 1998", price=4000, category=used_
cars.key)
accountant = Listing(title="Accountant for Factory", price=4000,
category=jobs.key)

accord.put()
civic.put()
crolla.put()
kia.put()
accountant.put()

for job in Listing.query(Listing.category == jobs.key).fetch(10):
    print job.title

for car in Listing.query(Listing.category == honda.key).fetch(10):
    print car.title

for car in Listing.query(Listing.category==used_cars.key).fetch(10):
    print car.title
```

Here's the output of the program:

```
Key('Category', 'used-cars')
Key('Category', 'honda')
Key('Category', 'toyota')
Key('Category', 'jobs')
Accountant for Factory
Honda Accord 2004
Civic 1995 mint condition
Kia Sportage 1998
```

Let's go through what we just did in detail. First, we introduced a new Kind called `Category`, which has only one string property called `name`.

Next we defined the `Listing` Kind, which is the same as before, except for a new property called `Category`, which is of the `ndb.KeyProperty` type. We will go through all the available properties later, but `ndb.KeyProperty` is what you use when you want to save the key of another entity in your entity. The `ndb.KeyProperty` property can store keys for any kind of entity, but here we want to make sure that only the keys of the `Category` Kind are stored. We have supplied an optional `Kind` keyword argument with the `Category` value to indicate that we only want to store the keys of the `Category` Kind. In case a key of another Kind is supplied, an exception will be raised. Just a gentle reminder: this validation is built into the `ndb` library, which is a part of the datastore and actually under the hood BigTable cares nothing about what you store and has no validation in place as it just stores plain old raw bytes.

Pretty simple so far. Next we create four entities of the `Category` Kind, but instead of letting the datastore assign it automatically generated unique integer identifiers, we decide to override this by supplying our own `ndb.Key` instance as a `key` keyword argument to the constructor. This will make things more intuitive and easy too. So, in case we want to retrieve a `Category` entity later, we can simply use the following code:

```
key = ndb.Key('Category', 'jobs')
jobs = key.get()
```

This will fetch the `jobs` category. Now we are going to create the actual `Listing` entities, where we supply the `category` property with a key for the respective categories and simply call `put()` to save these listings. The only new thing is the category property and the way we assign it the key values.

In the end, we are just iterating over the `jobs`, `Honda`, and `used-cars` categories. We will explore how queries work in datastore and the API that is available to us in the next chapter, but here, `Listing.query` is a method that takes a list of filters as the input. A filter is a reference for a property, an operator, and a value. So, in our first query, `Listing.query(Listing.category == jobs.key)`, `Listing.category` is the reference to a property reference, `==` is the operator, and `jobs.key` is the value that is being compared. We call the `fetch()` method to fetch entities, which takes a required integer parameter to indicate the maximum number of results that should be fetched. Because we are just playing around here, so opted for `10`.

Next, we printed the jobs, Honda cars, and all the used cars. This shows how you can model your data in a traditional way. However, it has a flaw, and we will fix it next.

The second approach – a category within a key

The second approach uses the sorted nature of the Bigtable row keys to its advantage and designs its data formation around it. This will be clearer with an example. Before you run this example in the interactive console, it is better to delete all the existing entries from the Datastore Viewer in the admin console.

The following code is what you need to type into the interactive console:

```
from google.appengine.ext import ndb

class Category(ndb.Model):
  name = ndb.StringProperty()

# Our simple listing model.
class Listing(ndb.Model):
    title = ndb.StringProperty()
    price = ndb.IntegerProperty()

used_cars = ndb.Key(Category, 'used-cars')
honda = ndb.Key(Category, 'used-cars', Category, 'honda')
toyota = ndb.Key(Category, 'used-cars', Category, 'toyota')
jobs = ndb.Key(Category, 'jobs')

Category(name="Used Cars", key=used_cars).put()
Category(name="Honda", key=honda).put()
Category(name="Toyota", key=toyota).put()
Category(name="Jobs", key=jobs).put()
```

```
print used_cars
print honda
print toyota
print jobs

accord = Listing(title="Honda Accord 2004", price=4000, parent=honda)
civic = Listing(title="Civic 1995 mint condition", price=4000,
parent=honda)
crolla = Listing(title="Crolla 2000", price=4000, parent=toyota)
kia = Listing(title="Kia Sportage 1998", price=4000, parent=used_cars)
accountant = Listing(title="Accountant for Factory", price=4000,
parent=jobs)

accord.put()
civic.put()
crolla.put()
kia.put()
accountant.put()

print "All the listing keys"
print "-------------------"
print accord.key
print civic.key
print crolla.key
print kia.key
print accountant.key

print "Just Honda cars"
print "--------------"
for car in Listing.query(ancestor=honda).fetch(10):
    print car.title

print "Just Toyota cars"
print "--------------"
for car in Listing.query(ancestor=toyota).fetch(10):
    print car.title

print "All the cars cars"
print "--------------"
for car in Listing.query(ancestor=used_cars).fetch(10):
    print car.title

print "And some jobs:"
print "--------------"
for job in Listing.query(ancestor=jobs).fetch(10):
    print job.title
```

Here's the output for the preceding code:

```
Key('Category', 'used-cars')
Key('Category', 'used-cars', 'Category', 'honda')
Key('Category', 'used-cars', 'Category', 'toyota')
Key('Category', 'jobs')
All the listing keys--------------------
Key('Category', 'used-cars', 'Category', 'honda', 'Listing',
6333186975989760)
Key('Category', 'used-cars', 'Category', 'honda', 'Listing',
4925812092436480)
Key('Category', 'used-cars', 'Category', 'toyota', 'Listing',
6051711999279104)
Key('Category', 'used-cars', 'Listing', 5488762045857792)
Key('Category', 'jobs', 'Listing', 6614661952700416)
Just Honda cars---------------
Civic 1995 mint condition
Honda Accord 2004
Just Toyota cars---------------
Crolla 2000
All the cars cars--------------
Civic 1995 mint condition
Honda Accord 2004
Crolla 2000
Kia Sportage 1998
And some jobs:---------------
Accountant for Factory
```

Let's see what we have done here. First, we declared the `Category` Kind as usual. Nothing new here. Next comes the `Listing` Kind. This is the same as our first approach, except that the `category` attribute is not used any more. Then, how can we keep track of the categories? We'll see in a while.

Once done with the definition of both kinds, we define the keys for the categories because we want to have separate slugs for each instead of automatically generated numeric identifiers from datastore. The first one is pretty simple. The category slug is `used-cars`, and it is defined in the following way:

```
used_cars = ndb.KeyProperty(Category, 'used-cars')
```

As we have already examined the `ndb.Key` class, this seems straightforward. Next we will define a key for another category with a `honda` slug. However, we decided that this category is a subcategory of `used-cars`. So, the following code demonstrates how we define its key:

```
honda = ndb.Key(Category, 'used-cars', Category, 'honda')
```

Now, this is interesting. As we learned before, the `ndb.Key` class constructor accepts a list of kind-identifier pairs to form a key. Hence, the first pair is exactly the same as the one that we supplied to define the key of the `used cars` category, whereas the last `Category` pair, `honda`, is the one that is the key for another category. The first pair is just an indication that it should be prepended to the last one. Next, another key is defined for the `Category` Kind and using the `toyota` slug in the same way. That's how these keys that including the key for `jobs` will end up in BigTable:

```
Category-used-cars
Category-used-cars-honda
Category-used-cars-toyota
Category-jobs
```

Note that this only created key instances, and nothing has been stored or written yet to the datastore at all. That's what we are going to do next. We will create instances of the `Category` Kind, mention the corresponding key instances as the `key` keyword argument and call the `put()` method on them:

```
Category(name="Used Cars", key=used_cars).put()
Category(name="Honda", key=honda).put()
Category(name="Toyota", key=toyota).put()
Category(name="Jobs", key=jobs).put()
```

As all is set by now, we can create listings. We will create four listings for cars in different categories and one job. While creating the instances, we will indicate the key that should be prepended to the keys of each listing via the `parent` keyword argument, as follows:

```
accord = Listing(title="Honda Accord 2004", price=4000, parent=honda)
```

This has an interesting side effect. Without mentioning the parent, the following will be the key for this listing:

```
Listing-<some-unique-autogenerated-number>
```

However, by indicating that the `honda` key is the parent of this entity, the key supplied as the `parent` keyword argument will be prepended to the key, as follows:

```
Category-used-cars-Category-honda-Listing-<some-unique-autogenerated-
number>
```

You can see how the the keys of each created listing look in a notation that the `ndb. Key` class will use, but here's how they will end up in the Bigtable:

```
Category-used-cars-Category-honda-Listing-4925812092436480
Category-used-cars-Category-honda-Listing-6333186975989760
Category-used-cars-Category-toyota-Listing-6051711999279104
Category-used-cars-Listing-5488762045857792
Category-jobs-Listing-6614661952700416
```

You may recall that keys are always stored in a sorted fashion in Bigtable. One of the operations that we learned when examining Bigtable was scanning rows whose keys start with a given prefix. This is exactly the trick that we will use to iterate over all the used cars with the following call:

```
Listing.query(ancestor=used_cars).fetch(10)
```

Under the hood, this actually starts a row scan for the keys that start with `Cateogry-used-cars`. Because of the way we modeled our data, by defining keys for categories and later indicating them as parents, so that they are welded together with the keys of the listings that we create, we are able to get all the used cars, as follows:

```
Category-used-cars-Category-honda-Listing-4925812092436480
Category-used-cars-Category-honda-Listing-6333186975989760
Category-used-cars-Category-toyota-Listing-6051711999279104
Category-used-cars-Listing-5488762045857792
   Category-jobs-Listing-6614661952700416
```

The rows starting with `Category-used-cars` are the ones that will be returned and are highlighted in the list of keys shown in the preceding code. So, it's our clever modeling around properties of Bigtable that yields this. In comparison to the first approach, you might argue that although it is a clever technique to model data, we don't see a category attribute on the created listings and hence, we cannot know the exact category which this is in.

That's not true. Each entity has a property `key`, which returns an instance of the `ndb.Key` class. The following is the key of the `honda` listing:

```
# Prints Key('Category', 'used-cars', 'Category', 'honda', 'Listing',
5066549580791808)
print honda.key
```

However, what category does it belong to? To find out, the `ndb.Key` class's `parent()` method can be put to use, which will return the parent `ndb.Key` instance:

```
# Returns Key('Category', 'used-cars', 'Category', 'honda')
print honda.key.parent()
```

This means that this car belongs to the `honda` category. Furthermore, if we want to get the root, then we can use the following code:

```
# Returns Used car: Key('Category', 'used-cars')
print honda.key.parent().parent()
```

To get the actual entity from the key, we can simply call the `.get()` method on the returned `ndb.Key` class's instances, as follows:

```
# Prints Used cars
print honda.key.parrent().parent().get().name
```

This concludes the second approach of modeling your data. In general, whenever you store related data in your system, you should form these kind of relationships via child-parent keys so that your data items end up together in datastore, due to the sorted nature of the Bigtable row keys. In an invoicing application, where you have categories, products, customers, invoices, and invoice items, you can form such a relationship between categories and products. Here, the key of the category entities will be the parent key of the related product entities. In this way, you will be able to scan through all the products of a category by just scanning all the rows that start with the key of the category, as follows:

```
# Fetch all the products in perfumes category. Note that perfumes is
# an instance of ndb.Key class.
Product.query(ancestor=perfumes).fetch(10)
```

Similarly, you can make such a relationship between the customers and orders, where the key of the customer entities end up as the parent of their orders, enabling you to iterate over all the orders of a customer, as follows:

```
Order.query(ancestor=jhon).fetch(10)
```

Because each order has many line items, you can use the key of the order entities as the parent on the line items while creating them, so that you can iterate over all the line items of a given order, as follows:

```
# Same as before
LineItem.query(ancestor=myorder).fetch(10)
```

With this, we conclude our discussion on how to model data around the Bigtable features to take the maximum advantage of Datastore. Next we will look into the property types that are available and how to use them.

Properties

We have been declaring a few Kinds with a few properties, so we have some idea about what they are. So far, we have used `ndb.IntegerProperty` to store prices, `ndb.StringProperty` to store various textual pieces of information, and `ndb.KeyProperty` once to store references to other entities. There are many more available property types. All of them accept a common set of keyword arguments with which we can modify their behavior. Let's go through these common options in turn. Here's the list; we will discuss each option in detail after this list:

- required
- default
- repeated

- choices
- indexed
- validator

The required option

This is a Boolean that is by default set to `False`. If you set it to `True`, not assigning a value to this property will raise an exception. We can revise the `Category` kind in light of this, as follows, because a category without a name makes no sense:

```
from google.appengine.ext import ndb

class Category(ndb.Model):
    name = ndb.StringProperty(required=True)


c = Category()

# Shall raise BadValue
c.put()
```

The default option

This keyword argument specifies the default value that you would like this property to have in case you do not specify a value. If a property is required, and then you indicate a default value as well, that does not make much sense, because when something is required, it will not fall to the default values. Therefore, we cannot use this with the `required` argument on the same property. In light of this, we can revise the `Listing` Kind by making the price have a default value, as follows:

```
from google.appengine.ext import ndb

class Listing(ndb.Model):
    title = ndb.StringProperty(required=True)
    price = ndb.IntegerProperty(default=0)
l = Listing(title="Bike for sale")

# Save it, price would default to 0
l.put()

#prints 0
print l.price
```

The repeated option

This is a Boolean and, by default, it is set to `False`. If it is set to `True`, the property accepts a Python list. Once assigned, you can modify the list in place or reassign a new list to it. One thing that differs from the Python lists (the Python `list` type) is that the Python lists can have values of any type, but, in this case, the list should have elements of the same type as the ones that are acceptable by the property. Let's add a `tags` property to our `Listing` class, as follows:

```
from google.appengine.ext import ndb
class Listing(ndb.Model):
    title = ndb.StringProperty(required=True)
    price = ndb.IntegerProperty(default=0)
    features = ndb.StringProperty(repeated=True)
car = Listing(title="BMW i530", price=25000)
car.features = ['DVD Player', 'Power Steering']
# Raises exception because last element not a string
car.features = ['DVD Player', 'Power Steering', 34]
```

In the next chapter, we will see how to query entities with multiple property values.

The choices options

By using this keyword argument, you can restrict the acceptable values to a given list of values. For example, in our case, let's suppose that we want to have a property called `make` with a limited set of choices. This is how we go about it:

```
from google.appengine.ext import ndb

class Listing(ndb.Model):
    title = ndb.StringProperty(required=True)
    make = ndb.StringProperty(choices=['Coup', 'Sedan', 'SUV'])

civic = Listing(title="Honda Civic")
civic.make = 'Sedan'
# Will raise exception.
civic.make = 'Whatever'
```

So, as you can see, it won't allow you to assign a value that is not in the list of choices that were given at the time of declaration.

The indexed option

This is a Boolean argument with a default value of `True`. We discussed in the previous chapter how querying works for single property values; we indicated that the value that is to be queried against is actually used as a key, and row scan operations are performed in a separate index BigTable table to locate the actual row that contains data. This will be clearer in the next chapter, when we examine how queries work. However, the main point here is that an index is built for every property that you declare, which takes up space.

It could be the case that you just want to store the property and never ever want to query it. In this particular case, setting `indexed` to `False` won't create the built-in default index for this property, and it will save you some space. However, on the other hand, you won't be able to filter your results on this property.

The validator option

You might want to have some validation in place for your declared properties. With this function, you can indicate a function that will validate the values for you. Let's put a validator in place for `price` to ensure that it does not get assigned a negative value. Try the following example in the interactive console:

```
from google.appengine.ext import ndb
def validate_price(prop, value):
    if prop._name != 'price':
        return None

    if value < 0:
        raise ValueError("Price cannot be negative")

class Listing(ndb.Model):
    title = ndb.StringProperty(required=True)
    price = ndb.IntegerProperty(default=0, validator=validate_price)


car = Listing(title="Mercedez Benz")
car.price = 34
# BadValue exception. Price cannot be negative.
car.price = -2
```

The first argument to the function is the property being validated and is an instance of ndb.Property or its subclasses, whereas value is whatever value was assigned. If you either return None or do not return anything from this function, the value will be used as it was supplied. If you modify the value and return it, the modified value will be used instead. If you raise an exception, well, you then know what to expect.

The available properties

Now that we understand the common options that can be supplied to properties, it is time to take a look at the kind of properties that we can declare. Let's go through them in turn:

Property type	Details
BooleanProperty	Stores either True or False.
IntegerProperty	Stores a 64-bit signed integer.
FloatProperty	Stores a double-precision floating-point number.
StringProperty	Stores up to 500 characters and is indexed.
TextProperty	Stores an unlimited unicode string, but is not indexed.
BlobProperty	A raw uninterrupted string of bytes. If indexed is set to True, this stores only 500 bytes, which are indexed. If it is set to False, you can store an unlimited amount, but it is not indexed. Optionally, if compressed is set to True, the contents will be compressed.
DateProperty	Stores date. More details on this later.
TimeProperty	This stores time. More details on this later.
DateTimeProperty	This stores both date and time. More details on this will be provided later.
GeoPtProperty	This stores a geometric point, longitude, and latitude. It is constructed by using ndb.GeoPt(34.43, 56.90) or like ndb.GeoPt("45.345, 64.34534").
KeyProperty	Stores a reference to another key of an entity. Optionally, supply the kind keyword argument, which accepts a class instance or a string. This will limit the types of keys that you can assign to it. We've seen an example of this earlier.
JsonProperty	You can assign any Python object that is serializable to JSON by using the json module. The assigned object or value is stored as a JSON string. Optionally, if you set compressed=True, data will be compressed. Compression will save disk space, but reading and writing will be slightly more time-consuming.

Property type	Details
PickleProperty	Like JSON, this takes the same values, except that they are serialized by using Python's pickle module. This takes a compressed keyword argument as well, just like JsonProperty.
GenericProperty	Catch all. Takes anything from int, float, bool, str, unicode, datetime, Key, ndb.GeoPt, or none.
ComputedProperty	A property whose value is computed by a function. More details on this later.
StructuredProperty	Allows you to nest entities inside others. So this will take a whole entity instance as a value. More explanation on this will be provided later.
LocalStructuredProperty	This is the same as StructuedProperty, except that the values are not indexed because the on-disk stored representation is just a plain string of bytes.

The date and time properties

When talking about dates and time, we usually have three levels of granularity. At times, we are only concerned about time and not about date at all. For such occasions, you should use TimeProperty, which accepts objects of the time class from Python's datetime module.

Then there's the case where you are not bothered about the time, but just the date, such as the date of an event or a holiday. In such cases, you should use DateProperty, which accepts instances of the date class from the datetime module.

Finally, there's the last case where you care about both the date and time. For these situations, you should use DateTimeProperty, which accepts instances of the datetime class from the datetime module.

All the three classes accept two keyword arguments. The first is auto_now_add. By default, it is set to False. If it is set to True, the property will be assigned the value of the current time when it is created, but when you update it, the value will be untouched.

The other optional argument is auto_now, which is the same as auto_now_add except that it will assign the current time irrespective of whether you are creating the entity or updating it. If both the arguments are set to True, auto_now will be considered instead.

There's one catch here. The two aforementioned options cannot be used if you set repeated=True. You may recall that with the repeated argument set to True, you can assign multiple values to a property.

Structured Properties

Structured properties is a feature of the `ndb` library, where it allows you to assign a whole entity to a property of your model. The entity that is assigned as a value is not stored independently and eventually does not have a row key as any independently created entity would have. This assigned entity can only be queried and accessed from the entity that it is assigned to. An example will clarify this. Let's suppose that we want to store the `Lister` class besides the listing as well. This is how you should do it:

```python
from google.appengine.ext import ndb

class Lister(ndb.Model):
    name = ndb.StringProperty()
    email = ndb.StringProperty()

class Listing(ndb.Model):
    title = ndb.StringProperty(required=True)
    price = ndb.IntegerProperty(default=0)
    lister = ndb.StructuredProperty(Lister)

lister = Lister(name="Mohsin", email="mohsin@appengine.com")
car = Listing(title="Mercedez Benz", price=50000, lister=lister)

car.put()
```

Just a gentle reminder so that there's no confusion: we are using the words entity and model interchangeably. The word model comes from the domain modeling where you represent your business concepts (such as products and orders) as classes. In the world of relational databases, an instance of such a class is actually a row in a database table. However, in the case of datastore, we call an instance of a model an entity.

We actually defined `Lister` as a separate model and created a new property of the `ndb.StructuredProperty` type by declaring that it will get the `Lister` model as a value. Next we created an instance of `Lister` and assigned it to an instance of `Listing`. Finally, we called `put` on the `Listing` instance, which actually stores the whole thing in datastore. All the properties of `Lister` will actually be stored as the properties of the `Listing` entity. As we know from our exploration of Bigtable and how datastore is built on top of it, all the properties are stored in a single column of Bigtable. So, all of these will end up in a single column after serialization. Here's the list of properties and their values as they will be stored:

The property name, as stored and serialized	The property value
title	Mercedez Benz
price	50000
lister.name	mohsin
lister.email	`mohsin@appengine.com`

The computed properties

There are situations where you realize that the value of a property is dependent on the value of other properties because it has to be computed in a certain way. For such situations, the ndb library provides us with ndb.ComputedProperty, which takes a function with a reference to the entity instance. You can point the entity instance to refer to the values of other properties if you want to, and compute the value for the property that is based on them and return it. Let's take an example. Let's suppose that we want to have another property that stores the half of the listed price. Clearly, it depends on the price property's value and can be computed from it. So, let's see how we do this:

```
from google.appengine.ext import ndb

def calculate_half_price(entity):
    return entity.price / 2

class Listing(ndb.Model):
    title = ndb.StringProperty(required=True)
    price = ndb.IntegerProperty(default=0)
    half_price = ndb.ComputedProperty(calculate_half_price)

car = Listing(title="Honda Accord", price=50000)
# Prints 25000
print car.half_price
```

Pretty self-explanatory. This covers our discussion of properties. Next we are going to elevate ourselves one step higher and look at models.

The model

We have been using `ndb.Model` so far, but didn't look at the class in detail. The following are the three groups of things that we need to look into:

- The constructor
- The class methods
- The instance methods

Let's look at these in turn.

The constructor

We have been using constructor throughout our examples, as follows:

```
Listing(title="Civic 1995 for Sale")
```

What can you pass to the constructor? Basically, all the properties that you declared on the `model` itself can be supplied as keyword arguments for initial values while creating the instance. Besides this, the following can be supplied:

- **ID**: This is either an integer or a string that you wish to use as an identifier instead of the autogenerated one using the `id` keyword argument. If an ID is provided, then the key cannot be specified. We have used it in some of our examples.
- **Key**: You can specify the whole key yourself using the `key` keyword argument. If you are supplying the `ndb.Key` instance, the ID and parent cannot be supplied and should be `None`. We have also done this in some examples.
- **Parent**: The `ndb.Key` instance should be used as a parent. You can specify it using the `parent` keyword argument. If the parent is supplied, the key should be `None`. We have also used this in a previous example and learned how it affects things.
- **Namespace**: By default, it will take the current namespace, but if you want to create it in some other namespace, you can mention it here using the `namespace` keyword argument. If the namespace is given, the key cannot be given, and it should be set to `None`.

Class methods

There are a few class methods that are available for various tasks. Let's take a look.

The allocate_ids() method

We discussed that, by default, datastore assigns autogenerated numeric identifiers to the entities that we create. It may be the case that you want to generate lots of entities and want their IDs to be consecutive. This method will allow you to allocate a range of consecutive IDs, which are guaranteed not to be assigned again once returned. We saw an example of this previously. There are three parameters here:

- **size**: This is the number of IDs that need to be allocated. If supplied, max cannot be given.

- **max**: The maximum number to which the identifiers need to be generated. For instance, if size=1000, all the identifiers that are available and under or equal to 1000 will be generated.

- **parent**: This parent key needs to be used while generating IDs. We have discussed the parent key in detail. This will be an instance of the ndb.Key class.

The get_by_id() method

Given an ID, this method returns the entity. As you know from the discussions so far, an ID is either an integer or a string, as we used for categories.

The get_or_insert() method

Given an ID, this method either gets an entity or creates one. You can specify arguments as the initial properties. Let's suppose that we want to create a Category entity only if it does not exist. Otherwise, we want to have it returned, if it already exists in the datastore:

```
Category.get_or_insert('used-cars', name="Used Cars")
```

This will return an entity if it exists. Otherwise, it will create it.

The query() method

This is the method that we have used to query entities so far. This basically takes a list of filters. We will explore this in detail in the next chapter.

The instance methods

There are a handful of instance methods that are available as well. Let's quickly go through them.

The populate() method

The function of this method is the same as supplying property values through a constructor or assigning them. That is how it looks like:

```
listing = Listing(title="Furniture for sale", price=200)
# Or this way
listing = Listing()
listing.populate(title="Furniture for sale", price=200)
```

The put() method

We have used this method a lot. This actually writes an entity to the datastore and only returns when the row key is generated and written.

The to_dict() method

This method converts a `model` instance into a dictionary. It accepts the `include` keyword parameter, which is a list of property names. If supplied, only the given properties are included. Similarly, it has an `exclude` keyword argument, which will exclude the properties listed:

```
listing = Listing(title="Furniture for sale", price=200)
# Only title
listing.to_dict(include['title'])
# Only price
listing.to_dict(exclude=['title'])
```

Asynchronous versions

The `allocate_ids()`, `get_by_id()`, `get_or_insert()`, and `put()` methods are blocking functions; that is, they don't return from execution until the thing that they are doing is complete. There are asynchronous versions of these functions as well, which are `allocate_ids_async()`, `get_by_id_async()`, `get_or_insert_async()`, and `put_async()`. These return a `Future` object instead of a result. This Future object has a `get_result` method, which can be called to obtain the results. This method will not return until the result is retrieved. Another method is `wait()`, which will block until the result is available; although, this method won't return a result. Instead, it always returns `None`. To check whether the result has arrived yet or not, you can call the `done()` method on the returned `future` object, which reruns immediately. Let's take a look at a quick example. Try the following in an interactive console:

```
from google.appengine.ext import ndb

class Category(ndb.Model):
```

```
    name = ndb.StringProperty()

future = Category.get_by_id_async('used-cars')

if future.done():
   print "Got the result"
   print future.get_result().name
else:
   print "Yet didn't get the result., will wait."
   # Can call future.get_result() as well if we want to because
   # that will wait too.
   future.wait()
   print "Finished waiting, now will collect the results."
   print future.get_result().name
```

Here's the output of the program:

```
Yet didn't get the result., will wait.
Finished waiting, now will collect the results.
Used Cars
```

Here we basically called the asynchronous version of get_by_id(), which returned a future object. We next checked whether the process of getting ID was done by calling done(). In the case it was done by calling done(), we collect the result. However, in the case it was not, we call wait() on it till we get the result.

This can be very useful when the operations that you are performing are pretty much independent. For instance, you can dispatch a get_by_id_async() call and do other stuff in the meantime. Once done with the other stuff, you can check whether the result is available and proceed in accordance. Thus, you can save some time.

Model hooks

There are four operations when it comes to entities—allocating IDs, getting an entity, putting an entity, and deleting an entity. The ndb library provides the facility of hooks for these operations. Each hook has two versions—a pre-call hook and a post-call hook.

These hooks have to be defined as an instance of the class methods on the Model class, which is inherited from ndb.Model. Here's the complete list:

```
from google.appengine.ext import ndb

class Category(ndb.Model):
    name = ndb.StringProperty()
```

```python
    @classmethod
    def _pre_allocate_ids_hook(cls, size, max, parent):
        """Hook that runs before allocate_ids()"""
        print "Going to allocate IDs", cls, size, max, parent

    @classmethod
    def _post_allocate_ids_hook(cls, size, max, parent, future):
        """Hook that runs after allocate_ids()"""
        print "Done allocating IDs", cls, size, max, parent

    @classmethod
    def _pre_delete_hook(cls, key):
        """Hook that runs before delete()"""
        print "Going to delete entity", cls, key

    @classmethod
    def _post_delete_hook(cls, key, future):
        """Hook that runs after delete()"""
        print "Done deleting entity", cls, key

    @classmethod
    def _pre_get_hook(cls, key):
        """Hook that runs before Key.get() when getting an entity of
this model."""
        print "Going to get the entity", cls, key

    @classmethod
    def _post_get_hook(cls, key, future):
        """Hook that runs after Key.get() when getting an entity of
this model."""
        print "Got the entity.", cls, key

    def _pre_put_hook(self):
        """Hook that runs before put()"""
        print "Going to put the entity", self

    def _post_put_hook(self, future):
        """Hook that runs after put()"""
        print "Done with putting entity", self


cars = Category(name="Used Cars", id=420)

# First put, pre and post hooks would be triggered.
```

```
cars.put()

# Now get it. Pre and post get hooks would be triggered.
c = Category.get_by_id(420)

# Now delete it, pre and post delete hooks would be triggered.
c.key.delete()

# Now allocate some IDs, pre and post hooks would be triggered.
Category.allocate_ids(10)
```

Excluding the hooks for the put() method, the others are class methods that receive the Model class as the first argument. Furthermore, because the synchronous and asynchronous methods have the same hooks, all the post_ methods take a future argument, which is an instance of Future in case the call was an asynchronous call. You may ask, "how do I prevent an operation from happening?" If you raise any exception in a pre-call hook, the related operation will be aborted. It's that simple.

Summary

In this chapter, we started with the need for data modeling and examined how to model data using the ndb's Model class. Then we dived into how it is stored internally, with all the properties serialized into a single column. Next we examined in detail how datastore constructs unique row keys for an entity by using the application ID, the current namespace, the Kind (the model's class name), and a unique identifier. We also studied how the identifier can be either a string or an integer. In the case it is an integer, we learned that datastore generates numeric IDs, and we can allocate our own range of IDs as well if we want to.

Next we examined the ndb.Key class and how it allows us to weld keys together to achieve some interesting effects. We introduced two approaches to modeling data. The first approach included the key of another entity as its property. The other approach included the key as a part of the entity's key itself. We compared both approaches briefly, and then moved on to exploring the available properties and methods of the model class. We examined the asynchronous methods and how to use them. We also briefly looked into the available hooks as to how we can plug in to various post and pre events, such as before the entity is stored to datastore, after it is stored, or deleted. With this, we concluded our discussion about data modeling.

We did not talk about how to query data in this chapter, which is what we will look at in the next chapter.

5
Queries, Indexes, and Transactions

Till now, we have examined the internals of datastore, how it is built on top of BigTable, and how we can model our data around it. This, of course, makes us store whatever we want to, but it is useless until we can retrieve what was stored. Datastore provides us with a way to query the stored data with two parallel interfaces. One is an API, which is used to query data, and another is an SQL-like language called **Google Query Language** (**GQL**).

In this chapter, we will learn the following:

- Querying your data
- The way queries work and the limitations of what can be queried
- The query API and GQL
- Transactions

So, that's a tall order. Let's start our journey.

Querying your data

Before we can query some data, we should have some data. So, our first step will be to generate some sample data on which we can experiment with the query API that is provided by datastore. We will take our old `Listing` model from the previous chapters and add a few more fields to it. Next, we will create some listings for cars from 1990 to 2000 that come with a random price assigned to each.

So, the following is the program that does this:

```
from google.appengine.ext import ndb
import random

class Listing(ndb.Model):
    title = ndb.StringProperty()
    year = ndb.IntegerProperty()
    price = ndb.IntegerProperty(default=0)

for year in xrange(1990, 2001):
    car = Listing()
    car.title = "Honda Civic %s" % year
    car.price = random.randint(4000, 50000)
    car.year = year
    car.put()
```

So, as you can see, we have a `Listing` model with `title`, `year`, and `price`. We created a `Listing` instance, assigned a title to it, set a random price, and the year was assigned in sequence. Next, we simply used the `put()` function to put the newly created instance in datastore.

To run this program, go to any existing App Engine app (we will use the `hello` application from the first chapter) and execute the following:

```
/path/to/gae/sdk/dev_appserver.py --clear_datastore true .
```

Just a reminder. We are running the local App Engine server. The `--clear_datastore` option will ensure that we get a blank datastore with no entities at all. This will ensure that we have a clean slate to experiment. The last `"."` symbol indicates that the current directory contains the app that we want to run. This directory must contain `app.yaml`, as explained in the first chapter.

Now go to the interactive console, paste the preceding code in it and execute it. The execution of the said code will create ten listings with different prices.

Now comes the part where we query the data. Go to the interactive console, remove the old code, and paste in the following:

```
from google.appengine.ext import ndb

class Listing(ndb.Model):
    title = ndb.StringProperty()
    year = ndb.IntegerProperty()
```

```
    price = ndb.IntegerProperty(default=0)

    def __str__(self):
        return "%s: $%s" % (self.title, self.price)

def p(items):
    for item in items:
        print str(item)

print "Cars of 1995 model:"
p(Listing.query().filter(Listing.year == 1995).fetch())
# Same with GQL sytax. Output not being printed intentionally
ndb.gql("SELECT * FROM Listing WHERE year = 1995").fetch()

print ""

print "Cars of price 7000 or above:"
p(Listing.query().filter(Listing.price >= 7000).fetch())
# Same with GQL syntax. Output not being printed intentionally
ndb.gql("SELECT * FROM Listing WHERE price >= 7000").fetch()

print ""

print "Cars between 7000 and 20,000:"
p(Listing.query().filter(Listing.price >=
  7000).filter(Listing.price <= 20000).fetch())
# Same with GQL syntax. Output not being printed intentionally
ndb.gql("SELECT * FROM Listing WHERE price >= 7000 AND price <=
  20000").fetch()

print ""

print "Cars of year 1995 between 7000 and 20,000:"
p(Listing.query().filter(Listing.price >= 7000).filter(Listing.price
<= 20000).filter(Listing.year ==
  1995).fetch())
# Same with GQL syntax. Output not being printed intentionally
ndb.gql("SELECT * FROM Listing WHERE price >= 7000 AND price <=
  20000 AND year = 1995").fetch()

print ""

print "Most expensive cars starting from $7000:"
```

```
    p(Listing.query().filter(Listing.price >= 7000).order(-
      Listing.price).fetch())
    ndb.gql("SELECT * FROM Listing WHERE price >= 7000 ORDER BY price
      DESC").fetch()

    print ""

    print "Most recent cars starting from $7000:"
    try:
        p(Listing.query().filter(Listing.price >= 7000).order(-
          Listing.year).fetch())
        ndb.gql("SELECT * FROM Listing WHERE price >= 7000 ORDER BY year
    DESC").fetch()
    except Exception as e:
        print "Query rejected, exception %s raised from datastore" %
    type(e)
        print "with message: %s" % str(e)

    print ""
    print "Cars between $7000 to $20000 but introduced in 1995 or later:"
    try:
        p(ndb.gql("SELECT * FROM Listing WHERE price >= 7000 AND price <=
    20000 AND year >= 1995").fetch())
    except Exception as e:
        print "Query rejected, exception %s raised from datastore" %
    type(e)
        print "with message: %s" % str(e)
```

Here's the output of the preceding code:

```
Cars of 1995 model:
Honda Civic 1995: $27531
Cars of price 7000 or above:
Honda Civic 1991: $7561
Honda Civic 1999: $13063
Honda Civic 1996: $17260
Honda Civic 1994: $18968
Honda Civic 1990: $20960
Honda Civic 2000: $26752
Honda Civic 1995: $27531
Honda Civic 1992: $30584
Honda Civic 1997: $35951
```

```
Honda Civic 1998: $37331

Cars between 7000 and 20,000:
Honda Civic 1991: $7561
Honda Civic 1999: $13063
Honda Civic 1996: $17260
Honda Civic 1994: $18968

Cars of year 1995 between 7000 and 20,000:

Most expensive cars starting from $7000:
Honda Civic 1998: $37331
Honda Civic 1997: $35951
Honda Civic 1992: $30584
Honda Civic 1995: $27531
Honda Civic 2000: $26752
Honda Civic 1990: $20960
Honda Civic 1994: $18968
Honda Civic 1996: $17260
Honda Civic 1999: $13063
Honda Civic 1991: $7561

Most recent cars starting from $7000:
Query rejected, exception <class 'google.appengine.api.datastore_
errors.BadRequestError'> raised from datastore
with message: The first sort property must be the same as the property
to which the inequality filter is applied.  In your query the first
sort property is year but the inequality filter is on price

Cars between $7000 to $20000 but introduced in 1995 or later:
Query rejected, exception <class 'google.appengine.api.datastore_
errors.BadRequestError'> raised from datastore
with message: Only one inequality filter per query is supported.
Encountered both price and year
```

Let's go through the code from top to bottom. In the `Listing` model, the only new thing is the `__str__` method, which is added so that the output can be more readable. It just prints the `Car name`, `year`, and `price`.

When we issue queries, we might get multiple entities that match our criteria. To print all of them, we will have to loop through them. Therefore, the code will have loops because we are going to execute many queries here. To avoid this, we have a small utility function named `p` that just goes through the list of entities and prints each of them.

Next, we will ask the following five queries:

- Give us the entities for cars of model 1995
- Give us the entities for cars that are priced at 7,000 or more
- Give us the entities for cars that are priced between 7,000 and 20,000
- Give us the entities for cars that are priced between 7,000 and 20,000 but later than year 1995
- Give us the entities for cars that are priced above 7,000 in such a way that the most expensive ones are listed first

We asked two more queries which are unfortunately met with exceptions:

- List the cars that are priced above 7,000. List the latest models first.
- Cars between 7,000 and 20,000, but which were on the market post 1995 or beyond.

We will see why these queries failed. Each of the preceding queries is posed in two different dialects:

- As the Query API that is provided by datastore
- GQL, an SQL-like language

There's one interesting point to note. The actual API of datastore is the query interface that is shown in the code. The GQL language is built on top of this. When you write a GQL query, it is transformed into the equivalent API calls. This is the reverse of the situation from the ORMs, such as Active Record for Rails, Django's ORM, or SQL Alchemy, where the API calls are translated into SQL. Here, GQL is translated to the API calls instead.

Now, let's explore how the listings are queried. The ndb.Query is the main class that is used to query the datastore. You can create its instance and apply few filter() and order() calls on this instance for the ordering. Once satisfied, you can simply call the fetch() method, which will get you a list of matching entities.

So, for example, we want to get the entities for cars that are priced greater than or equal to 7,000. Here's how we do this:

1. First, we create a Query instance by using the following command:

```
q = ndb.Query(kind='Listing')
```

   The kind keyword argument in the above statement specifies what kind we want to filter. However, you can create the query instance in the following way too, as we have done in the preceding code:

```
q = Listing.query() # Same as ndb.Query(kind='Listing')
```

This statement above is the same as before, but it is probably more readable. Therefore, this is what we have used in our code. The next thing that we have to do is apply some filters.

2. You have to call the `filter()` method with an expression, as follows:

```
q.filter(Model.property operator value)
```

So, in our case, it will be like this:

```
q = q.filter(Listing.price >= 7000)
```

Note that we have assigned q back to q because each invocation to the `filter()` method returns a new instance of the `Query` object. If we want to add another condition that needs to be applied, it will be the second argument, which is as follows:

```
q = q.filter(Listing.price >= 7000, Listing.price <= 10000)
```

This shows all the listings where the price of the car is between 7,000 and 10,000.

3. So now, our query object is ready and we can call the `fetch()` method on it. But before that, you can apply some ordering to it as well, using the `order()` method. To do this, you can call `order()` method, as follows:

```
q = q.order(Model.property)
```

So, if we want the prices listed in the ascending order, we will use the following command:

```
q = q.order(Listing.price)
```

However, if we want order in the descending order, we will simply use the following command:

```
q = q.order(-Listing.price)
```

4. Now, putting all of the above together in a single statement, we will get the following:

```
q = ndb.Query(kind='Listing').filter(Listing.price >= 7000).
order(-Listing.price)
```

Alternatively, we can get something that looks like the following:

```
q = Listing.query().filter(Listing.price >= 7000).order(-Listing.
price)
```

5. If you prefer something that is SQL-like, you have the `ndb.gql()` method at your disposal to construct the same. Here's how you can do this:

```
q = ndb.gql("SELECT * FROM Listing WHERE price >= 7000 ORDER BY
price DESC")
```

6. Now, we have to process the results after we are done with all the filtering and ordering. We will learn more about GQL later but whichever method you use to build your query object, you have to call the `fetch()` method to retrieve the entities. Here's how it works:

```
listings = q.fetch()
for listing in listings:
    print listing
```

Now, after the preceding explanation, you should be able to understand what is going on in the code. All that we are doing is asking the aforementioned questions. Results from all the returned listing objects are printed. Here's the breakdown of the different operations for each question:

1. First, we asked for the cars of the 1995 model, which means that we have to filter by the year property. So this is a filter on a single-property.

2. Next, we looked for cars that were priced at 7,000 or above. So, the price is the property of concern. This is again a filter for a single-property.

3. Next, we asked for cars between 7,000 and 20,000, which again is filtered according to a single-property, which is the price of the car in this case.

4. Next, we got bold in our questioning. We asked for the cars between price range 7,000 and 20,000 but those manufactured from the year 1995. In abstract terms, we have inequality filters for a single-property and an equality filter for a single-property.

5. Then, we asked for not only the cars that are priced at 7,000 or above, but we also wanted the results sorted by price in the descending order. So, we filtered on a single-property and ordered on the same property, which is the price of the car. In abstract terms, inequality filters on a single-property and sorting the results by the same property. We get the results, and all goes well.

6. After this, we asked for cars that are priced at 7,000 or above, but we wanted them to be sorted by year in the descending order. So, we filtered on a single property price, but ordered our results by another property. In abstract terms, inequality filter on a single-property, but sort order on another property. This will fail, and we will encounter an exception.

7. Next, we asked the last question. We looked up for cars between price 7,000 and 20,000, but besides this, the year should be 1995 or later. We do not want our results to be sorted in any way; it's just the two filters. So eventually, we have a filter for the price of the car and another filter for the year. In abstract terms, there are inequality filters on two different properties. In response, we encounter an exception.

As you can see, for the last two questions, we didn't get an answer, rather we encountered some exceptions. That's interesting. Why did the two queries fail? We will have to look under the hood to understand this. Let's explore.

Queries under the hood

In the previous two chapters, we learned that datastore is built on top of BigTable. We also learned the BigTable operations. You may recall from our discussion in the third chapter on BigTable that while reading data from BigTable, operations fetch either a row whose key is known, or a set of rows by using a starting and ending key, which is also known as a **range scan**. We also learned that the rows in BigTable are always stored sorted in the lexicographic order of the row keys. Hence, scanning the range is very efficient because all the rows are consecutive on the disk.

You'll also recall that our entities are stored as rows in BigTable, with all the properties serialized into a single column. Now, we have a situation where all the properties end up in a single BigTable column and on top of that, the only operations that are available are fetching a single row by key or a range of rows by giving a starting and an ending key range.

So, when this is how data is stored and only these limited operations are available on BigTable, how are we able to filter by price range and even add a year to filter in one of the cases? The idea is simple. We actually have another BigTable table, which has its keys as the values for the property that we want to filter on. Because BigTable is a key-value store, the value is the key of the row that has the property to be searched for in the actual table. Read the previous sentence carefully because it explains 80 percent of the datastore that you need to understand while working with it.

So, we had a lot of abstract discussion here. Let's make our understanding more concrete by looking at actual examples. To better understand how the search operation works using indexes, we will first have a look at the simplest case, where we are trying to filter rows on a single-property. Once this is clear, we will move towards the case where more than one property is involved in queries.

Single-property queries

Let's take example of price. We know that the price ends up as a serialized value in a single column in BigTable. If we want to filter our entities by price, datastore will create another BigTable index table behind the scenes with the following structure:

Key (of form kind-property-value)	Value (the entity key)
Listing-price-4277	Listing-6333186975989760
Listing-price-4298	Listing-5910974510923776
Listing-price-10311	Listing-6473924464345088
Listing-price-14227	Listing-5348024557502464
Listing-price-15418	Listing-6192449487634432
Listing-price-15919	Listing-4785074604081152
Listing-price-26506	Listing-5770237022568448
Listing-price-38419	Listing-5207287069147136
Listing-price-47041	Listing-5066549580791808
Listing-price-49035	Listing-4644337115725824
Listing-price-49237	Listing-5629499534213120

This is the same index table from the list of six tables that we discussed in *Chapter 3, Understanding the Datastore*. In this table, the row keys are in the [kind]-[property-name]-[property-value] format. So, Listing-price-47041 means that the entity with a price has a value of 47041. Also, in the value column, we have the row key for this entity, which is Listing-5066549580791808. You may recall from the last two chapters that in Listing-5066549580791808, the long number is the entity ID, which is automatically generated by datastore. However, you can specify your own as well to form a key.

With the preceding index table in place and the BigTable operations of fetching a row by key and scanning a range of keys, we can support the following types of queries:

- price = some value: This simply means a key lookup in the index table and picking up an actual row key

- price > value, price >= value: This simply means starting from the Listing-price-value key and scanning until the end because all values are in a sorted order

- Order by price: Because BigTable stores keys in the lexicographic order, to sort entities by price, all we have to do is to read the records in order, as stored in this table

The following are the three operations that are not yet addressed:

- `order by price` descending
- `price != value`
- `price <= value`

Let's start with the first one. To support the sorting of price in descending order, another table is created. This table is exactly the same as the `Index` table that we saw earlier, except that the entities are sorted in descending order instead of ascending order, as shown in the first table. So, this is how the second index table looks:

Key (of form Kind-property-value)	Value (entity key)
Listing-price-49237	Listing-5629499534213120
Listing-price-49035	Listing-4644337115725824
Listing-price-47041	Listing-5066549580791808
Listing-price-38419	Listing-5207287069147136
Listing-price-26506	Listing-5770237022568448
Listing-price-15919	Listing-4785074604081152
Listing-price-15418	Listing-6192449487634432
Listing-price-14227	Listing-5348024557502464
Listing-price-10311	Listing-6473924464345088
Listing-price-4298	Listing-5910974510923776
Listing-price-4277	Listing-6333186975989760

Nothing is different from the first table except that it is sorted by the row key in descending order.

Now, if we want to get all the entities sorted by price in descending order, we simply start reading from the start of this table and keep on collecting the corresponding rows until the end by fetching them with the keys listed. Eventually, everything will be sorted by price in descending order.

The next operation is `price <= value`. Again, this is pretty simple. Because the table is sorted in the descending order by price, we start with the row scan operation with the `Listing-price-value` prefix and read until the end of the table. For instance, we are looking for cars that are priced under 20,000, that is, `Listing.price <= 20000`. So, our starting key will be `Listing-price-20000`. Now, from the preceding table, the value of the `Listing-price-15919` row key is less than `Listing-price-20000`. Therefore, this is where the scan starts from and keeps on moving until the end, collecting all the rows that we encounter.

Now, we are left with the final case, where `price != value` is to work. How will this work? Well, `price != value` means that the price is not equal to the value. In other words, anything greater than or less than price So, we can say that `price != value` is the same as `price > value` and `price < value`. We have already learned that `price > value` is supported by the index table in the ascending sort and the `price < value` case is supported by the second index table, which is sorted by price in the descending order. Now, if we execute the corresponding range scan operations on both the tables and merge their results, we will get the results for `price != value`.

We have explored these internal workings of datastore in the previous chapters as well. Therefore, we will keep it brief here. However, to explain how this works under the hood, we'll now examine our own queries from an earlier code example.

Examples of single-property queries

After all the theory on how queries work on a single-property, let's look at the code that we wrote earlier to better understand how indexes enable us to search for entities:

```
Listing.query().filter(Listing.year == 1995).fetch()
ndb.gql("SELECT * FROM Listing WHERE year = 1995").fetch()
```

This translates into a single-key lookup for a row in the `index` table for the `year` property. So, we're looking for a row in the `index` table for the year with the `Listing-year-1995` key. Once picked up, we read its value, which will be the key for the entity that will be read and returned.

Now, let's look at the next example:

```
Listing.query().filter(Listing.price >= 7000).fetch()
ndb.gql("SELECT * FROM Listing WHERE price >= 7000").fetch()
```

Here, we will look in the `index` table for the price. We will scan for rows with keys that are greater than or equal to `Listing-price-7000` until the end of the table. For each row that is being read, we will read its value, which is a key for the actual entity that needs to be fetched. Thus, listing will be fetched and collected and the whole result set will be returned.

Now, let's move on to the next example where two filters exist on the same property:

```
Listing.query().filter(Listing.price >= 7000).filter(Listing.price <=
20000).fetch()
ndb.gql("SELECT * FROM Listing WHERE price >= 7000 AND price <=
20000").fetch()
```

This is the same as the previous one, except that instead of reading until the end, we only scan until we reach the row with the `Listing-price-20000` key.

In summary, for each property of your entity, index entries end up in two tables. Their keys are in the `Kind-property-value` form. One of these two tables is sorted in the ascending order, and the other table is sorted in the descending order by the `Kind-property-value`. It is appropriate to mention here that the disk space consumed by the rows in these tables counts towards your datastore storage quota. Because the aforementioned space counts towards your quota, there might be a case where you do not want to query a property and hence, do not need to be recorded into these tables. You can prevent this from happening by setting `indexed=False` by defining the property in the following way:

```
price = ndb.IntegerProperty(indexed=False)
```

We already have examined the `indexed` keyword argument in the previous chapter. There's one major difference between traditional databases and datastore. In relational databases such as MySQL, Postgres, and others in the same league, the index is not required if you wish to query the data. So, for example, if you stored the same data in MySQL, you will still be able to query it if there's no index. It is just that the performance will be poor. Adding an index will speed up things to a much greater degree. In contrast to this, because of the way BigTable works, you cannot query by a property if an index is not created for it, and you will encounter an exception instead.

Now that we understand how this works for single-property filters, let's expand our case towards multiple properties.

Multiple property indexes

When more than one property is involved in a query, nothing much changes from the operational standpoint. It is just a row scan operation, as we have seen so far. It is only the row key formation of the `index` tables that change. One of the queries that spanned over multiple properties, which was issued in the previous code example, was where we asked for cars between the price range of 7,000 and 2,000, but of year 1995. As you can see, this query clearly spans over two different properties, `price` and `year`. How does this work then? It's pretty simple. Another BigTable is created, whose row key has the following pattern:

```
[Kind]-[property-with-equality]-[property-with-inequality]
```

So here, the property with an equality filter is the `year`, whereas the property that has inequality filters is the `price`. Let's fill in the blanks to see how such a row looks:

```
Listing-year-1995-price-22000
```

Such a key is generated for each row in the index table. Let's look at five such example rows in the multiple property index tables. Please note that the data in this example is made up to explain how things work, and it is not from the original example data generator program that we saw earlier in this chapter:

Key (contains multiple properties)	Value (key of the actual row)
Listing-year-1995-price-6700	Listing-6473924464345088
Listing-year-1995-price-9000	Listing-5770237022568448
Listing-year-1995-price-11000	Listing-6192449487634432
Listing-year-2000-price-25000	Listing-4785074604081152
Listing-year-2000-price-28000	Listing-4644337115725824

Now, when you ask for cars of year 1995 within the price range of 7,000 to 20,000, datastore will form a row key prefix to scan value. In this case, the properties with equality will be prefixed first to the key that needs to be searched. So, we are only interested in cars of model 1995. Listing-year-1995 will be a part of the key that we are looking for. Next, because the price range starts from 7,000, the starting key range will be Listing-year-1995-price-7000. Next, because the maximum price for the car that we are looking is 20,000, the ending key for a key range scan will be Listing-year-1995-price-20000.

The next steps are pretty simple:

1. A row range scan will be performed on the preceding index table from the Listing-year-1995-price-7000 key to the Listing-year-1995-price-20000 key.
2. The row keys in the value column will be collected along the way. These rows are highlighted in the preceding table.
3. The actual entities will be read from the entities table (you may recall the six tables from the *Chapter 3, Understanding the Datastore*) and their data will be serialized and returned.

There is an interesting thing to note here. We had the following condition:

```
year = 1995 AND (price >= 7000 AND price <= 20000)
```

However, let's suppose that we exchange the operators and the following is our query:

```
price = 20000 AND (year >= 1996 AND year <= 2000)
```

Now, instead of the `year` having equality filters and the `price` having inequality filters, the reverse is the case—the year has the inequality filters and the price has an equality filter. Will the preceding rows in the `index` table be able to accommodate this query? No, it won't be able to do so. The property with an equality filter needs to appear first in the row key of the `index` table so that the part stays constant and the rows can be scanned for the other property that has the inequality filters. In this case, the rows will look like this:

```
Listing-price-20000-year-1995
Listing-price-20000-year-1996
Listing-price-20000-year-1998
Listing-price-20000-year-1999
Listing-price-20000-year-2002
```

As you can see, the cars with the same price point but different year end up closer. Now, for a query such as `price = 20000 AND (year >= 1996 AND year <= 2000)`, datastore is going to start scanning from `Listing-price-20000-year-1996`, the ending range will be `Listing-price-20000-year-2000`, and all the rows within this range will be returned.

As we will discuss in detail later, these indexes are to be mentioned in the `index.yaml` file so that when an application is deployed, App Engine will start building them. On the development server, `index.yaml` is automatically generated. When we run `year = 1995 AND (price >= 7000 AND price <= 20000)`, the following is added to `index.yaml`:

```
- kind: Listing
  properties:
  - name: year
  - name: price
```

Please note that the property with an equality filter is listed first. That's how the row key of an index table is composed, as we saw in the preceding explanation. For the `price = 20000 AND (year >= 1996 AND year <= 2000)` query, the following is generated in `index.yaml`:

```
- kind: Listing
  properties:
  - name: price
  - name: year
```

Because the `price` property had an equality filter, it is listed first. These details are just mentioned to show how things work. Otherwise, you don't need to bother about these entries, as these are automatically taken care of by the development server for you. Generally speaking, this is how the queries and row scans for the multiple properties relate to each other:

- Selection of multiple properties:

  ```
  Year = 1995 AND model = Civic AND (price >= 10000 AND price <=
  20000)
  ```

- Starting key range for scan:

  ```
  Listing-year-1995-model-Civic-price-10000
  ```

- Ending key range for scan

  ```
  Listing-year-1995-model-Civic-price-20000
  ```

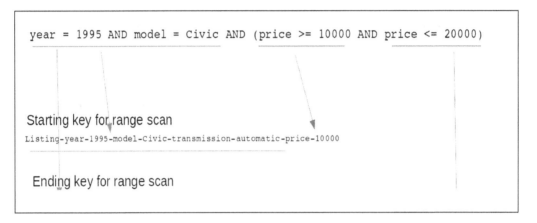

Working with indexes

As you are well aware by now, all queries, including even the simple ones, require a corresponding index. Unless you explicitly specify not to, two indexes for each property are automatically generated for you — one is in ascending order and the other is in descending order.

Beyond this, Google App Engine has no idea what questions you might have about your data. So, it is up to you to specify other indexes that need to be built, and the way to do this is by listing them in a file called `index.yaml`, which resides in the root of your application. Every time you upload your application to App Engine, this file gets uploaded. Any new indexes mentioned therein are built for you.

This index building takes lots of time depending on your data, usually in hours. It may take several days, again depending on how much data you have. Eventually, they occupy disk space that counts towards your storage quota. When an entity is deleted, updated, or created, these corresponding indexes containing the affected properties are updated. These write operations also count towards your write quotas besides the fact that these index updates also affect the write performance. That is, the more indexes you have, the more the write operations and hence, the slower the write operations.

As we mentioned previously, to specify the indexes, you do not have to do it manually. The index.yaml file on your local machine gets updated whenever the App Engine SDK encounters a new query. However, it won't delete any entries in this file for indexes that you might not be using. So, this housekeeping responsibility of removing any index entries in this file that are not being used falls on your shoulders. When you upload your app the next time, this will not only free up the storage space occupied by these indexes that are no longer needed, but will also boost the performance a bit because now, writing new entities won't have to update those removed indexes.

Adding new indexes is pretty much an automated operation that you do not have to worry about. But while deleting index entries from the index.yaml file, make sure that your code really is not using these index entries by running queries on the local system. For this, perform the following steps:

1. Delete the entries in index.yaml that you think you do not need anymore.
2. Run the development server (the dev_appserver.py file) with --require_indexes true flag.
3. Now, try interacting with your app to check whether any NeedIndexError exceptions are being thrown.
4. If no exceptions are thrown, everything is fine. Otherwise, you have deleted an index entry that was required, and this will be suggested in the exception message.

For example, I deleted all the entries in index.yaml and ran the development server with the following arguments:

```
$ /path/to/sdk/dev_appserver.py --datastore_path ./ --require_indexes
true /myappdir
```

Next, I opened the interactive console in the browser and ran the following query:

```
Listing.query().filter(Listing.price == 7000, Listing.year>=1995).
order(-Listing.price).fetch()
```

When executed, the following exception was thrown:

```
NeedIndexError: This query requires a composite index that is not
defined. You must update the index.yaml file in your application root.
The suggested index for this query is:
- kind: Listing
  properties:
  - name: price
  - name: year
```

While being at the root of your application directory, you can update the application indexes with the following command:

$ /path/to/sdk/appcfg.py update_indexes

But a better and recommended way of cleaning up is to first clean the index.yaml file locally and test it. Once all of this is done, run the following command:

$ /path/to/sdk/appcfg.py vaccum_indexes

This will check the indexes on the server and compare with the local index.yaml file. If it finds any indexes that are present on the server but not in the local index.yaml file, you will be prompted about it and asked whether you want to delete them.

The query API

Now that we understand how queries work under the hood, along with its their limitations and workarounds, it is time to learn more about the query API. As we have already seen briefly, there are two interfaces through which you can query your data. One is the object-oriented way where you can create query objects, call methods on them to tailor them according to your needs, and fetch results. The other is the SQL-like interface, which only allows you to read data. Thus, the only available statement is SELECT. This language is called **GQL**. Whatever queries you issue in GQL are translated into its equivalent object-oriented API.

Previously, the datastore API was available under the db package and was not very intuitive. Besides this, there was no caching available. So, every query that you issued would hit the underlying datastore, thus counting towards the quota limits. You could use the Memcahce API to manually store the fetched results on your own and invalidate the cache.

Then came along the new `ndb` library, where n stands for new. This library's most beautiful aspect is its simplicity along with its elegant, intuitive design. With a minimal number of calls, you can get what you want. This is beautiful because Python's creator, *Guido van Rossum* himself, is the author of this library and of course brings his insights into the API design. Besides its design, this automatically handles caching for you so your code is far simpler because you do not have to deal with the caching yourself.

We will first review the object-oriented API, its options, and operations. Later, we will look into the GQL API. In order to make queries by using the object-oriented API, the following are the steps that you have to perform:

- Obtain an `ndb.Query` instance
- Apply filters on the query instance by using the `filter()` method
- Apply ordering, if required, by using the `order()` method
- Fetch the results by using the `fetch()` method or iterate over it with iterators and cursors

Let's first look at how you can create an `ndb.Query` object.

The Query object

All the questions that you have for datastore are represented by the `ndb.Query` class. Create an instance of this class and modify it as per your requirements. To obtain all the listings, this is how you will go about it:

```
q = ndb.Query(kind='Listing')
```

The `kind` is one of the keywords that you can supply to customize the behavior of the query object. The following is a list of arguments that you can supply to the query object:

- `app`: This describes the app from which you wish to query data.
- `namespace`: This describes the namespace from which the entities are to be fetched.
- `kind`: This narrows down the kind of the entities that need to be fetched.
- `ancestor`: This limits the retrieval to only the entities with the given key as a part of their keys. We've already seen an example of this while talking about how to model our data.

- projection: This limits the number of properties that are returned. By default, all the properties are returned.
- filters: This is used to specify the filtering criteria.
- orders: This is used to specify the sort order for the returned results.

Let's examine in turn all of these in detail.

App

This is your app ID. You rarely need to supply this because this is automatically picked from your app.yaml file. However, if you want to supply a different app ID in case you have multiple apps, you can do this.

Namespace

We discussed namespace in the previous chapter. You can simply partition your storage and data into multiple namespaces. By default, the query object will pick up the current namespace when you create an instance of it. However, in case you want to query in some different namespace, you can mention it here in the constructor using namespace keyword argument. We'll have more to say about namespaces in *Chapter 9, Working with the Google App Engine Services*, when we will examine various Google App Engine services.

Kind

This is not required, but in case you don't specify the kind, the query will go through all the entities of all the kinds. As you can see, we provided the kind name, which is simply the name of the class as a string, which is used to limit our queries to the entities of only a particular kind. You do not need to specify the kind if you get the query object from the query() method of the ndb.Model class, such as Listing.query().

The ancestor

We discussed the idea of row keys of the BigTable in detail. We also learned that row keys can prefix other row keys as well. This is the key that you'd like to indicate as the prefix so that all the keys that have this key as their prefix will be queried. You can refer to our discussion on ancestor keys in the context of the Category, Listing, Products, and Order example in *Chapter 4, Modeling Your Data*.

The projection

By default, all the properties of an entity are read and returned. This means that because all the properties are serialized and stored in a single BigTable column, they need to be not only deserialized, but returned as well, which will count towards your CPU and data in/out quota from datastore. Instead, you can provide a list of properties that need to be returned. Now, deserialization will still happen, but only the indicated properties will be returned. So when you ask for few properties to be returned, data in/out quota will be consumed far less than returning all the properties indiscriminately. Here's an example that demonstrates this:

```
q = ndb.Query(kind='Listing', projection=('price', 'year'))
```

Alternatively, you can use the following way:

```
q = Listing.query(projection=('price', 'year'))
```

Now, when you fetch the results and try to access a property that is not in the projection list, you will get the `UnprojectedPropertyError` exception.

In the GQL syntax, you will do the following, which is just like what you would do to specify the columns that need to be selected in the SQL SELECT statement:

```
listings = ndb.gql("SELECT year, price FROM Listing").fetch()
```

Filters

These are the actual filters that you'd want to apply. When you create a query object and apply the `filter()` calls (discussed later), these are all available as a single instance of `ndb.FilterNode`, which is accessible as a property on the query object, as follows:

```
filters = q.filters
```

In case you already have a filter object whose filters you'd like to copy, you can use the following command:

```
newq = ndb.Query(kind='Listing', filters=q.filters)
```

We will explore the filters in detail later.

The orders

Besides filtering, you can order your results too, and one or more orders can be specified. This keyword argument is your chance at supplying an order from an existing query object just like the filters that were mentioned before. We will look at ordering in detail later.

Further query options

There are many more keyword arguments such as how many maximum results need to be fetched, from where to start fetching the results, and so on. There are two ways by which you can supply these arguments. The first way comprises constructing the `ndb.QueryOptions` instance, supplying the required values as keyword arguments, and later passing this instance to the `ndb.Query` constructor or the `Model.query()` method as the `default_options` keyword argument, as follows:

```
options = ndb.QueryOptions(projection=('price', 'year'), offset=5)
listings = ndb.Query(kind='Listing', default_options=options).fetch()
listings = Listing.query(default_options=options).fetch() # same as
above.
```

The other way is to supply these options directly to the `fetch()` method as keyword arguments, as follows:

```
listings = ndb.Query(kind='Listing').fetch(projection=('price',
'year'), offset=5)
```

So here, we directly supplied these arguments to the `fetch` method. Now that we know how to use them, let's review what is available to us:

- `keys_only`: If this is specified, only the keys of the entities will be returned
- `projection`: This is the same as before, and only the listed properties will be returned
- `offset`: This determines how many entities need to be skipped while fetching values
- `limit`: This determines the number of maximum entities that need to be returned
- `batch_size`: This specifies the number of entities that are required to be processed together
- `prefetch_size`: This determines the number of entities that need to be prefetched
- `produce_cursors`: This cursors are like bookmarks. They represent a position in the rows in BigTable (so in entities in Datastore). If you set this keyword argument to `True`, results would return the cursor as well indicating the position of the last entity returned. We'll examine this along with `start_cursor` and `end_cursor` arguments in detail when we examine how to iterate over the results.
- `start_cursor`: This can have a starting point where from you want to start reading data, and you can specify that cursor here.

- `end_cursor`: If you have a cursor indicating a point to which you'd like to read data, you can specify it here.

The keys_only function

Because all the properties are serialized and sorted in a single BigTable column, fetching columns will not only count towards CPU utilization due to deserialization, but will also count towards your data in/out limits. However, a situation may arise where you'd only want the keys and not the rest of the properties. So, you can specify this here.

This option has a counterpart in GQL as well. The following statements achieve the same thing:

```
options = ndb.QueryOptions(keys_only=True)
listings = ndb.Query(kind='Listing', default_options=options).fetch()
listings = Listing.query(default_options=options).fetch()
listings = Listing.query().fetch(keys_only=True)
# Note instead of SELECT *, we are using SELECT __key__
listings = ndb.gql("SELECT __key__ FROM Listing").fetch()
```

The result from the preceding code will not be the instances of `Listing` kind. Instead, these will be the `ndb.Key` instances.

The projection

The projection is the same thing that we saw before—a list of property names that will be returned instead of everything. Just a reminder. This has a GQL equivalent as well.

The offset

The offset is similar to what you have in SQL. The given number of records will be skipped from the result. For example, let's assume that you execute the following code:

```
options = ndb.QueryOptions(offset=5)
listings = Listing.query(default_options=options).fetch()
listings = ndb.gql("SELECT * FROM Listing OFFSET 5").fetch() # Same
as above.
```

The first five entities will be skipped and from that point onwards, whatever you get is the output.

The limit

The limits again similar to what you may have seen in SQL — limiting the number of results. Here's an example:

```
options = ndb.QueryOptions(limit=10, offset=5)
listings = Listing.query(default_options=options).fetch()
listings = ndb.gql("SELECT * FROM Listing LIMIT 10 OFFSET  5").fetch()
# Same as above.
```

This code will skip the first five entities and return a maximum of ten entities no matter how many matching entities exist.

The batch_size entities

The batch_size entities is more of an optimization thing. When you process entities — fetch or write them — **remote procedure calls** (**RPC**) are executed. By default, 20 entities are processed in a batch. If you increase this number, more memory will be consumed, but a lesser number of RPC calls will be executed. This will result in a slight performance boost.

The prefetch_size entities

The `prefetch_size` entities are also about optimization. Let's suppose that you want to fetch some entities from the datastore, but you limit the number of entities by supplying a `limit` argument, as previously discussed. This `prefetch_size` will still fetch the number of entities in the memory so that they can be later returned without invoking the RPC calls. If `prefetch_size` entities are not supplied, this takes the value of `batch_size`.

The produce_cursors entities

Cursors are like bookmarks in a book. When reading through your data, you place bookmarks, and you start your next reading operation from where you left. You will see how to manage cursors later in detail.

The start_cursor entities

If you already have a cursor, you can supply it as `start_cursor`, and datastore will start reading data from that point onwards.

The end_cursor entities

In case you already have a cursor and supply it as `end_cursor`, entries only up to that point will be read.

Filtering entities

We have already seen how to filter entities using the `filter()` method. But now, we will take a closer look at what it is all about. Basically, all the queries are represented by the `ndb.Query` class, and the filtering is represented by the `ndb.FilterNode` class. When you apply various filters (such as the `price` and `year` in our examples), these eventually result in a single `ndb.FilterNode` object that has all the operations nested beneath it like a tree.

If you want to apply a filter, you have to supply an instance of `FilterNode` to the `filter()` instance method of an `ndb.Query` instance. This method takes one or more `ndb.FilterNode` instances and if two or more instances are supplied, they are AND together. However, how do you create an `ndb.FilterNode` instance? We didn't do this in our earlier examples.

The magic is implemented by overloading operators on `ndb.Property` and its subclasses. Consider a case where the following kind of statement gets executed:

```
ApropertyInstance AnyOperator Value,
```

This statement returns an instance of `ndb.FilterNode`. So, as an example, let's suppose that we have the following statement:

```
Listing.year == 1995
```

This statement will return an `ndb.FilterNode` function. This is exactly what we pass to the `filter()` method when we write the following statement:

```
Listing.query().filter(Listing.year == 1995).fetch()
```

When more than one filters are to be applied, they can be supplied together to the `filter()` method, as follows:

```
Listing.query().filter(Listing.price >= 7000, Listing.year == 1995).
fetch()
```

In the preceding example, we actually created two `ndb.FilterNode` instances, and both were passed to the `filter()` method. Both were applied so effectively that a logical AND is happening here.

The following command is another way that can be used to achieve the same thing:

```
Listing.query().filter(Listing.price >= 7000).filter(Listing.year ==
1995).fetch()
```

This chaining of the `filter()` methods has the same effect. Now that you understand the `ndb.Query` and `filter()` method, which are important when you're working with datastore, let's move further. We'll examine the following:

- Filtering repeated properties
- Filtering structured properties
- Applying the AND and OR operators
- Iterating over the results

So, let's get started and study each of these one by one.

Filtering repeated properties

You may recall that you can have multiple values for a single-property. All that you have to do is set `repeated=True` while defining the property. Let's suppose that the listings that we are saving have a property called `features` that has one or more values. This is how the model will look like:

```
# All list of possible features.
FEATUERS = ('ac', 'radio', 'dvd', 'power window', 'keyless entry')

class Listing(ndb.Model):
    title = ndb.StringProperty()
    year = ndb.IntegerProperty()
    price = ndb.IntegerProperty(default=0)
    features = ndb.StringProperty(repeated=True)
```

Let's suppose that you want all the listings of cars that have air conditioner in them. This is how we will do it:

```
Lisitng.query().filter(Listing.features == 'ac').fetch()
```

However, if you want a car with an air conditioner, a radio, a DVD, and power windows, this is how you will do it:

```
Listing.query().filter(Listing.features.IN(['ac', 'dvd', 'radio', 'power window'])).fetch()
```

So, this is how you can query for repeated properties. Pretty simple? Let's move on to the next item then.

Filtering structured properties

You may recall that an entity might have properties that have properties as well. These are called **structured properties**. Let's suppose that in our listings, instead of adding `manufacturer`, `model`, and `year` as three separate properties, we bundle everything together as a single structured property, as follows:

```python
from google.appengine.ext import ndb
import random

MODELS = {
  'Honda': ['Civic', 'City', 'Accord'],
  'Toyota': ['Crolla', 'Camery', 'Pirus']
}

MANUFACTURER_COUNT = len(MODELS.keys())

# The nested structured property
class Make(ndb.Model):
    model = ndb.StringProperty()
    manufacturer = ndb.StringProperty()
    year = ndb.IntegerProperty()

class Listing(ndb.Model):
    title = ndb.StringProperty()
    make = ndb.StructuredProperty(Make)
    price = ndb.IntegerProperty(default=0)
```

Now, you can generate some random data as we have been doing all along in our previous examples just like this:

```python
# Delete everything that exists already there.
for listing in Listing.query():
    listing.key.delete()

for i in xrange(0, 100):
    make = Make()
    make.year = random.randint(1980, 2015)
    make.manufacturer = MODELS.keys()[random.randint(0,
      MANUFACTURER_COUNT - 1)]
    make.model = MODELS[make.manufacturer][random.randint(0, 2)]
```

```
listing = Listing()
listing.price = random.randint(5000, 200000)
listing.make = make
listing.title = "%s %s %s" % (make.manufacturer, make.model,
   make.year)
listing.put()
```

Now, if you want to list all the Honda Civic cars that were introduced in 2000 or later, this is how you the query will be:

```
cars = Listing.query().filter(Listing.make.model == 'Civic', Listing.
make.year >= 2000).fetch()
for car in cars:
    print car.title
```

This is all that you need to know about how to structure properties in logical groups and query them.

The AND and OR operations

Until now, we didn't talk about logical operations on queries. We just mentioned that the conditions we have been applying get ANDed together. But what if we want to OR multiple conditions together? As you already know, there's no such operation that will allow you to perform an OR operation on a BigTable because all we have is a scan of row ranges. OR is actually implemented at the datastore level by merging algorithms. The basic idea is that datasets are fetched for both the conditions separately and efficiently merged together while removing any duplicates that might pop up because they satisfied both the conditions somehow.

Let's see how to do this in code and later discuss the whole thing in detail. Let's suppose that we are looking for a Honda Accord or a Honda Civic that was introduced in 2000 or later. So in pseudo code, the following is our logical expression:

```
(model = 'Accord' OR model = 'Civic) AND year >= 2000
```

Pretty straightforward. This is how you will actually do it using datastore's ndb library:

```
Listing.query().filter(ndb.AND(Listing.make.year >= 2000, ndb.
OR(Listing.make.model == 'Civic', Listing.make.model == 'Accord'))).
fetch()
```

If you execute this query on the dataset that was generated in the previous example, you'll get the matching results. If you followed the discussion on BigTable and how datastore is layered on top of it, you may have already figured out that such composite conditions with logical operators will consult a lot of indexes. For more details on this subject, you can refer to an article on the same by visiting `https://cloud.google.com/appengine/articles/indexselection`.

As we just mentioned how the OR operation works by in memory merger of results, you'd want to reduce the number of the OR clauses in your conditions so that such merges are reduced in number. One way to do this is by rewriting the logical condition in such a way that there's a big OR operation on the outside and all the AND operations are inside it. This comes from Boolean algebra and is called the **Disjunctive Normal Form (DNF)** of a Boolean expression, or DNF for short. But fortunately, you don't have to learn all the rules and apply them, as we will tell you about a shortcut. Let's work on our example expression and turn it into a DNF. We have the following:

```
(model = 'Accord' OR model = 'Civic) AND year >= 2000
```

For each equality/inequality expression, we replace it with a letter. So, we have the following:

```
(a OR b) AND c
```

Simply go to WolframAlpha computational knowledge engine and type in the preceding expression. Alternatively, you can just visit `https://www.wolframalpha.com/input/?i=%28a+OR+b%29+AND+c` directly, as it has the same expression.

Under the DNF, you'll see the following clause:

```
(a AND c) OR (b AND c)
```

This clause is actually the following statement:

```
(model == 'Accord' AND year >= 2000) OR (model == 'Civic' AND year >= 2000)
```

So, plunging it in the ndb library's API, you get something like this:

```
a = ndb.AND(Listing.make.model == 'Accord', Listing.make.year >= 2000)
b = ndb.AND(Listing.make.model == 'Civic', Listing.make.year >= 2000)
c = ndb.OR(a, b)
print 'Rewritten:'
print Listing.query().filter(c).fetch()
```

You'll see that both the forms have the same results except that the order might be different in case you didn't specify any order.

Iterating over the results

Before we can iterate over the results, we need to look at two concepts — cursors and iterators. Let's start with cursors. A cursor is just like a bookmark in a book. You leave it within the pages and resume reading from the same point afterwards. We already have generated some 50 entities in one of our previous examples. What if we want to iterate through them and process five entities at a time? How do we go about it? Let's look at an example:

```
more = True
cursor = None

while more:
    listings, cursor, more = Listing.query().fetch_page(5, start_
cursor=cursor)

    for listing in listings:
        print listing.key

    if not (more and cursor):
        print 'Thats the end'
        break
    else:
        print 'So far at ', cursor.urlsafe()
        print 'More records to follow:'
```

At the heart of the program is the `fetch_page` method instead of `fetch()`. This method takes one required argument, which is the number of results that need to be returned. The other arguments are all optional and are the same as those that we discussed and which can be base to the `ndb.Query` object's constructor. One of the interesting arguments here is the `start_cursor`, which indicates the position from where the read operation will start.

In the very beginning, we assume that we have more records. Hence, we set the `more` flag to `True`. However, because we haven't read anything yet, we set `cursor` to `None`. Next, we enter a `while` loop, which will repeat until the `more` becomes `False`.

Immediately, we call the `fetch_page` method on the `ndb.Query` object while providing it with the page size and the start cursor. In response, we get a tuple that contains the following three elements:

- A list of entities

- The cursor for the position after the last record that was returned in the aforementioned list
- A flag that indicates whether there are any more records or not

We assigned all of entities to separate variables in a single statement, as shown in the preceding example. Next, we simply processed the fetched records in another for in loop and do whatever we are pleased with. Then, the interesting part starts. If the more and cursor both are None, this means that there are no more records. That's what the not (more and cursor) expression exactly means. In this case, we need to do nothing, and the external while loop will automatically get terminated because the value of more is None. Otherwise, simply print the cursor by calling its urlsafe() method, which prints a string representation.

This urlsafe() form of the ndb.Cursor class comes in handy when you are rendering results on a web page. In that case, for the next set of records, you can print the cursor in a link, as follows:

```
link_template = '<a href="/listings?next=%s">Next</a>'
link = link_template % cursor.urlsafe()
```

Now, when you get a request when someone clicks on such a link, you can reconstruct a cursor object, as follows:

```
next = self.request.get('next')
cursor = ndb.Cursor(urlsafe=next)
```

Now, you can pass this cursor object to the fetch_page() method to start reading from where the user left the last time. You can take a look at such an example in the reference documentation by visiting https://cloud.google.com/appengine/docs/python/ndb/queries#cursors.

There are a few interesting limitations of cursors and iterators. If your query uses !=, IN, OR, then you cannot obtain cursors unless you sort the results by key. For example, consider the following query:

```
Listing.query().filter(Listing.year != 1995)
```

You won't be able to use cursors unless you modify the query in the following way:

```
Listing.query().filter(Listing.year != 1995).order(Listing.key)
```

So now you can fetch results and process them. A common pattern for web applications that shows a list of results with options to navigate back and forth in a dataset is to have two query objects, one for backward and the other one for forward, as follows:

```
forward = Listing.query().filter(Listing.year != 1995).order(Listing.
key)
backward = Listing.query().filter(Listing.year != 1995).order(-
Listing.key)
```

Showing the next and back options as and when required. The aforementioned link on the official documentation has an example. Reproducing this example here will make an unnecessary repetition of different concepts that we have been discussing for a while now.

Closely related to this is the concept of iterators. When you have an `ndb.Query` object and you call `fetch()` on it, all the matching records are loaded into the memory and returned as a list that you can process. However, when you directly use the `for loop` over an `ndb.Query` object, you use iterators instead. Let's take a very simple example:

```
forward = Listing.query().order(Listing.price).iter()
while forward.has_next():
    print forward.next()
```

So here, we iterated over the results ordered by price. The Iterator object has some interesting methods. The first one is `has_next()`. This will return `True` if there is another entity in datastore. Otherwise, it will return `False`. This is a blocking call. The corresponding `probably_has_next()` call is also available, which is much quicker but slightly inaccurate, as it might return `True` when there are no more records. This works on some probability magic, which makes it slightly inaccurate. However, it will never return a `False` when a matching entity in datastore actually exists.

The next interesting method is `next()`, which returns the next entity from datastore and advances to the next position in the matched set of entities. If there are no more matching entities, a `StopIteration` exception is raised, which can be handle as per your requirements. In order to traverse in the backward direction, you will have to create another query object with the reverse order, as follows:

```
backwards = Listing.query().order(-Listing.price).iter()
```

The other interesting methods are `cursor_before()`, which returns the `ndb.Cursor()` instance for the records just before the last entity was read, and the `cursor_after()` method, which returns the cursor after the last entity is read.

Conclusions

So, this ends our discussion on querying datastore to retrieve results. You might feel a bit disappointed with a few limitations that are inherent due to the way BigTable operates under the hood. The main goal of BigTable, and eventually datastore, is to scale to petabytes of data without sacrificing the performance. Your queries will run efficiently no matter how much data you have unlike the traditional RDBMS databases, where as the table size grows, the query performance degrades.

About the search limitations, you can perform many sorts of queries, but whenever you hit the wall, there's another solution in Google App Engine's arsenal, which is the efficient and powerful search service. And this search is what we are going to look at in the next chapter.

Transactions

There are cases where you'd want a number of operations to succeed or fail altogether and nothing in between. This is called a **transaction**, and App Engine's datastore offers support for transactions. In App Engine, you do this by encapsulating all the steps that you want to fail or succeed together in a function and decorate it with the `ndb.transactional` decorator.

Let's suppose that it so happens that we add a new property called `city` to indicate the city that the car is in. Sometimes, two cars are exchanged between two dealers in two difference cities. In that case, we need to update the cities of these two listings and basically swap them. There are multiple datastore operations involved here, given that we have keys for both the listings. First, we read both the listings from datastore, then modify the cities, and finally, we write them back. All of these operations shall either fail altogether, or succeed altogether. This is how we will do this by wrapping the function in a `ndb.transactional` decorator:

```
# We will look into this xg=True in a while.
@ndb.transactional(xg=True)
def swap_cities(key1, key2):
    """
```

```
Given two nbd.Key objects for two listings,
swaps their cities. All of these shall
fail or succeed together.
"""
# Fetch. Two datastore operations.
first = key1.get()
second = key2.get()

# Swap
temp = first.city
first.city = second.city
second.city = temp
# Write back. Two operations.
first.put()
second.put()
```

If any exception is raised during the execution of the preceding code, it will be handled by the ndb.transactional decorator and all the operations will get canceled, whereas the exception raised will be raised again so that the original calling function can get the original exception. But if you want to make it fail silently instead of propagating the exception to the calling code, you can raise the ndb.Rollback exception within this function, and it will fail silently. You might want to check whether your code is executing inside a transaction or not. So for this, you can call ndb.in_transaction().

There are times when you don't want to give up on what you are trying to do and might want to retry the same steps yet again in case they fail. This is simple to accomplish. You can simply apply the decorator in the following way:

```
# After first, 3 more tries so this gets executed 4 times at max
before failing
ndb.transactional(retries=3)
def swap_cities(key1, key2):
# .. rest of the function code.
```

In the preceding code, we told the datastore API to retry a maximum of three times after the first failure. So, this function will get executed a maximum of four times until it succeeds.

We discussed in much detail that datastore is just a layer on top of BigTable, which is just a distributed key-value store where keys are sorted. We also saw that we can prefix a key of another entity to another entity's key. You may recall the examples of `Listing` and `Category` modeling from the previous chapter. When we created a `Listing` entity, we supplied the key of `Category` as a parent in an argument, as follows:

```
category = Category(name='Used Cars'')
category.put()
honda = Listing(name='Honda Accord', parent=category.key)
```

Later, while browsing through all the used cars, we could specify the key of the category as its ancestor to get only the listings that have this key as a prefix to its key, as follows:

```
Listing.query(ancestor=category.key).fetch()
```

So, these are the ancestor queries, and that's only what's allowed inside transactions. The explanation will span several pages and refer back to all the material that we discussed as regards how BigTable works and datastore is modeled on top of it. But still, to summarize, because the BigTable (and eventually the datastore entity) row keys are sorted, they are spread over several machines. When you perform ancestor queries over very large datasets, due to the sort order of the row keys, the machines will be closer to each other. This makes it possible for you to make changes to the data being read and altered together in a transaction. For more clarification, you can review the discussion on how BigTable scales in the previous chapters.

When a set of entities have a common key as their prefix, this collection of entities is called an **entity group** in datastore's parlance. So, in the preceding case, all the entities of the `Listing` kind that we created, as shown previously, form a single entity group. In case you specify a different key for some entities, they will form a different entity group. In case you don't specify any parent while creating an entity, each entity has its own entity group that contains only one entity, that is, itself.

Now, the limitation of a datastore transaction besides only being able to issue ancestor queries is that you cannot touch entities from more than one entity group. This is why we had to set `xg=True` (where `xg` stands for cross group) in the first example that we showed in this section. Remove `xg=True`, and you will be greeted with the `BadRequestError` exception. When you set `xg=True`, you can touch a maximum of 25 entity groups in a single transaction. If you don't have any entities with parent keys, then it means only a maximum of 25 entities, because every entity without any parent key is an entity group that has only one entity in it.

That's all that you need to know about transactions in datastore. With this, we are done with datastore, from its internal workings to data modeling, querying, and transactions.

Summary

We started out discussion by asking some questions in the form of queries about the data stored in datastore. Some of the questions were answered and for some, we met with exceptions. Next, we embarked on the journey of how queries actually work under the hood. We learned that all queries are actually just translated into the BigTable row scans and for this, separate BigTable tables are maintained, which are updated whenever you write any new entities or modify or delete any existing ones. We learned the role of indexes and how they are not an optional thing but a required component unlike indexes in the RDBMS world.

Armed with this understanding, we went on to explore the Query API. We learned that all the magic happens around the `ndb.Query` object with its `filter()` method. We learned how to query for repeated and structured properties. We next focused on how to perform the logical AND, OR operations, how they work under the hood, and how an OR operation just merges two different row scan result sets into one. We learned that the OR operation is performed in the main memory. We also examined how we can rewrite our logical expressions into DNF in order to reduce the number of OR operations.

Next, we focused on how to iterate over results, what cursors are, how they can be obtained, how to iterate over results, and how iterators provides us with various methods to determine whether there are any more records in datastore that match our criteria.

Finally, we turned our attention towards transactions—the operations that should either fail or succeed altogether. We also had a look at the limitations of transactions, such as only the ancestor queries are allowed. We also studied entity groups. We learned that an entity without any ancestor key is in its own entity group and each transaction is limited to a maximum of 25 entity groups.

This wraps up the discussion about datastore that spanned over the past three chapters. As you have discovered some limitations regarding what you can query from datastore, it is time to address this in the next chapter, which is all about integrating search.

6
Integrating Search

In the previous chapters, we explored how the persistence solution offered by Google App Engine, known as datastore, works under the hood, how we can model data around it and how we can query that data. But we did hit some limitations when it came to performing searches, because of the way datastore works internally. It is time to address those limitations now. App Engine provides us with a separate search service where we can index our data and can later perform complex queries on it.

In this chapter, we'll look at:

- Indexing datastore entities
- Querying datastore entities
- Sorting, filtering and other operations
- Faceted search

This is a tall order so let's get started with our discussion of that. Before we dive into details, it would be better to have some context around how searches works and some background history.

Background

As the amount of information contained by computers grew, so came the need to search for desirable pieces of information, which led to a whole separate field of information retrieval in computer science. Based on those principles, one of the most famous and dominant implementations is a Java library called Lucene, which was written by Doug Cutting back in 1999. This man actually wanted to build a search engine so he first went out to create this library. Doug Cutting is also the man behind Hadoop, a distributed large scale data processing solution. Anyway, this Lucene library was later used in an open source search engine called **Nutch**, which was yet again a brainchild of Doug Cutting.

Later, people came up with brighter ideas around Lucene and added some web interface and RESTful API around this library and the result was SOLR. A similar product is ElasticSearch and both provide RESTful APIs, the ability to have a very large data set to be searched by distributing over multiple machines among other features. Nowadays, from LinkedIn, Facebook, to Twitter and everywhere where there is searches, Lucene is at its core in one form or the other. Probably one of the most prominent users of Lucene would be Wikipedia.

This library has been ported to many other languages such as PHP, Python and there's even a .NET implementation called `Lucene.NET`. The search facilities provided by Google App Engine that we are going to learn about in this chapter are based on this wonderful Java library called Lucene as well.

The underlying principle

The underlying principle is very simple. Suppose you have some text files that you want to be able to search. All the text contained in these files would be tokenized (broken into words and atomic units if you will) and a list (called an `index`) of these words is created that has all these words in a sorted order along with their position and location in each file.

So suppose that we have three files like this:

```
ages.txt
    The age of Internet is upon us.
tech.txt
Technology changes often in age of Internet.
goal.txt
To build a technology product.
```

Now all these files would be tokenized and each word (called a `term`) would have its corresponding location like this:

```
age [ages.txt:5, tech.txt:27]
build [goal.txt: 3]
change [tech.txt: 11]
internet [age.txt:11, tech.txt:34]
product [goal.txt:22]
```

Now, this is what we call an index. A few important things that we should take note of are:

- First, all the listed words (tokens or terms) are sorted in alphabetic order.

- The next thing is that the location on which this word occurs is listed in square brackets next to it. So, if a word appears in multiple documents or more than once in a single document, all the occurrences are listed.

- The other important thing is that all the terms are in lower case.

You will have noticed that many of the words are not in the index, such as `the`, `of`, `is`, `upon`, `in`, and so on. This is on purpose; the process of tokenization discards all the conjunctions and prepositions. How you tokenize your input is configurable if you are using Lucene or some serveries form of it such as SOLR and ElasticSearch. Sometimes, different languages have different tokenization algorithms and unlike English where space indicates boundaries between the words, it might not be the case with other languages such as Thai.

The other thing that you might have noticed is that while the document has word changes, it is recorded as a change in the index. This is another aspect of indexing where the words are reduced to their very root, such as colored would turn into color, timely would become into time, and so on. This process is called `stemming`. Yet again, different languages have different stemming rules and there are many approaches to how stemming is implemented (rule based or statistical modeling) and in short, is a vast area of computational linguistics. But apart from all the above discussion, you get the idea of how this works.

When it comes to information, Lucene thinks in terms of documents and fields. A document might have one or more fields, each possibly of different type (number, string and so on) and it is not necessary for all the documents to have the same number of fields or for that matter same type of fields. This flexible model makes it possible to index different types of data such as PDFs and spreadsheets. All you have to do is create a document, add various sections as fields (or different fields for different cells in case of a spreadsheet), and submit it to Lucene, which would tokenize and store it in an index for later retrieval.

Indexing your data

Now that we understand some of the background about searches and how the indexing works, it is time to index some of our own data. In the case of developing applications on top of Google App Engine, our source of data to be indexed would most likely be datastore. In this section, we will first generate some sample data with interesting characteristics and next we will see how we can index that data using the App Engine's search API.

Sample data

We have being using our `Listing` class for a while now for modeling a classified website. This time around, we are more focused towards real estate and hence some relevant attributes are added. Here's how our `model` class looks like this time:

```
class Listing(ndb.Model):
    title = ndb.StringProperty(required=True)
    ref_no = ndb.StringProperty(required=True)
    beds = ndb.IntegerProperty(required=True)
    size = ndb.IntegerProperty(required=True)
    price = ndb.IntegerProperty(required=True)
    location = ndb.GeoPtProperty()
    facilities = ndb.StringProperty(repeated=True)
    posted_on = ndb.DateProperty()
```

Let's take a look at interesting properties in order of appearance:

- The first one is `ref_no`, which is just a simple string property. There's nothing fancy about it but we will use to demonstrate a specific aspect of the indexing process.

- Secondly, we mentioned in our data modeling discussions in previous chapters that you can store geo coordinates in datastore as well but this is the first time `location` property is having them. We have added it to demonstrate how the locations can be indexed and searched for.

- Next, we also mentioned that a property might have multiple values. This `facilities` property is such an example that lists what facilities are available in the apartment being offered such as if it has balcony, parking and a gym and things like that. We have added this field to demonstrate how you can index multiple values and how to query for them.

To search, we should have lots of data to be searched so that's why our plan is to have about 5000 listings in datastore spread across five cities, where each listing in each city would be randomly within a radius of 50 kilometers. To do that, you just have to run the program in the interactive console. Before running the code you should start your development server assuming that you are in the application directory that contains `app.yaml`:

```
$ /path/to/appengine/sdk/dev_appserver --storage_path . .
```

So what we are trying to explain about the `--storage_path` option is that all the entities and indexes created on the local server should be stored in the current directory. The last . indicates that the current directory contains the application so that app.yaml can be looked up there. This is how you will be running your development application on server to run all the examples in this chapter. The code generates the following data:

```
from google.appengine.ext import ndb
import random
import datetime
import math

TODAY = datetime.date.today()

# Some cities from the world with latitude, longitude.
CITIES = (

    (40.7033127,-73.979681),    # New York
    (48.8588589,2.3470599),     # Paris
    (25.092076,55.15207),       # Dubai
    (51.5286416,-0.1015987),    # London
    (33.6691345,72.9849773),    # Islamabad
)


# Facilities an apartment might have
FACILITIES = (
'24 hour security',
'Central AC',
'Gym',
'Swimming pool',
'Balcony',
'Private Garden',
'Maids room' ,
'Built in wardrobes',
'Landmarks',
'Study',
'Parking'
)

class Listing(ndb.Model):
```

```
"""
Our listing class.
"""
title = ndb.StringProperty(required=True)
ref_no = ndb.StringProperty(required=True)
beds = ndb.IntegerProperty(required=True)
size = ndb.IntegerProperty(required=True)
price = ndb.IntegerProperty(required=True)
location = ndb.GeoPtProperty()
facilities = ndb.StringProperty(repeated=True)
posted_on = ndb.DateProperty()


def random_date(within=90):
    """
    Returns the next date within the past number of days..
    """
    global TODAY
    past = TODAY  - datetime.timedelta(days=within)
    days = random.randint(0, within)
    next_one = past + datetime.timedelta(days=days)
    return next_one



def random_point(point, within=50):
    """
    Returns a random geo location within given
    radius. The radius is given in kilometers.
    Inspired from:
    http://gis.stackexchange.com/questions/25877/how-to-generate-
      random-locations-nearby-my-location
    """
    lat = point[0]
    lon = point[1]
    # Pick two random factors
    u = random.random()
    v = random.random()

    # Convert kilometers to meters and then to degrees.
    meters = within * 1000
    degrees = float(meters / 111300.0)

    w = degrees * math.sqrt(u)
```

```
        t = 2 * math.pi * v

        x = w * math.cos(t)
        y = w * math.sin(t)

        x = x / math.cos(lat)

        return (lat + y, lon + x)

def get_one(options):
    """
    Out of the given options, returns
    one randomly.
    """
    MAX = len(options)
    index = random.randint(0, MAX - 1)
    return options[index]

def get_many(options, how_many=None):
    """
    Out of the given options, returns many
    options. how_many specifies how many
    at max shall be returned. If None,
    randomly decided how many to return.
    """
    selection = []
    MAX = len(options)

    if how_many is None:
        how_many = MAX

    max_selections = random.randint(0, how_many)

    for i in xrange(0, max_selections):
        selection.append(options[random.randint(0, MAX - 1)])

    return list(set(selection))

def round_to(number, boundary=1000):
    """
    Rounds the numbers to given boundaries.
    """
```

```
        return number if number % boundary == 0 else number + boundary -
    number % boundary

    # Generate and save 5000 listings in 5 cities randomly.
    for i in xrange(0, 5000):
        listing = Listing()
        listing.ref_no = "REF-%04d" % random.randint(0, 10000)
        listing.beds = random.randint(1, 6)
        listing.price = round_to(random.randint(8000, 250000))
        listing.size = round_to(random.randint(300, 5000), 25)
        listing.title = "%s Bedroom Apartment for %s/year" %
            (listing.beds, listing.price)
        listing.facilities = get_many(FACILITIES)
        listing.posted_on = random_date()
        listing.location = ndb.GeoPt(*random_point(get_one(CITIES),
            within=50))
        listing.put()
```

There are many small utility functions at the beginning. The `get_one()` helps in
randomly selecting a value from a list of available. The `get_many()` function does
the same thing but it selects multiple values from the list of choices. Near the top,
we have a list of cities with each city's latitude and longitude listed. Given that city
as center point, the `random_point()` function returns a random point within 50
kilometers of radius. This way, we spread our 5000 listings randomly across five
cities, each listing within 50 kilometers of each city.

The main workhorse of the whole program is the loop at the very end that is
generating the `Listing` objects, populating them using utility functions wherever
required, and putting them in the datastore.

Now that we have finished generating the data, we will move towards indexing it.

Indexing thyself

Just like the database is the most major unit of storage and processing in the RDBMS
world and then come tables, and columns, similarly in the search service provided by
App Engine the first major unit of storage is the index, which contains documents and
documents have fields. In order to index, you first have to create an index like this:

```
from google.appengine.api import search
index = search.Index(name='property')
```

This returns you the `index` named property. If this `index` does not exist, it will be created when you put your first document in it. There's no limit to how many indexes you might have but the size of each index is limited to 10 GB.

The `storage_limit` shows how much you can store and `storage_usage` shows the size of your index. These properties are always set to `None` if you get the index as shown above. The `search.get_indexes()` method returns all the indexes that your application has so the following code snippet prints the size consumed by 5000 listings after they are indexed:

```
for index in search.get_indexes():
    print index.storage_usage / (102*1024), " MB of ", index.storage_
limit  / (1024*1024*1024), "GB"
```

And the output of this is:

```
13 MB of 1 GB
```

This is listed as 1 GB because that's the limit on the local development server.

One catch with the `get_indexes()` is that it takes a limit argument, which limits how many indexes to be returned in a single call. This argument can take a maximum value of 1000, which effectively means you can only return a maximum of 1000 indexes. The other keyword argument is offset, which defines how many indexes to skip so that yet again we can have a maximum value of 1000. These two facts combined mean that because you can get only 1000 indexes in a single call and can only skip 1000 indexes using offset, this method returns a maximum of 2000 indexes:

```
first_thousand = search.get_indexes(limit=1000)
next_thousand = search.get_indexes(limit=1000, offset=1000)
```

This limitation means that you cannot iterate over all your indexes using this method if you have more than 2000 but you can still have as many indexes you want to have. A better method to deal with this situation would be to store the index names elsewhere such as in the datastore and get them whenever required:

```
my_indexes = ['property', 'rental', 'motors'....'up to 5000 or
whatever entries in this list']
```

For the index in `my_indexes`:

```
    search.Index(name=index) # No limitation now!
```

Documents

Coming back to the process of indexing a document, you first create the index as shown above, next you create documents by creating objects of `search.Document` class. And that's how you do it:

```
document = search.Document(doc_id='myunique-id', fields=list_of_
fields)
```

Here the `doc_id` is an optional argument and this is the unique identifier to the document. You can think of it as the primary key in the RDBMS world. It is a string that must not be greater than 500 characters (visible, printable ASCII characters) and must not start with exclamation! mark. Also, it cannot begin or end with double underscores. As mentioned earlier, this is optional and in case you don't supply one, it would be created automatically. In our case, we will use the entity key as `doc_id` so this way, each document will have a logical link to the entity in datastore. If you do not supply the `doc_id`, the search service will automatically create a unique one for you so you don't have to worry about that.

The other important but optional attribute of the `Document` class is called `rank`. This is a number and when you specify any query without mentioning any sort order on results, the returned results are sorted by decreasing `rank`. By default, the value of `rank` is set to the number of seconds since January 1, 2011. So as a result of this, when you specify a query without any sorting, results would be returned by the date they were put in index so recent results would have priority.

In our particular case of adding `Listing` objects to search index, this behavior is good enough because when no sort order specified, the recently posted listings would show up first.

Now comes the most important argument for the `Document` class, which is `fields`. This is actually a list of `search.Field` instances or its descendant classes. Let's look into it in more detail.

Fields

A document can have many fields and each field has a name, a type, and a value. The field name again must be printable in ASCII within a limit of 500 characters but it should start with a letter and might contain digits and underscores afterward. About the type, you can store the following types of data in a document:

- Text (more on that later)
- Numbers represented by `search.NumberField`

- Dates represented by `search.DateField`
- Geo location represented by `search.GeoField`

So if you have a number such as price in our `Listing` class, that's how you will create the field:

```
price = search.NumberField(name='price', value=listing.price)
```

For the date, you need to have a `datetime.date` or `datetime.datetime` object so that's how you mark 1 day of the new millennium:

```
date = search.DateField(name='posted_on' = datetime.date(2000, 1, 1))
```

There's one catch with the dates. No matter whether you supply a `datetime.date` or `datetime.datetime` object, internally the dates are always stored as number days since January 1, 1970. This means that the time part of the date is never stored and it is not possible for us to get granular to the level of hours, minutes and seconds. This is easy to fix; you can convert the `datetime.datetime` object into seconds (or even smaller unit) andstored that as a number which than can easily be processed. in relation to the Geo location, this expects an instance of `search.GeoPoint` class like this:

```
location = search.GeoField(name='location', value=search.
GeoPoint(24.84, 10.34))
```

The text fields

And that's all – it's pretty simple. Now we are only left with the textual types of fields. When it comes to text, you have three types of fields:

- `AtomField` for text that should be matched as is
- `TextField` to store normal text
- `HTMLField` text with markup

Recall that when you store some text, it is tokenized. All the above fields store text just the difference is in how and if they are tokenized or not.

For the `AtomField`, text is not tokenized at all and stored as is. Eventually, when it comes to search, only an exact match can be made. We will discuss this in detail when we look into queries but the only thing for you to remember right now is that text is not tokenized at all and stored as is.

About `TextField`, the text that you store is tokenized as per the rules of the language. In English, space and other punctuation mark the boundaries of the words. So if you have string *Slow, steady and calm*, it would be broken down into three tokens *slow*, *steady* and *calm*. Three tokens you say? Where did the *and* go? There's a list of words that are ignored and removed while tokenizing and in information retrieval's parlance; these are called **stop** words such as *if, which, and, on* and *so on*. You can read more about stop words here: `http://en.wikipedia.org/wiki/Stop_words`.

The `HTMLField` is exactly the same as `TextField` except that it might have markup in it so you can store HTML based text into it. While tokenizing, the tags would be ignored so if you have some marked up text like:

```
I feel <strong>about</strong> future.
```

So the tokens would be *feel* and *future* whereas the *strong* would be ignored because it is a tag. *I* and *about* of course are dropped because they are stop words.

So now we've explained about the text fields, the variety available and the differences between them. Now that's how you create a `TextField`, not very different from what you've seen earlier:

```
title = search.TextField(name='title', value='20 bedroom Mansion')
```

And that's it. Now when you have created all the fields, you have to put them in a list and can pass on to the document constructor like this:

```
# A list of all the fields that we created above:
document_fields = [title price, date, location]
# Ignoring doc_id, letting search service generate one for us.
document = search.Document(fields=document_fields)
```

Now you have a document. All you have to do is to put it into the index.

Placing the document in an index

So let's make some more progress. Now we know how to create fields of various types and how to create a document using text fields. But it is not yet added to the index. For that, first you need to get or create the index in which you'd like to place the document like this:

```
index = search.Index('property')
```

And then just the magical command:

```
index.put(document)
```

And you are done. But how do you know that the document was really placed in the index? This method returns an instance of `PutResult`, which has a property called `code`. So a safer way would be this:

```
result = index.put(document)
if result.code == search.PutResult.OK:
    print 'All went well'
elif result.code == search.PutResult.TRANSIENT_ERROR:
    # Temporary failure, try putting the document again
    index.put(document)
```

Or you can wrap the whole thing in an exception handling code like this:

```
try:
    index.put(document)
    except search.Error as e:
    if e.result.code ==  search.PutResult.TRANSIENT_ERROR:
        # Failed due to congesion so let's retry:
        index.put(document)
    else:
        print 'Oh God!' # Log the error here
```

So that completes how you would add the document to the index. But there's one more thing about it. Adding one document at a time is slower because each addition entails overhead of RPC calls. Therefore, batch operations are better. It is recommended to batch documents together. So the `Index.put()` method accepts a list of documents as well up to a maximum of 200 documents. That way, it would be more efficient. We'll see how to do that later.

Now only three things remain:

- How do you get a document?
- How do you update a document?
- How to do you delete a document from the index?

Let's examine these three things in order.

Getting a document

If you know the ID of a document, it is pretty simple to get it just with a single call like this:

```
document = index.get('REF-100')
```

The other thing you can do is get a range of document IDs. For instance, if we are using our own provided document IDs instead of relying on auto-generated ones, we can get a range starting from `REF-100` like this:

```
documents = index.get_range(start_id='REF-100', limit=10)
```

And you may iterate over the results like this:

```
for document in documents:
    # do something.
```

Basically, `Index.get_range()` returns a `GetResponse` object which has a `result` attribute, a list of `search.Document` instances. This object implements Python's iterator object protocol and that's why you can directly iterate over the returned object as well.

Of course, this is not very useful to get documents by IDs or get by a range of IDs. We'll look at more sophisticated ways of querying indexes later on in this chapter.

Updating documents

Once added to the index, a document cannot be changed at all. All you can do is first delete it and then create it again. The only thing that comes close to updating a document is when you have a document with an ID and you add yet another document with the same ID. In that case, the contents of the existing document would be replaced by the contents of the new document.

Deleting documents

Deleting documents is possible. This is the `Index.delete` method that takes a document ID and will delete the document for you just like this:

```
index.delete('my-doc-id')
```

But deletion just like all other calls invokes RPC calls behind the scenes, which entail a certain overhead; therefore if you have to delete lots of documents, you're better off batching them together up to 200 document IDs like this:

```
index.delete(['doc-1', 'doc-2', 'doc-3'])
```

And all the documents will be deleted.

Indexing the documents

Now that we understand how indexes work, how to get indexes, how to add, remove, and update documents in them, it's time to put all this together and index all the data that we generated earlier. Below is the program that picks up all the 5000 listing entities, creates fields for each property and then creates a Document out of these fields. Finally, we place them in the index in a batch of 200 entities at a time. Execute this in the interactive console:

```python
from google.appengine.ext import ndb
from google.appengine.api import search

import random

class Listing(ndb.Model):
    """
    Our Listing Model
    """
    title = ndb.StringProperty(required=True)
    ref_no = ndb.StringProperty(required=True)
    beds = ndb.IntegerProperty(required=True)
    size = ndb.IntegerProperty(required=True)
    price = ndb.IntegerProperty(required=True)
    location = ndb.GeoPtProperty()
    facilities = ndb.StringProperty(repeated=True)
    posted_on = ndb.DateProperty()

index = search.Index(name='property')

more = True
cursor = None

# Process in batches of 200 using datastore cursors.
while more:
    listings, cursor, more = Listing.query().fetch_page(200,
        start_cursor=cursor)
    documents = []

    for listing in listings:
```

```
    # Construct the fields.
    fields = [
        search.TextField(name='title', value=listing.title),
        search.AtomField(name='ref_no', value=listing.ref_no),
        search.NumberField(name='beds', value=listing.beds),
        search.NumberField(name='size', value=listing.size),
        search.NumberField(name='price', value=listing.price),
        search.DateField(name='posted_on',
          value=listing.posted_on),
        search.GeoField(name='location',
          value=search.GeoPoint(listing.location.lat,
            listing.location.lon)),
        search.TextField(name='facilities',
          value=",".join(listing.facilities))
    ]
    document = search.Document
      (doc_id=str(listing.key.to_old_key()), fields=fields)
    documents.append(document)
index.put(documents)
print "Indexed 200 documents"
```

When executed, this shall index all the entities in batches of 200 as advertised. There are a few things that need some explanation though.

First is the `ref_no`. This is supposed to be a reference number which should be treated atomically. We have a convention of REF-[number] and we do not want it to be tokenized. Otherwise it would be broken into two halves, which we do not want because when we want it to be looked up, we want it as a whole. So that's why we are using `AtomicField` here instead of a `TextField`.

Next thing requiring explanation is a minor one about geo location. When you set a value for a geo location property on an entity, it is an instance of `db.GeoPt`. Whereas the `search.GeoField` expects `search.GeoPoint`, this instance is created and supplied as the value.

The last thing that needs further explanation is a bit more interesting. Recall that the facilities property is multivalued, which means that it might take more than one value that end up as a list. How do we index that kind of thing? Simple, we form a comma separated list of values and use that as the value. Because it is a `TextField`, it would be tokenized on boundaries, which includes punctuation. This will enable us to search for certain listings with certain features such as `parking`, `gym` and so on as we'll see later.

Queries

Now that we have some data indexed, it is time to get it back and that's where
queries fit in. Queries can be as simple as a single word and might be complex by
including various Boolean operations. Let's expand our understanding gradually.

Simple queries

The simplest form of a query is a single term like this:

```
q = "gym"
```

Now there's a simple algorithm at work. First of all, because no field name is
mentioned here and it is just a string so this word gym would be searched in all
the document fields. All the document fields, you say? What's the point of searching
this gym in a number field or a date field for that matter because they won't contain
such content, you might ask. You're right. Basically, there are few simple rules for
this as follows:

1. If the search term looks like string, first TextField, HTMLField are searched
    and lastly AtomField is looked up. In case of HTML and Text fields, the
    string might appear anywhere in them but in case of AtomField, the whole
    search string must be as shall match the value of the AtomField.

2. If the search term looks like a number such as 5, first the NumberField is
    searched that has a value of 5 then TextField and HTMLField and lastly,
    AtomField is looked up. Whereas for the NumberField, the value should
    be 5. For Text and HTML fields, the 5 might appear anywhere. So a
    TextField having value Rate is 5.23 would match it. In case of
    AtomField, the value should match as is.

3. If the search term looks like a date such as 2015-05-06 then first
    DateField would be searched then TextFiled, HTMLField and if
    nothing matches, AtomField would be considered with the same
    rules stated for AtomFields before.

So to summarize, based on type of the search token (whether it is a string, number
or date), first the fields of its type are searched and as the last resort AtomField is
looked up. Whereas searching text and HTML fields comes in between except in
case where input itself looks like text where it would be first looked in TextField,
HTMLField and lastly in AtomField.

If you want all the documents that do not have the word gym in them, you simply put NOT before the search term, like this:

```
q = "NOT gym"
```

Boolean operators are always written in upper case and this query would return all the documents that do not contain the word gym anywhere. So that was the case with single queries. Next move a little to more complex multi-value queries.

Multiple value queries

If you have this string:

```
q = "gym playground"
```

you would expect that this would return the documents that contain the string gym playground but that's not the case. The space between the two strings is considered as a Boolean AND operator and all the documents that contain both words in any of the fields would be returned. This means that even if single field contains both words in any order, it would be returned as well as the case where they occur in different fields, that document would be returned as well.

Basically, the way it works is that the search string is tokenized and in our case, it would contain two tokens gym and playground. Now all the rules that are applicable to the single value queries that we just learned in the previous section would be applicable except for one additional thing that once all the rules are exhausted for a single search, the whole search string is looked up for in AtomFields as is. So in this particular case, we would have gym playground and if any AtomField has as it as is, that document would be returned.

Logical operations

So that's pretty primitive for now. You can say that you want documents having both word gym and parking written as gym parking but what if you want either of them instead of both? It's pretty simple. You have logical operators AND, OR, and NOT at your disposal and you can get as specific as you want to be in your demands such as:

```
q1 = "gym OR parking"
```

Or you can get more demanding and can put parenthesis around the terms for both readability and grouping things together:

```
q1 = "(gym OR parking) AND balcony"
```

So here, we're looking at all the documents having `balcony` with either `gym` or `parking`. You can negate things too like this:

```
q2 = "(parking OR balcony) AND NOT \"swimming pool\"
```

Here, we want all those documents that don't have `swimming pool` and have either `parking` or `balcony`. Note that swimming pool is in double quotes. This is because this search term contains a space and as we know that spaces would be considered as an implicit `AND` operator. So if we do not have quotes here, it would be considered as following:

```
q = "(parking OR balcony) AND NOT swimming AND pool"
```

Which is, of course, not what we want.

Being specific with fields

Till now, we had general search terms and didn't mention about fields at all. But you can be more specific like this:

```
q = "facilities: gym AND price <= 500"
```

So here, we are looking for documents that contain `gym` in facilities field and having `price` field with a value less then or equal to `500`. The `:` means equal and you can use the `=` sign as well so it can be written as:

```
q = "facilities= gym AND price <= 500"
```

Both are the same so it's just a matter of personal preference as there's no difference between the two in any way except the appearance. All the things that we talked about queries are applicable here such as Boolean operators. Now that we can be specific with fields, let's go through each field type to look into what operators are available to us and how to use them. Besides using Boolean operators between fields as shown above, you can do the same within field values like this:

```
q = "facilities: (gym OR parking)"
```

This is the same as:

```
q = "facilities: gym OR facilities: parking"
```

The implicit nature of `AND` also stays the same so the query:

```
q = "facilities: gym parking" (or for better readability facilities:
(gym parking))
```

actually means:

```
q = "facilities: (gym AND parking)"
```

which yet again, can be rewritten as:

```
q = "facilities: gym AND facilities: parking"
```

And this is applicable to all the field types that we are going to talk about next. So, do you know what's next? Yes, it's time to review what operators are available for each field type.

Operators on NumberField

In case of number fields, you have all the relational operators available such as =, >, >=, <, <= except the not equal != which is not available but there's a way to just express that too. The value can be written as integer, a floating point number or in an exponential form. Some examples are shown below:

```
q = "beds: 4"
q = "size = 725"
q = "price <= 29.5"
q = "distance_from_earth > 2.5E10"
```

But what about if you want all the documents that don't have four beds? There's no != operator so how you'll do that? With Boolean operators, it's pretty simple:

```
q = "NOT beds = 4"
```

And that's it.

Operators on DateField

The date fields have all the same operators as available for NumberField such as =, >, >=, <, <= except the != operator for which you will have to use Boolean NOT just as we showed in previous examples. The date should be specified in yyyy-mm-dd format where the leading zeros for month and date might be skipped:

```
q = "posted_on = 2015-05-08"
```

Because the leading zeros for month and day can be skipped, so the above can be rewritten like this:

```
q = "posted_on = 2015-5-8"
```

Pretty simple.

Operations on AtomField

`AtomField` has only one operation available, which is equality and for that too, the contents of the field must match the query value exactly except that the match is case insensitive:

```
q = "ref_no = PR781"
```

But if you field contains any special characters, you will have to quote the query value in quotes just like this:

```
q = "ref_no: \"NT&271\""
```

And it would return documents that contain the field having the exact value.

Operations on TextField and HTMLField

Just like `AtomField`, there's only one operator available for `TextField` and `HTMLField`, which is equality. The only difference is that whereas the equality operator for `AtomField` means that the value should exactly match, for text and HTML fields it means that the query value might occur anywhere in the field value.

```
q = "description: flowers"
```

This would match any document with `description` field having the word `flowers` anywhere in it. The implicit `AND` operator works here to just as with other fields:

```
q = "description: flowers roses leaves"
```

It is exactly as this:

```
q = "description: flowers AND roses AND leaves"
```

This would return all the documents with `description` field having `flowers`, `roses` and `leaves` anywhere within the field and in any order, just that all the three words must be present in the value. But often it could be the case that this is not what you want and instead you are looking for exact the phrase *flowers roses leaves* so how about that? It's pretty simple; just enclose the whole value in double quotes like this:

```
q = "description: \"flowers roses leaves\""
```

Now this will return only those documents with `description` field having exact whole phrase in them.

Recall that when talking about indexing, we mentioned that besides tokenizing the input, the words are reduced to their root, a process called **stemming**, which would reduce the word colors to color and things like that. You can search for variants of a word too, like with a query such as:

```
q = "description: ~flower"
```

Now this won't only return the documents with the word flower in their description field but also those with words such as flowery, flowers, flowered and flowering. Unfortunately, at present this feature is only available in the production environment and you cannot do that on a local server provided by App Engine SDK.

Operations on GeoField

So now we are left with the last type of field and one of the most interesting. This field contains no relation operators and therefore you cannot mention them in your queries directly. The only thing that you can do is call a function on them, which is called `distance` and looks like this:

```
distance(point1, point2)
```

This would return the distance between two points in meters. Assuming that our documents contain a `location` field along with another field called `nearest_bustop` that stores the location of the nearest bus stop:

```
q = "distance(location, nearest_busstop) < 5000" #Wrong, won't work!
Read along.
```

This would return all the documents that have a bus stop within 5 kilometers (the value is in meters) but there's a catch in the above query: Both the arguments to `distance()` function cannot be field names. At least one has to be constant. So for just this precise reason, we come to the other function called `geopoint` which takes two numbers and returns a `geopoint` number:

```
geopoint(34.56645, 23.56765)
```

So that way, you can query something like this:

```
q = "distance(location, geopoint(34.56645, 23.56765)) < 5000"
```

So this would return all those documents that have location within 5 kilometers radius of the given point. We will see this in action shortly.

Putting it all together

Now that we understand the field types, what operators are available and how they can be combined with Boolean operators, it is time to put this all in practice. The program below asks some interesting questions from the search services and the results are printed. Execute this on an interactive console:

```python
from google.appengine.ext import ndb
from google.appengine.api import search

index = search.Index(name='property')

def query(query_string):
    """
    Prints the query and its results.
    """
    result = index.search(query_string)

    print "Query: ", query_string

    for document in result.results:
        print_document(document)

    print "============="

def print_document(document):
    """
    Prints all the fields of a document.
    """

    fields = []
    for field in document.fields:
        fields.append("%s: %s" % (field.name, field.value))

    print ", ".join(fields)

query('beds = 2 AND facilities: gym parking balcony "central ac"
"built in wardrobes"')
query('facilities: gym parking balcony "central ac" "built in
wardrobes" NOT "swimming pool"')
query('beds = 2 facilities: gym parking balcony "central ac" "built in
wardrobes" distance(location, geopoint(25.092076,55.15207)) <=50000')
```

At the heart of the program is the `query()` function that given a query, submits to the search service, retrieves results and iterates over the returned list of documents. We have already discussed that the `index.search()` method returns a `SearchResult` object that has a `results` property containing a list of results and `num_found` as the number of results returned. By default, a maximum of 20 documents are returned no matter how many are found as indicated by `num_found`.

Next, the `query()` function uses a utility function called `print_document()` that given a document, will print all the fields. The results array contains objects of `ScoredDocument` type, which has an attribute called `fields` that contains all the fields. Each field is actually an instance of the relevant field class and has two properties – `name` and `value`.

We are printing all the fields of the document in `print_document()` function but what if we are interested in any particular field instead? That's possible too:

```
print document.field('price').value
```

The `field()` method takes the field name and would return the field object the same as mentioned earlier. But for the sake of demonstration, we are printing all the fields instead of using `field()` method.

Finally, we ask three tough questions. First, we want to have two-bedroom apartments with a gym, parking, balcony, central AC and built-in wardrobes so the query in compact form looks like this:

```
q = 'beds: 2 facilities: gym parking balcony "central ac" "built in wardrobes"'
```

To avoid escaping the double quotes, we have enclosed the query in single quotes. Now this query contains filters on two fields and there are spaces between values after the field names. As we have already discussed that the space is considered as an AND operator so the same query could be written like this as well:

```
q = 'beds: 2 AND facilities: gym AND parking AND balcony AND "central ac" AND "built in wardrobes"'
```

But because we can skip AND and replace them with spaces, we opted for that. Note that some values in the value part for the `facilities` field are quoted. This is because the values we want to match themselves contain spaces and without quotes would be interpreted as AND operator by the query operator.

Next, we ask for apartments that have a gym, parking, a balcony, central AC, built-in wardrobes but not the swimming pool:

```
q = 'facilities: gym parking balcony "central ac" "built in wardrobes" NOT "swimming pool"'
```

Now again, space is interpreted as an AND operator and because it is considered as AND operator, some of the values with having space in them are quoted to avoid that. The same query can be written like this:

```
q = 'facilities: gym AND parking AND balcony AND "central ac" AND
"built in wardrobes" AND NOT "swimming pool"'
```

Now we go to the next level and ask our last questions. We want a two-bedroom apartment within 50 kilometers of Dubai having a gym, parking, a balcony, central AC and built-in wardrobes:

```
q = 'beds: 2 facilities: gym parking balcony "central ac" "built in
wardrobes" distance(location, geopoint(25.092076,55.15207)) <=50000'
```

Again, because space is considered as an AND operator, the same query can be written like this:

```
q = 'beds: 2 AND facilities: gym AND parking AND balcony AND
"central ac" AND "built in wardrobes" AND distance(location,
geopoint(25.092076,55.15207)) <=50000'
```

Note that the geopoint hard-coded in the query are the geo coordinates for Dubai and the distance() function returns the distance between two points in meters so 50 kilometers means 50,000 meters.

The rest of the program is self explanatory and hence is the output. Next, we are going to refine some refinements to the same.

Selecting fields and calculated fields

Sometimes, when pulling the datastore from a storage solution, not all fields are of interest. In that case, if there's a way to limit what is being returned can not only improve efficiency but can make the code more readable and deterministic as we know for sure what we have asked for. Currently our search results return all the document fields just as in an RDBMS something like:

```
SELECT * FROM listings;
```

This would do. But what we want instead is something like:

```
SELECT title, beds, size, price FROM listings;
```

So how do we do that? That's one thing that we will learn how to do that. The other thing is that not all the fields are available in the storage solution but are calculated on the fly such as following query:

```
SELECT price, (price / 2) AS half_price FROM listing;
```

So as you can see, the `half_price` field actually doesn't exist in the underlying table but is being calculated on the fly based on another field. How do we do that? We'll learn that too.

Up to now, we have been just issuing queries and getting results. In that case, we only get 20 documents sorted by their rank (recall that rank is a number assigned by search service and is actually in number of seconds since January 1, 2011) and all the fields are returned. Turns out that we might want not only to get more then 20 documents but might want to limit number of fields or calculate new fields. Or we even might want to sort results differently.

How do we do that? For that, we would need more expressive power in our code then just passing around the query strings. That's where the `search.Query` class comes in, which takes two arguments:

```
query = search.Query(query_string="beds: 2", options=query_options)
```

So as you can see, this class constructor takes two keyword arguments. First is the plain old query string that we know very well as `query_string` and the other is the `options` keyword argument. What is that? It is actually an instance of `seach.QueryOptions` object that takes several optional keyword arguments. Currently of interest are two of them: `returned_fields` and `returned_expressions`.

Let's focus on `returned_fields`. This is just a simple list of field names that you want to return and only those would be returned to you. That's how your query building would look like:

```
fields = ['title', 'price'] # Only give us two fields
query_options = search.QueryOptions(returned_fields=fields)
query = search.Query(query_string="beds: 2", options=query_options)
# Now process the results as usual.
```

You even might want to be more sparse and might want only the document IDs. In that case, you'll set the `ids_only` keyword argument as `True`:

```
query_options = search.QueryOptions(ids_only=True) # instead of
returned_fields
```

But what about the fields calculated on fly? That's simple too. You have to pass a list of expressions as `returned_expressions` keyword argument to the function. Each element in this list is instance of the `search.FieldExpression` class which is instantiated like this:

```
half_price = search.FieldExpression(name='half_price',
expression='price/2')
```

As you can see, the first argument to the constructor is the `name` you'd want to give this calculated field to. The other argument `expression` describes how you'd want to calculate the value for this field. You can use field names, mathematical operators in this expression as you like to. Next, you pass this to the constructor of the `search.QueryOptions` so the whole thing looks like this:

```
# Prepare expressions
half_price = search.FieldExpression(name='half_price',
expression='price/2')
distance = search.FieldExpression(name='distance',
expression='distance(location, geopoint(12,23))')
expressions = [half_price, distance]
# Prepare query options
query_options = search.QueryOptions(returned_expressions=expressions)
# Prepare query
q = search.Query(query_string="beds: 2", options=query_options)
# Now execute.
results = index.search(q)
```

As you can see, we create expression objects, put them in a list, pass them to query `options`, those query options then are passed to the the query object and finally, that query object ends up being passed to the `index.search()` method. Now these would appear as `expressions` property on the returned document where as the fields would have the document fields:

```
for field in document.fields:
    # Do something
# And these are the calculated fields
for calculated_field in document.expressions:
    # Do something
```

In the second expression called `distance`, you might have noticed that we have used a couple of functions besides a field name such as `distance()` and `geopoint()`, which we have already discussed. So turns out that you can use functions too and below are some functions that are at your disposal:

- `max()`: This will return the maximum of the given values such as `max(3, 4, 1)` returns 4.
- `min()`: This is same as above except that it will return a minimum of all.
- `log()`: This returns a natural logarithm.
- `abs()`: This returns an absolute number so `abs(-3)` would return 3.
- `pow()`: This calculates the x to the y power. So `pow(2,8)` returns 256.

- `count()`: This returns the number of fields in a document. Recall that a document might have multiple fields of the same but different type. So `count(fieldname)` would return the number of fields named `fieldname` in the document.

So that's all that we need to know about selecting and calculating fields. Let's put this all into practice:

```
"""
Demonstrate return fields, calculated fields, expressions
"""
from google.appengine.ext import ndb
from google.appengine.api import search

index = search.Index(name='property')

def query(query_string):
    """
    Prints the query and its results.
    """

    fields_to_return = ['title', 'beds', 'size', 'price']
    price_per_sqft = search.FieldExpression(name='price_per_sqft',
expression='price/size')
    distance = search.FieldExpression(name='distance',
expression='distance(location, geopoint(25.092076,55.15207))/1000')

    query_options = search.QueryOptions(
        returned_fields=fields_to_return,
        returned_expressions=[price_per_sqft, distance])

    query = search.Query(query_string=query_string,
        options=query_options)
    result = index.search(query)

    print "Query: ", query_string

    for document in result.results:
        print_document(document)

    print "============="

def print_document(document):
    """
```

```
    Prints all the fields of a document.
    """

    fields = []
    for field in document.fields:
        fields.append("%s: %s" % (field.name, field.value))

    for field in document.expressions:
        fields.append("%s: %s" % (field.name, field.value))
    print ", ".join(fields)

query('beds = 2 facilities: gym parking balcony "central ac" "built in
wardrobes" distance(location, geopoint(25.092076,55.15207)) <=50000')
```

Important parts of the code are highlighted and we have already explained much of the program. The `fields_to_return` is the list of fields that we want to return so this list is passed as `returned_fields` keyword argument of the `search.QueryOptions`.

Next, we are creating two expressions:

- First is `price_per_sqft`, which simply divides the price on square feet to determine price per square feet.

- The other field is distance, which calculates how far is the listed property from center of the Dubai city using `distance()` and `geopoint()` functions. Because `distance()` returns the result in meters, it is divided by 1000 to convert it into kilometers.

These expressions are placed in a list named `expressions`, which is passed as a `returned_expressions` keyword argument of the `search.QueryOptions`.

Finally, the query options are passed to the `search.Query` object as `options` keyword argument. Now the returned results contain the document fields under `fields` property for each document object where as calculated fields are under `expressions` property of the same. That's why we have modified the `print_document()` function to iterate over the `expressions` property while printing the document fields as highlighted in the example above.

Sorting

Now we are comfortable with querying the data, it is time to put it in some desirable order. That is, sorting the results. How do we do that? Our old friend `search.QueryOptions` takes a keyword argument called `sort_options`. We just have to supply that and we are done. Okay, so the question is what this `sort_options` argument would be?

It's actually an instance of `search.SortOptions` class which takes a single argument called `expressions`. What is expressions then? It is just a list of `search.SortExpression` instances where `search.SortExpression` constructor takes some keyword arguments which define the sorting behavior.

All this seems bit complicated so let's take another look.

- Whenever you are going to sort, you are either going to sort on a field or a calculated value. For example, you might want to sort on `price`, which is just a field or price per square feet that is a calculated field obtained by dividing `price` to `size` field.

- But that was just for the value but as we know it is not mandatory for all the documents to have all the fields so we'd like to specify some default value as well in case the field we want to sort on is missing in the document.

- Lastly, you would also want to specify whether sort should be ascending or descending.

All this information is captured by the `search.SortExpression` class which takes three keyword arguments for its constructor:

1. The `expression` is the value to sort by. It can be a field name or an arithmetic expression just we had in case of calculated fields.

2. The `default_value` will be used in case value cannot be calculated from the given `expression`, this `default_value` would be used instead.

3. The `direction` whether the sort should be descending (indicated by specifying `search.SortExpression.DESCENDING` as value for the `direction` argument) or ascending (using `search.SortExpression.ASCENDING` as value)

Let's take an example. Suppose that we want to sort by the number of bedrooms in descending order so that's how we'll express it:

```
by_beds_descending = search.SortExpression(expression='beds',
direction=search.SortExpression.DESCENDING, default_value=0)
```

Now here, we are creating a `search.SortExpression` and stating that the sort should be on the beds field in descending direction and in case the field is missing, assume `0` as the value.

We might also want to sort by the average price per bedroom for each listing. As we have only `beds` and `price` in the documents, we will have to calculate this on the fly. So this is what it looks like:

```
by_price_per_bed_descending = search.SortExpression(expression='price
/ beds', direction=search.SortExpression.DESCENDING, default_value=0)
```

Note that the `expression` argument is no more just a field but an arithmetic expression composed to two fields: `price` and `beds`. The rest of the things are same.

So, now suppose that we want to sort our documents first on price and then on price per bedroom. How do we go about that? Pretty simple, the next logical step is to create a `search.SortOptions` instance like this:

```
sort_orders = search.SortOptions(expressions=[by_beds_descending,
by_price_per_bed_descending])
```

So what we have done here? We simply created an instance of `search.SortOptions` and passed the list of sort expressions as a list in order we want the sort order to occur as `expressions` keyword argument. Okay so now what do we do next? Just one more step, pass this `sort_orders` to the `search.SortOptions` constructor under `sort_options` keyword argument like this:

```
query_options = search.QueryOptions(sort_options=sort_orders)
```

And the rest as you already know, will be passed to the `search.Query` like this:

```
# Find all the apartments having parking ordered by beds and price per
bed.
query = search.Query(query_string="facilities: parking",
options=query_options)
index.search(query)
```

And that's all, you are done. Now is the time to put all this into practice. The program below issues four queries. The first one sorts by price, the next sorts by price per square feet, next to that by distance from the center of city. And lastly, we sort on three sort orders first by price per square feet, then price and finally by distance so multiple sort orders are there. So there's the program:

```
"""
Demonstrate return fields, calculated fields, expressions
"""
from google.appengine.ext import ndb
from google.appengine.api import search

index = search.Index(name='property')

def query(query_string, sort_orders=None):
    """
    Prints the query and its results.
    """

    fields_to_return = ['title', 'beds', 'size', 'price']
    price_per_sqft = search.FieldExpression(name='price_per_sqft',
        expression='price/size')
```

```python
        distance = search.FieldExpression(name='distance',
            expression='distance(location,
                geopoint(25.092076,55.15207))/1000')

        orders = []
        for order in sort_orders:
            orders.append(search.SortExpression(
                expression=order[0],
                direction=order[1],
                default_value=order[2]
                ))

        sort_opts = search.SortOptions(expressions=orders)
        query_options = search.QueryOptions(
            returned_fields=fields_to_return,
            returned_expressions=[price_per_sqft, distance],
            sort_options=sort_opts)

        query = search.Query(query_string=query_string,
            options=query_options)
        result = index.search(query)



        for document in result.results:
            print_document(document)

        print "============="

def print_document(document):
    """
    Prints all the fields of a document.
    """

    print document.field('title').value
    fields = []
    for field in document.fields:
        if field.name == 'title':
            continue
        fields.append("\t%s: %s" % (field.name, field.value))

    for field in document.expressions:
```

```
        fields.append("\t%s: %s" % (field.name, field.value))

    print "\n".join(fields), "\n"


q = 'beds = 2 facilities: gym parking balcony "central ac" "built in
wardrobes" distance(location, geopoint(25.092076,55.15207)) <=50000'

# Each sort is a tuple - expression, sort direction and default value.
by_price = ('price', search.SortExpression.DESCENDING, 0)
by_price_per_sqft = ('price/sqft', search.SortExpression.DESCENDING,
0)
by_distance = ('distance(location,
geopoint(25.092076,55.15207))/1000',
    search.SortExpression.DESCENDING, 0)
query(q, [by_price])
query(q, [by_price_per_sqft])
query(q, [by_distance])
query(q, [by_price_per_sqft, by_price, by_distance])
```

This is actually almost the same program that we showed to demonstrate the field selection and calculation. The `query()` function is modified to take a list of sort specification, whereas each sort specification is three element tuples containing the `expression`, sort direction and default value.

So that's what `by_price`, `by_price_sqft` and `by_distance` are, just sort specifications. The `query()` function is the one that creates instances of `search.SortExpression` from these tuples as can be see from the code above. Each instance of the `search.SortExpression` is appended to a list named orders. This list is then passed to `search.SortOptions` as the expressions argument, which in turn is passed to `search.QueryOptions` as explained.

The rest of the program is pretty self explanatory.

Pagination

The last piece of the puzzle is pagination. So let's look into that. By default when you issue an `index.search()` call, the first 20 matching documents are returned and the result is actually a `search.SearchResult` instance, which has the following properties:

- `results`: This are the list of `ScoreDocument` instances. Each object in this list has `fields` property that we already have seen. The number of items by default are 20 but you can increase that number by supplying a `limit` keyword argument to `search.QueryOptions`.

- cursor: This is a pointer to the last document in the results list above. So the next time you execute `index.search()` with the same query and pass this as `cursor` keyword argument, the read operation will start from that point. More on this later.

- number_found: This is the total number of matching documents. This value is an estimate if the number of matching documents is more the `number_found_accuracy`. More on that later.

There's a keyword argument to the `search.QueryOptions` called `number_found_accuracy`. This is a number that when not specified defaults to `limit` keyword argument of the same class and `limit` in turn defaults to 20 as we already know. So because the value for this `number_found_accuracy` defaults to 20 (because it is not specified so it defaults to value of `limit` which is 20) therefore if there are more then 20 matching documents, the `number_found` property's value will be an estimate.

The point here is that the `number_found` is always an estimate and only accurate up to either `number_found_accuracy` (maximum value for which is 25,000) or to `limit` if not specified which itself defaults to 20. A higher number for `number_found_accuracy` would impact performance negatively so it is better not to go for it unless you absolutely need to.

The `cursor` is always `None` and is only set if there's a `search.Cursor` instance specified as a `cursor` keyword argument to `search.QueryOptions` class. We will see how this works in a while.

When it comes to pagination, there are two main approaches. Let's go through each of them.

Offset-based pagination

Out of the available approaches, one is the plain old limit, offset technique. You can specify how many documents to fetch (limit) after skipping how many of them i.e. the offset. When not specified, the limit defaults to 20 (just as discussed) and the offset defaults to 0 so only the first 20 matching documents will be returned.

This is somewhat similar to how you would use LIMIT and OFFSET clauses in an SQL statement like this:

```
SELECT * FROM listings LIMIT 25 OFFSET 25
```

So the same thing for our search index (which contains 5000 documents in all) would look like this:

```
query_options = search.QueryOptions(limit=25, offset=25)
query = search.Query(query_string="beds: 2", options=query_options)
```

```
result = index.search(query)
print len(result.results) # Would print 25
print len(result.number_found) # Would be an estimate if more then 25
matching documents were found.
```

And in order to iterate over all the documents, it's pretty simple. Each time you advance the `offset` by the number of results fetched and issue the query again:

```
returned_results = 1
offset = 0

while returned_results > 0:
    query_options = search.QueryOptions(limit=200, offset=offset)
    q = "beds: 2"
    query = search.Query(query_string=q, options=query_options)
    result = index.search(query)
    returned_results = len(result.results)
    offset += returned_results
```

But there are two issues with this approach:

- The first one is that from the perspective of performance, it is not a good approach because whenever you issue an `offset` such as `200` then all the matching documents still get loaded and then the first 200 would be skipped. So that's not very good from performance perspective.

- The second issue is a big limitation and that is that the `offset` cannot take a value more then 1000, which effectively means that you cannot skip beyond the first 1000 documents hence you are limited to iterate over only the first 1000. If the `offset` value is more then 1000, the `search.QueryOptions` constructor will throw a `ValueError` exception.

Let's look at the other approach.

Cursor-based pagination

The other way to iterate over results is cursor-based approach. This is similar to what we learned about datastore cursors. You create an initial cursor that is an instance of `search.Cursor` and supply it to `cursor` keyword argument of the `search.QueryOptions` class. Now when you issue the query, `SearchResult` object returned by `Index.search()` method's `cursor` property would contain a cursor pointing to the last document returned under results property. And that's how you would iterate over the data:

```
cursor = search.Cursor()

while cursor != None:
```

```
query_options = search.QueryOptions(limit=200, cursor=cursor)
q = "facilities: balcony"
query = search.Query(query_string=q, options=query_options)
result = index.search(query)
cursor = result.cursor
```

So as you can see, we create a new cursor instance and then the `while` loop continues till the cursor is not `None`. Each time, we supply the cursor to `search.QueryOptions` as `cursor` keyword argument and call `Index.search()` method. The `cursor` property of the returned `SearchResult` object is assigned to cursor again.

Now let's put all this in practice. Below is the program that iterates over all the documents using both approaches one at a time:

```
from google.appengine.ext import ndb
from google.appengine.api import search

index = search.Index(name='property')

def iterate_over_documents_using_offset():
    """
    Iterates over matching documents using offsets
    """
    returned_results = 1
    offset = 0

    # Cannot go much longer without cursor.
    while returned_results > 0:

        try:
            query_options = search.QueryOptions(limit=200,
offset=offset)
        except ValueError as e:
            print "Error occured: ", str(e)
            break

        q = "facilities: balcony"
        query = search.Query(query_string=q, options=query_options)
        result = index.search(query)
        returned_results = len(result.results)
        offset += returned_results
```

```
        print "Total matching documents: ", result.number_found, "
Fetched ", returned_results, " documents"


def iterate_over_documents_using_cursor():
    """
    Iterates through matching documents using cursors.
    """
    cursor = search.Cursor()

    while cursor != None:

        query_options = search.QueryOptions(limit=200, cursor=cursor)
        q = "facilities: balcony"
        query = search.Query(query_string=q, options=query_options)
        result = index.search(query)
        returned_results = len(result.results)
        cursor = result.cursor
        print "Total matching documents: ", result.number_found, "
Fetched ", returned_results, " documents"
iterate_over_documents_using_offset()
iterate_over_documents_using_cursor()
```

There are two functions `iterate_over_documents_using_offset()` and
`iterate_over_documents_using_cursor()`, which are called at the bottom.
Note that in the function using offset-based iteration, we have wrapped the
instantiation of the `search.QueryOptions` in exception handling code and
in case of exception, we break out of the loop:

```
    try:
            query_options = search.QueryOptions(limit=200,
offset=offset)
        except ValueError as e:
            print "Error occurred: ", str(e)
            break
```

And this exception mainly occurs when the value of `offset` is greater then
1000. The other function simply uses cursors as explained. As you know that
the `SearchResult` contained cursor under `cursor` property, you can make it be
attached to each returned document as well by creating the initial cursor like this:

```
cursor = search.Cursor(per_result=True)
```

Now instead of the `SearchResult`, each returned document will contain its own cursor under `cursor` property. When you issue a query with a cursor of a document, a search would start after that specific document.

Lastly, you can save the cursor value somewhere by obtaining its string form like that for later use:

```
cursor_str = cursor.web_safe_string
# Save it and do some other stuff.
cursor = search.Cursor(web_safe_string=cursor_str)
```

And that's all you need to know about the pagination options available to us.

Facets

Have you ever been to Amazon or eBay? While searching for an item, you will have noticed on the left a set of filters that tell you how many items of each type are available. For instance, if we're looking for TVs, they'll have a section where a list of brands and number of items in each brand would be listed. One section would be for the screen size with each screen size and number of available items in that. Similarly, one would be for TV features, whether it is a SmartTV, has 3D features and so on.

So you get the idea, categorized, summarized information on your left that lets you filter your results should you choose to go for a Sony Smart TV in 60 inches with 3D capabilities. You make appropriate choices by ticking the check boxes and the listed items will be filtered by your selection.

Certainly, you'll want such capabilities in your own application. How does that work and how can we implement it? This is pretty simple actually, but there are few steps:

- Mentioning facets when indexing data. This alters the indexing process a little bit. It is just that we have to specify what fields we'd like to see facets for so that data for them can be preprocessed and arranged for us.

- Requesting facets when querying data. We have been querying our indexes for a while now. These queries won't return facet information such as how many TVs of each brand are out there and things like that. We have to request that and there are few options here for us that we'll examine in a while.

- Filtering data by selected facets when requested. So that's when a user selects that they want a 55-inch TV (size facet) in Sony (brand facet) so we have to filter the items as requested.

Now let's take a look at each of these steps in more detail.

Indexing facets

We have been indexing documents and we know that to index a document, all we have to do is to create an instance of search.Document and provide it a list of search.xxxField instances where xxx isn't what you think it is or people go to torrent sites for, it is just the type name and we've seen all the available field types and available operations on them.

Indexing facets is similar as well; we have to provide a list of facet field instances under a facets keyword argument like that:

```
search.Document(fields=list_of_fields, facets=list_of_facets)
```

OK, so what is this list of facets? This is a list of objects that can be instance of either of these classes:

- search.NumberFacet
- search.AtomFacet

The first class is for specifying facets for fields that are numeric in nature like TV size in inches, wattage, number of bedrooms in an apartment and so on. The second type is for indivisible strings. We have already discussed what atomic strings are. So, this can be useful for things that have string values such as if we have a features field for our TVs that can take values such as Wi-Fi, SmartTV, 3D, DLNA and like that.

This seems limited. What about dates you say? Well, nothing stops you from creating facets of dates as strings. It is just that everything else has to be converted to a string. Now comes the question: how do we create facet instances? Here's how:

```
size = search.NumberFacet(name='screen size', value=55)
wifi = search.AtomicFacet(name='features', 'WiFi')
```

Each facet instance expects two keyword arguments. First is name and other is value. The value is pretty obvious. The name can be anything that is valid as a field name and we've discussed the rules for field name already. It is not necessary that if you are creating a facet for field size should have the name size as well. You can give it any name that you want but it would be overall easier for you to manage things if field and facet names are the same.

So now that we have created two facet instances, we have to mention them under a facets keyword argument while creating the document like this:

```
document = search.Document(fields=list_of_fields, facets=[size, wifi])
```

And you put the document in the index. It's pretty simple. But there's one thing left. A TV does not have only a single feature. It usually has more than one feature such as 3D, USB ports and things like that. So this means that features is a field that takes multiple values. We know how to deal with it while creating fields for indexing fields but how do we do it here while creating facets?

It turns out that you can have as many facets fields of the same name as much you want and there's no restriction. It is not even required that the facet fields of the same name must be of the same type and you can mix NumberFacet and AtomicFacet types together. So in order to create facets for a very capable TV, that's what we have to do:

```python
size = search.NumberFacet(name='screen size', value=55)
# All the TV features:
wifi = search.AtomicFacet(name='features', 'WiFi')
three_d = search.AtomicFacet(name='features', '3D')
smart = search.AtomicFacet(name='features', 'SmartTV')
dlna = search.AtomicFacet(name='features', 'DLNA')

tv_facets = [size , wifi, three_d, smart, dlna]
document = search.Document(fields=list_of_fields, facets=tv_facets)
```

Now you are finished. This TV has all the facets in it and now it can be added to the index. So how about we revise our indexing of our classified listings example that is about property listings? There are a few interesting fields that are good candidates to have facets such as number of bedrooms, apartment size, and facilities. Let's take a look at the revised program and then we will discuss it in detail:

```python
from google.appengine.ext import ndb
from google.appengine.api import search

import random

class Listing(ndb.Model):
    """
    Our Listing Model
    """
    title = ndb.StringProperty(required=True)
    ref_no = ndb.StringProperty(required=True)
    beds = ndb.IntegerProperty(required=True)
    size = ndb.IntegerProperty(required=True)
    price = ndb.IntegerProperty(required=True)
    location = ndb.GeoPtProperty()
```

```
    facilities = ndb.StringProperty(repeated=True)
    posted_on = ndb.DateProperty()

index = search.Index(name='property')


more = True
cursor = None

# Process in batches of 200 using datastore cursors.
while more:
    listings, cursor, more = Listing.query().fetch_page(200, start_
cursor=cursor)
    documents = []

    for listing in listings:
        # Construct the fields.
        fields = [
          search.TextField(name='title', value=listing.title),
          search.AtomField(name='ref_no', value=listing.ref_no),
          search.NumberField(name='beds', value=listing.beds),
          search.NumberField(name='size', value=listing.size),
          search.NumberField(name='price', value=listing.price),
          search.DateField(name='posted_on', value=listing.posted_on),
          search.GeoField(name='location', value=search.
GeoPoint(listing.location.lat, listing.location.lon)),
          search.TextField(name='facilities', value=",".join(listing.
facilities))
        ]

        facets = [search.NumberFacet(name='beds', value=listing.beds),
                  search.NumberFacet(name='size', value=listing.size)]

        for facility in listing.facilities:
            facets.append(search.AtomFacet(name='facilities',
value=facility))

        document = search.Document(doc_id=str(listing.key.to_old_
key()), fields=fields, facets=facets)
        documents.append(document)

    index.put(documents)
    print "Indexed 200 documents"
```

Important portions of the code are highlighted above. We are just creating two `NumberFacet` instances for `beds` and `size` fields putting them in `facets` list. Next, for all the `facilities` of a listing, we create one `AtomicFacet` and append it to the `facets` array. Finally, when all this facet construction is done, we supply this `facets` list as `facets` keyword argument to the `search.Document` constructor. Lastly, `index.put(document)` is the normal business.

Now if you run this example in console, it will actually pick up all the entities from the datastore, and will create document instances with all the fields and facets as specified as shown above. Because we are using the entity key as the document ID, each document will be replaced by the newer version of the document. That's because when you create a document with an existing ID, it replaces the existing document. Run this in an interactive console and then we will move on to the next steps.

Fetching facets

Now that we have indexed data, we would like to fetch the facets so that we can display this information to the user. This will actually contain information such as we have 20 TVs of 42-inch size, 17 TVs of 48-inch size and things like that. It is the usual breakdown of the items that you as a user of various e-commerce websites are used to.

We know how to query data from a search index. This querying doesn't bring facets and we have to request that information. How do we do that? There are actually four modes to it:

1. The first option is called automatic facet discovery. You just ask for facets and it returns most frequent occurring facets and their values.

2. The next option is that instead of returning all the facets, you specifically ask for certain fields to be returned in facets.

3. The next option is that you just don't indicate the facets to be returned but you also provide values. So you can say return me `facilities` with `wifi` and `dlna` values.

4. You can be even more specific and can ask for not just fields and values but can specify the value ranges.

This all seems pretty complicated, so let's look into each option in detail.

Asking facets via automatic discovery

Automatic facet discovery returns all the frequently used facets. But this has a limitation. Only the first top ten fields will be returned and for each value for these fields, the top ten most occurring values will be returned. Sounds complicated? It is not. The idea here is that suppose there are 100 documents that mention the `size` field, 70 mention `features` and so on and so forth. So, only the top ten fields with respect to the count will be returned. Now for the values against each of the returned fields, yet again only the top ten values will be returned. So, for instance, if `size` field is being returned and it has values such as 55 inch occurring 200 times, 48 inch occurring 180 times and so on, only the top 10 values with respect to count will be returned. If there are five 14-inch TVs in your document index and they don't make their way into the top 10 values, this won't be returned.

So how do we request that? We just set the `enable_facet_discovery` keyword argument to `True` to the `search.Query` instance like this:

```
results = index.search(search.Query("",enable_facet_discovery=True))
```

We have supplied an empty query string here because we do not want to filter the results and get facets for the filtered set, rather we want to get it for the whole indexed data.

What's next and where are the returned facets? The returned object has a property called **facets** that contains the instances of `FacetResult` class. Each instance has two properties. The first is `name`, which is the face name (the one we gave when creating it during the indexing process) and the other is `values`, which, of course, has all the values for that facet/field. This is because there can be many values for a facet (such as `size` so there are many different sizes of TVs) therefore `values` is actually a list of `FacetResultValue` instances. Each instance contains just three properties:

- `label`: This is actually the value such as 55 inch in case of size or Wi-Fi in case of features
- `count`: This is the number of documents that are in index for this value
- `refinement_token`: This is a magic string that if supplied while query in an index would only contain the documents that fall under face value. We'll take a look at it later.

To summarize the above structure, that's how you can look at it:

- `results.facets`: This is a list of `FacetResult` instances, which has two properties:

  - `name`: This is the name of the facet that was given when creating facet during indexing
  - `values`: This is a list of FacetResultValue instances with each instance having three properties:

    `label`: This is the actual value such as wifi, 55 and so on

    `count`: This is the number of documents we have in index with the above value

    `refinement_token`: This is a key that we can specify and results would be filtered by the facet under consideration

In the next few sections, we are going to print the output of facets over and over so we encapsulate the whole thing in a function like this:

```
def print_facets(facets):
    """
    Prints the facets.
    """
    # For each facet, print its name
    for facet in facets:
        print '%s\n:' % facet.name
        # Now for each value for a facet
        # print label, count and refinement key
        for value in facet.values:
            print'  %s: count=%s, refinement_token=%s\n' % (value.
label, value.count, value.refinement_token)
```

In our forthcoming discussions about facets, we'll just refer to this function and you should assume that it will print the returned facets. So, coming back to the automatic face recovery, how do we retrieve facets based on automatic discovery? Let's execute the following in the interactive console:

```
from google.appengine.api import search

index = search.Index(name='property', namespace='')
results = index.search(search.Query("",enable_facet_discovery=True))
print_facets(results.facets)
```

And here's the output from the `print_facets()` function:

```
facilities:
  Maids room: count=410, refinement_token=CgpmYWNpbGl0aWVzEgpNYWlkcyB
yb29t
  24 hour security: count=405, refinement_token=CgpmYWNpbGl0aWVzEhAyNC
Bob3VyIHNlY3VyaXR5

  Balcony: count=399, refinement_token=CgpmYWNpbGl0aWVzEgdCYWxjb255
  Gym: count=380, refinement_token=CgpmYWNpbGl0aWVzEgNHeW0=
  Study: count=376, refinement_token=CgpmYWNpbGl0aWVzEgVTdHVkeQ==
  Landmarks: count=374, refinement_token=CgpmYWNpbGl0aWVzEglMYW5kbWFy
a3M=
  Swimming pool: count=374, refinement_token=CgpmYWNpbGl0aWVzEg1Td2lt
bWluZyBwb29s
  Private Garden: count=370, refinement_token=CgpmYWNpbGl0aWVzEg5Qcml2
YXRlIEdhcmRlbg==
  Parking: count=370, refinement_token=CgpmYWNpbGl0aWVzEgdQYXJraW5n
  Central AC: count=366, refinement_token=CgpmYWNpbGl0aWVzEgpDZW50cmF
sIEFD

beds:
  [1.0,6.0): count=1000, refinement_token=CgRiZWRzGgoKAzEuMBIDNi4w

size:
  [325.0,5000.0): count=1000, refinement_token=CgRzaXplGg8KBTMyNS4wEg
Y1MDAwLjA=
```

Lets' examine the output in detail starting from the `features` facet. If you recall, this is an `AtomicFacet` when indexed. So here in the output we have each value listed along with a count of how many documents having that value are in the index. Lastly, there's a `refinement_token` that when supplied to the `search.Query` will return only that documents that have the listed value.

The next two facets are interesting. Both are numeric and we used `NumericFacet` while indexing them. Now instead of the actual values listed, what we have here is a list of range. So for the beds, we have `[1.0, 6.0)` and the count 1000. The `[1.0, 6.0)` is a mathematical notation for denoting ranges. The square bracket on the left means that `1.0` is included in the range whereas the closing parenthesis on the right after `6.0` means that this range is up to 6.0 but 6.0 itself is not part of the range. And all in all, the documents that have values of `beds` field in range 1.0 to 6.0 (which is not included) is 1000.

So the key thing here is that when you ask facets for numeric fields without any specifications of your own, you get the ranges for numeric values. But we can change that can be refine things more as you'll see in a while.

Asking specific facets

Now, as you know the automatic feature discovery returns the top 10 facets and their top 10 values. You might not want all the facets and would be interested in only few of them or some specific facets even if they are not the most frequently occurring ones. That's possible to control. You have to specify the name of the facets that you want under `return_facets` keyword argument to `search.Query` like this:

```
results = index.search(search.Query("",return_facets=['beds',
'size']))
print_facets(results.facets)
```

And the output this time would be:

```
beds:
    [1.0,6.0): count=1000, refinement_token=CgRiZWRzGgoKAzEuMBIDNi4w
size:
    [325.0,5000.0): count=1000, refinement_token=CgRzaXplGg8KBTMyNS4wEg
Y1MDAwLjA=
```

So as you see, pretty simple. Just list the facets that you are interested in and that's it.

Asking facets with specific values

Now the thing is, that we can limit only the facets we are interested in but the values for numeric facets are always being returned as a range. That's not very useful. Even for the atomic facets, we might not be interested in all the values but only in a handful of them. So how do we control that? Pretty simple, the same `return_facets` keyword argument that we specified with facet names will do the trick. But this time, instead of just listing the name of the facet, we will have to give an instance of `search.FacetRequest` instance like this:

```
search.FacetRequest('beds', values=['1', '2', '3', '4'])
```

The first argument is the name of the facet we are interested in and the `values` keyword argument is a list of values we want to be returned. Even if it is a numeric facet, the values should be specified as strings and that's why we have the values in single quotes. So the whole thing looks like this:

```
facets=[search.FacetRequest('beds', values=['1', '2', '3', '4'])]
results = index.search(search.Query("",return_facets=facets))
print_facets(results.facets)
```

And here's the output from the above:

```
beds:
  3: count=183, refinement_token=CgRiZWRzEgEz
  1: count=175, refinement_token=CgRiZWRzEgEx
  4: count=158, refinement_token=CgRiZWRzEgE0
  2: count=154, refinement_token=CgRiZWRzEgEy
```

So this time, instead of just listing the facet names in `return_facets`, we used `search.FacetRequest,` which takes both the facet name and a list of values to be returned. It's pretty simple. Congratulations! You've almost made it to the finish line for faceted search, there's just last mile left.

Asking facets in specific ranges

So by now, we know that we can limit not only the facets to be returned but can also limit what values to be returned. But what if instead of the values to be returned, we want some custom ranges? For instance, for the `size` we might want a range from 300 to 550 and from 550 to say 900 and like that? How do we do that? Our newly discovered friend `search.FacetRequest` again comes to the rescue. It will take the facet name as usual but instead of `values`, we specify a new keyword argument called `ranges` that lists the ranges we want to be returned. Each range is represented by a `search.FacetRange` instance, which takes just two parameters:

- `start` means the start of the range
- `end` means the end of the range

You can specify any of the above or both, so for example:

- This means that the documents with a value starting at 200 whereas:
  ```
  search.FacetRange(start=200)
  ```

- This means that the documents have a value less than 500 and finally:
  ```
  search.FacetRange(end=500)
  ```

- This means that the documents have values in range starting from 200 and ending with 500, whereas 500 is not included in the range:
  ```
  search.FacetRange(start=200, end=500)
  ```

Now, armed with this knowledge, we want to return a facet about apartment sizes in the following ranges:

- 300 to 550
- 550 to 1000
- 1000 to 1500
- 1500 and above

So, equipped with this knowledge, we arrive at the following to have our custom ranges:

```
range1 = search.FacetRange(start=300, end=550)
range2 = search.FacetRange(start=550, end=1000)
range3 = search.FacetRange(start=1000, end=1500)
range4 = search.FacetRange(start=1500)

size_ranges = [range1, range2, range3, range4]
size_facet = search.FacetRequest('size', ranges=size_ranges)


results = index.search(search.Query("",return_facets=[size_facet]))
print_facets(results.facets)
```

And here's the output of the above:

```
size:
  [1500.0,Infinity): count=772, refinement_
token=CgRzaXplGggKBjE1MDAuMA==
  [550.0,1000.0): count=101, refinement_token=CgRzaXplGg8KBTU1MC4wEgY
xMDAwLjA=
  [1000.0,1500.0): count=91, refinement_token=CgRzaXplGhAKBjEwMDAuMBI
GMTUwMC4w
  [300.0,550.0): count=36, refinement_token=CgRzaXplGg4KBTMwMC4wEgU1N
TAuMA==
```

How to count against each of the specified range is listed along with the refinement key, which we are going to refine next.

Filtering by facets

We have been ignoring the `refinement_token` returned by facets up to now. There's nothing complicated about it. You just specify a list of refinement tokens as `facet_refinements` keyword argument to `search.Query` instance like this:

```
results = index.search(search.Query("",facet_refinements=[token1,
token2, token3]))
```

The results will contain only the documents that have the facet values corresponding to the refinement tokens specified. If the tokens contain the same facet (such as `size`), these are combined by OR together, whereas the refinement tokens for different facets are combined by AND together.

Now what is the use of all this? Whatever facets and however we retrieve them, probably we are going to display them to the user on interface where they can make selections by ticking the check boxes like this:

```
# Template for a checkbox
checkbox = '<input type="checkbox" name="%s" value="%s">%s [%s]<br>'
# Fetch results
facets=[search.FacetRequest('beds', values=['1', '2', '3', '4'])]
results = index.search(search.Query("",return_facets=facets))

for facet in facets:
    for value in facet.values:
        filling_values = (facet.name, value.refinement_token,
                          value.label, value.count)
        print checkbox % filling_values
```

And that's the HTML out of it:

```
<input type="checkbox" name="beds" value="CgRiZWRzEgEx">1 [175]<br>
<input type="checkbox" name="beds" value="CgRiZWRzEgEy">2 [154]<br>
<input type="checkbox" name="beds" value="CgRiZWRzEgEz">3 [183]<br>
<input type="checkbox" name="beds" value="CgRiZWRzEgE0">4 [158]<br>
```

Now when users make one or more selections from the above, we can easily read it in our request handlers and filter our results in accordance like this in our handlers:

```
class SearchHandler(webapp2.RequestHandler):

    def post(self):

        # Step 1: Read all the selected values.
```

```
brands = self.request.get_all('brand')

# Step 2: Obtain index
index = search.Index(name='my-index', namespace='')

# Step 3: Construct query and fetch results
query = search.Query("",facet_refinements=brands)
results = index.search(query)

# Now render the processed results to the user.
```

It's pretty self explanatory. Go, build the best out of it!

Summary

We started our journey from the need to search for information that we have stored. We looked at the history of information retrieval and learned about a Lucene library and products based on it. Next, we turned our attention to generate some data to index. Then we learned how indexing works, what an index is, document and what fields are and how many types of fields are available. After that, we turned our attention towards indexing the data. After indexing, we moved to querying the index. We learned that there are global queries and we can be specific by naming the fields we want to filter on. We also learned about Boolean operations and operators available for each field type. After all that, we looked into sorting and iterating over results.

We then looked into faceted search where we can categorize and summarize the documents that we have. Lastly, we mentioned the prospective search and how it reverses the direction of search.

In the next chapter, we are going to take a look at how to do time-consuming things in the background.

7
Using Task Queues

When you open a URL, usually you get a text document in response that usually contains marked up text with HTML (and CSS, JavaScript), which in turn is either generated on the fly or is fetched from the file system as is. In any case, the time it takes for such a computational activity is pretty small, in the order of a few hundred milliseconds. But there are things that need and take more time than just milliseconds and can't be appropriately done within such time frame.

For more computationally expensive tasks, it's best if they are executed in the background. And that's where the task queues comes in where you queue computationally expensive tasks and process them later at your convenience in the background or in case there are batches of data that need to be processed and cannot be done in a single request. Google App Engine provides you with this functionality to enqueue your longer tasks and process them in background. That's what this chapter is all about.

In this chapter, we will look into:

- The need and background of queues
- Push queues
- Pull queues

So let's explore what these task queues are, why they are needed, and how they can be helpful to our application development. But before we jump to that discussion, it is better to take a look at why we need background processing and queues at all. Let's get started.

The need to queue things

The web started as a simple document-based system with a text-based protocol called HTTP. You have a URL that contains a name of a machine (which gets resolved using another protocol called DNS) and the path of the required document and the software running over the host machine (called an HTTP server because it could parse the HTTP protocol and carry out the required) and will return that document back to you.

HTML was the language to mark text within those documents, sections, headings and links to other documents along with some formatting tags. Formatting within documents turned out to be tedious to maintain across hundreds of documents so it moved out as separate style documents called style sheets written in a notation called CSS.

Then came the interactivity part, someone from Netscape included a small language resembling Java called JavaScript enabling you to respond to events such as mouse clicks and key presses on certain elements and the rest, as they say, is history.

But things have changed a lot and people started to do more complicated stuff than just rendering text documents in response to user requests. Even when rendering text documents, there are times in the life span of a web application when it needs to perform certain tasks that are computationally expensive. Examples include resizing images, and other computationally expensive processing on user uploaded files. One prime example would be video processing since the advent of YouTube. You upload video in any format but it is converted to a single base format, which requires video encoding, a computationally expensive operation.

People started to realize that these kinds of computationally expensive tasks are best done in the background instead of putting our web servers under stress and performing them right there. That's where the whole idea of message queues and independent workers came to life. The main idea is that any computationally expensive tasks are added as a message to a queue and there are multiple worker machines that pull out the messages from the queue, process them as described by the message and store the results.

There are many messaging queues available with different configurations, options and the ones that you can host yourself such as ActiveMQ, RabitMQ, ZeroMQ and so on. Then there are hosted versions of queues such as **Amazon Simple Queue Service** (**SQS**) that comes as part of the Amazon Web Services or Google Cloud Pub/Sub for that matter.

Google App Engine provides its own version of messaging queues where you can enqueue messages and process them later.

There are two modes of operations available; one is the push queue where you enqueue the messages and they are pushed to your application as HTTP calls to the URLs that you specify in your messages that you enqueue. That's called the **web-hook** model. The other version is pull queues, where you have to pull the tasks (messages) yourself and delete them when you've finished processing them.

The queue

The queue model in App Engine is little bit different and it's best to take a look at the model before we go into exploring things further. The discussion in this section mainly pertains to push queues, some of which is applicable to pull queues as well but we'll note the differences when we come to pull queues. Basically, you have a queue where you can enqueue as many messages (called tasks from now onwards). This queue then fills up a fixed size bucket (configurable) at a fixed (that too, configurable) rate.

A task is just a URL (which is handled by and is within your application) optionally with query parameters, payload, and headers. Whenever something needs to be done in the background, you simply put it in the queue as a task. Google App Engine will then dispatch HTTP POST call to the URL mentioned in the task along with mentioned query parameters, headers and payload if any. This model of processing is called web hook, which is pretty standard now.

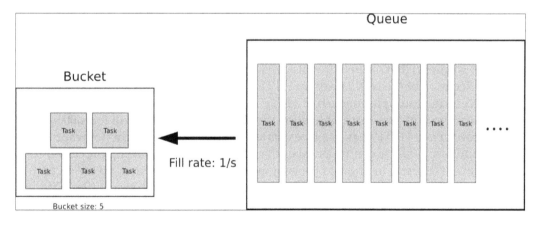

Let's elaborate all this in more detail. In the figure above, we have a queue on the right which is filling a bucket that contains five tasks and it is being filled at a rate of one task per second. The tasks are added to the queue, they reside there. So you can see that in five seconds, the bucket will be full and tasks are always fetched and executed from the bucket and not directly from the queue.

Let's examine the queue first. There are three aspects of the queue that are configurable:

- One is the name of the queue; every application comes with a queue named default and you can have more than one queue. We'll see how to do that.

- The other aspect is the capacity of the queue. Each task that you add to the queue certainly occupies some space. You can set a storage limit to the queue. The free apps have a limit of 500 MB, whereas paid apps have no such limits until you set one yourself.

- Third is the rate at which the bucket is filled from queue. We have here one task per second but you can configure to a higher rate such as five tasks per second, which would mean that every one second, the bucket would be full because its size is just five.

Now we are left with the bucket. As you know, the tasks keep falling into bucket from the queue at a configurable rate. From the bucket, they are immediately processed all at once until the bucket is empty. When the bucket is empty, Google App Engine waits until the bucket fills up. The bucket also has two configurable aspects:

- Firstly, the bucket size. By default, the bucket size is five but you can configure it. The maximum is 100. The larger the bucket, the slower it will fill but more tasks would be in execution as you can imagine because of the larger number of tasks falling into the bucket and going into execution.

- The system will pick up as many tasks as possible from the bucket, will process them and will pick more until the bucket is empty and in case it is empty, that's where it will wait for it to fill it up with tasks. Because execution of the task means an HTTP call, this means that your app would be receiving multiple concurrent HTTP requests, which would, of course, lead to more rapid resource utilization. By default, the system will let 1000 such concurrent HTTP requests be executed per queue. You might not want that and bring the maximum number of concurrent requests being processed to say 10 requests in order to prevent faster resource depletion. So the second aspect, how many concurrent tasks can be processed, is also configurable.

So this was all about good scenario so far where whatever task enqueued got executed successfully. That won't always be the case; some would certainly fail. So what about that? Such a failed task remains in the queue, not deleted and would be retried. So the retry is the last thing we need to look into while looking at the queue model. You can configure the following things about retries:

- The maximum number of times a task can be retried before giving up. For instance, if you set it to seven, the task would be tried a maximum of seven times, after which it won't be retried and would be removed from the queue.

- The maximum time limit for a task to be retried before giving up. For instance, if you set it to five days, any task that's older than five days would be given up and won't be executed again. If both the maximum retry count and maximum retry age are specified, Google App Engine would exhaust both options before finally giving up on a task.

- The minimum and maximum time between trying failed tasks. We will take a detailed look into that when exploring the actual queue configurations.

Now that we have reviewed the queue at a much abstract level, let's look at how to define one.

Defining queues

Up to now, we have been talking about what the queue is and what the options are around it, the processing model and all. But how do we define one? That's pretty simple; all the queue definitions reside in a file called queue.yaml. This file can be anywhere but typically it is at the root directory of the application.

Every application comes with a default queue, also called default. When enqueueing a task, you don't specify any specific queue, it goes to the default queue. But you can define as many queues you want to, depending upon your needs up to 10 for free apps and 100 for the paid apps as these lines are being written but that might change in future.

Mostly, you would do that to group tasks into logical collections such as those pertaining to image processing in one queue, others about compressing files in another and like that. All this is defined in the `queue.yaml` file and this is how such a configuration file will look:

```
# This is applicable to all the queues.
total_storage_limit: 100M

# All the queue definitions here.
queue:
# This one is for images.
- name: images
  rate: 10/s
  bucket_size: 20
  max_concurrent_requests: 5
# We want to change the default queue:
# 1. Change the bucket size
# 2. Max concurrent requests
# 3. Retry parameters.
- name: default
  bucket_size: 10
  max_concurrent_requests: 10
  retry_parameters:
    task_retry_limit: 10
    task_age_limit: 5d
# This last one for processing zip files.
- name: zip-files
  rate: 10/s
  bucket_size: 50
  max_concurrent_requests: 50
  retry_parameters:
    task_retry_limit: 50
    task_age_limit: 7d
    min_backoff_seconds: 30
    max_backoff_seconds: 21600 # 6 Hours
    max_doublings: 0.2 #2**(max_doublings - 1) * min_backoff_seconds.
```

And this is what these queues would look like in a development console:

Queues as the appear on local development server

Let's try to understand this bit by bit. At the very top, we are defining the storage limit for all the queues using `total_storage_limit` directive. This defaults to 500 MB for free apps and is unlimited for paid apps. This can be useful at times to limit your queue size in case of a programming error where each task recursively keeps adding more tasks and they in turn add more tasks, something called a *fork bomb*. The value of the directive is a number followed by unit. `B` for bytes, `K` for kilobytes, `M` for megabytes, `G` for Gigabytes, and finally `T` for terabytes. So in the example file above, we are setting the size for all the queues to 100 MB.

The first queue is called `images`. The queue name can be anything between 100 characters and can contain upper and lower case characters including numbers and hyphens. Let's pretend that this queue is supposed to do some image processing related stuff hence the name.

The messages are placed into the bucket at a rate of 10 tasks per second (defined by rate directive), which if you don't specify, defaults to five tasks per minute. The rate is actually a number followed by unit where s is for seconds, m for minutes, h for hours and d for days. If you specify the value to be 0 such as 0/s, no tasks would be processed from the queue. That's a way to pause a queue so that no further tasks are processed.

The size of the bucket (defined by `bucket_size`) is 20 tasks, which if not specified defaults to 5. Next we allow only five tasks to be executed at once by specifying this under `max_concurrent_requests`.

So in summary, this queue puts tasks at a rate of 10 tasks per second into a bucket of size 20 and allows a maximum of 5 tasks to be executed concurrently.

As we mentioned earlier, every application comes with a default queue, which will have its own configuration. What if you want to modify those parameters pertaining to the default queue? That's very much possible; you just have to put `default` as the queue name and the configurations will be applied to the default queue.

In the configuration file above, besides modifying the bucket size and maximum concurrent tasks, we modify the retry attempts under the `retry_parameters` directive for the `default` queue. In case of failure, we want the tasks to be retried for a maximum 10 times (which is specified using `task_retry_limit`) and only those tasks that are a maximum of 5 days old. That's specified using `task_age_limit` directive. This directive takes an integer followed by time units same as the ones for rate directive we saw earlier.

So in summary, for the default queue, we are setting the bucket size to 10 with maximum concurrent tasks set to 10 as well. Besides that, we are specifying that tasks up to five days old should be retried or those tasks should be retried that are already tried for a maximum of 10 times. If you specify both the maximum retries and maximum retry age, Google App Engine will exhaust both limits before finally giving up on the task.

Now comes the last queue, which let's pretend is being created to ZIP large files and store them somewhere. This queue is named `zip-files` with a larger bucket size of 50 and which is filled at a rate of 10 tasks per second. We allow a maximum of 50 tasks to be in concurrent execution from this queue. And for the retries, we allow a maximum of 50 retries before giving up plus any tasks that have not succeeded in seven days are finally given up and won't be tried again. Pretty good – we know all the configurations up to this point.

Now comes the newer bit. When you try something and it fails, you'd better not try again right away, rather you should wait for a while, let things cool down, and try again under different circumstances hoping for it to succeed. That's exactly what `min_backoff_seconds` is about. This is the minimum number of seconds that Google App Engine would wait for before retrying a failed task again.

If the task fails again even after retrying, when it should be tried again? After the same amount of time as before? No, that's not how it is done if you get a no for something in real life. You're supposed to wait longer before trying yet again hoping that circumstances have changed. That's exactly what `max_doublings` is for. After each failed attempt, the following is calculated:

```
2 max_doublings - 1 * min_backoff_seconds
```

And this amount is added to an internal counter after every retry. This makes sure that the gap between consecutive retries keeps expanding. If you specify a bigger number here, you can make the gap grow even bigger in successive retries. If you specify 2, it will be twice the `min_backoff_seconds` every time because the expression will yield 2 whereas if you specify 1 as `max_doublings`, the expression will yield 1 hence only the `min_backoff_seconds` will be added to the counter. So let's take the `max_doubling` to be 1 and `min_backoff_seconds` to be 1 then it will generate the series:

1, 2, 3, 4, 5... and like that

Now as we just learned that the time between retries keeps increasing. But up to what extent because if we keep adding the gap, we might end up with millions of seconds amounting to years of gap between failed attempts. That's where the `max_backoff_seconds` comes in. It specifies a top limit between two failed attempts and once that is reached, further failed attempts will happen with that much gap between them always and never more. Here, we've set it to 21600 seconds, which amounts to six hours so two failed task attempts will never be more than six hours apart.

There are few more configuration options that go into `queue.yaml` but they mainly pertain to the pull queues. There are just two directives that we haven't talked about as yet. The first is the mode directive that goes under the queue directive. This defines what kind of queue we are defining and whether it is a pull queue or a push queue. The value defaults to push therefore all the queue definitions above are actually push queues. But if you want to define a pull queue, you simply specify pull as a value like this:

```
queue:
- name: my-pull-queue
  mode: pull
```

We will look into pull queues later in this chapter. We've thoroughly examined all the directives available to us when configuring the queues except one directive: target. This defines what version and what module of your application shall handle the tasks from this queue. We will ignore this for now and will come back to this topic in the last chapter while examining deployments.

Let's move further on, adding tasks.

Adding to a queue

Now that you understand how task queues work in Google App Engine and how to configure one, it is time to add some tasks to the queue. In case of push queues, which are our primary focus for now, adding a task is just simply a matter of specifying a URL path within your application, which would handle processing that task. This URL, of course, would have a request handler that you would have to implement yourself to do whatever you'd like to do with the task.

Before you add the task, you need the queue. So that's how you obtain a queue:

```
from google.appengine.api.taskqueue import Queue

queue = Queue('zip-files')
```

So this would give you the queue named `zip-files`. This must be defined in `queue.yaml` file as discussed earlier. If you do not specify a queue name to the constructor, you will get the default queue:

```
default_queue = Queue()
```

There are few interesting methods of the `Queue` class that we will take a look at later on but the most important one is `add()`, which adds a task to the queue. This method takes an instance of the `Task` class. You create an instance like this:

```
from google.appengine.api.taskqueue import Task, Queue
queue = Queue('zip-files')
task = Task(url='/tasks/zip-files')
queue.add(task)
```

The `Task` constructor accepts many keyword arguments and all of them are optional and have defaults, even the `url` argument. If we didn't specify any URL, Google App Engine would make an HTTP POST call to `/_ah/queue/zip-files` whereas `zip-files` is the queue name and would vary in what queue you add the task to. Of course, you would have to write a handler for this task.

You might not want to use the default URL, therefore you can specify one like this:

```
task = Task(url='/tasks/zip-files')
queue.add(task)
```

The `Task` class has an `add()` method as well that optionally takes a `queue_name` keyword argument that defaults to `default` if not specified. So instead of the above, you can do this too:

```
task = Task(url='/tasks/zip-files')
task.add(queue_name='zip-files')
```

This would add the task to the `zip-files` queue. So either you can instantiate a queue and then a task and call the `add()` on queue giving it the task object or you can bypass creating the queue instance and directly calling the `add()` method on the task giving it the queue name. But there's a third method as well, which is even shorter:

```
from google.appengine.api.taskqueue
taskqueue.add(url='/tasks/zip-files', queue_name='zip-files')
```

This is a shortcut method that would instantiate a `Task` object, would add it to the mentioned queue under `queue_name` argument. This function takes all the keyword arguments that the `Task` class would take therefore we would focus on the `Task` class in our discussion from this point onwards but keep this in mind that both functions the `taskqueue.add()` and `Task` constructor take the same arguments except the `queue_name`, which is actually passed to the `Task` object's `add()` method just as we saw earlier.

Now once this task is added to any queue, it will be dispatched to `/tasks/zip-files` by Google App Engine as a HTTP POST call. As this is HTTP POST request, you might want to send request body as well so that it can be processed by the request handler. For that, you can use `payload` parameter like this:

```
task = Task(url='/tasks/zi-files', payload='Hey, this is the message
for you.')
```

But you might not want to use a HTTP POST request. That's possible too using the `method` keyword argument:

```
task = Task(url='/tasks/zi-files', method='GET')
```

Now instead of HTTP POST, this would be delivered as HTTP GET. But that might not be enough. You might want to send some further parameters too. That's perfectly possible. You specify a list of parameters as a dictionary like this under the `params` keyword argument:

```
task = Task(url='/tasks/zi-files', params={'id': 27, 'delete': True})
```

The same effect can be achieved by this as well:

```
task = Task(url='/tasks/zi-files?id=27&delete=True', method='GET')
```

Although we had to change the HTTP request method from POST to GET because if you specified query string with HTTP POST, the constructor would throw an exception at you as that's now allowed. So, it is better to use the `params` dictionary unless and until you have a very strong reason not to.

Now depending upon the HTTP method, this `params` dictionary will end up differently. Here's how:

- In the case of HTTP POST (which is the default if you don't specify), these would end up in the request body as `application/x-www-form-urlencoded`. So, if you are specifying `params` while the method is set to POST, do not specify payload and vice versa.

- Similarly, if the method is PUT this `params` dictionary will end up with the query string if the payload is specified as well because there would be no room for your specified payload and these `params` to be in the request body at the same time. This `params` dictionary would end up in query string if you've already specified a query string regardless of the payload.

- Lastly, if the method is HTTP GET, these `params` would end up as a query string but you can't do both: specifying a query string of your own and specifying `params` dictionary as well. You will have use only one way out of the two.

 Besides everything, with a GET request, you certainly have a limit on URL length which in turn would limit how many query parameters with how much data can be sent. If you're curious, the HTTP standard itself imposes no limit on URL length but in practice, various pieces of software have different limits such as for Internet Explorer, it is roughly 2048 characters. For more interesting discussion and details on the subject, you can go through this `http://stackoverflow.com/questions/417142/what-is-the-maximum-length-of-a-url-in-different-browsers`.

Quite an elaborate discussion on how to specify request parameters and request body but that was really needed because without specifying some information with the task that you are adding the queue, nothing much can be accomplished.

Lastly, what if you want to specify some request headers as well? That's pretty simple; you use the `headers` keyword argument to specify a dictionary of headers like this:

```
task = Task(url='/tasks/zi-files', headers={'id': 27, 'delete': True})
```

Now these key value pairs will end up as HTTP request headers and can be processed as such at the receiving end. To summarize what kind of information you can specify, here's a list of all the things in order:

- `url`: This specifies a URL. If not specified, it defaults to `/_ah/queue/queue-name`. The URL might contain a query string as well in case of HTTP `GET`, `PUT` methods.

- `method`: This can specify the HTTP method as well which can be `GET`, `PUT`, `POST`, `DELETE` and `Defaults to` `POST` method.

- `payload`: In case the HTTP method is `PUT` and `POST`, you can specify a payload to be sent as the request body.

- `headers`: You can specify request headers to be sent.

- `params`: You can specify `request` parameters, which would end up as either a query string or as a HTTP request body depending upon various conditions that have been discussed in detail above.

We have covered most of the arguments that you can pass to the `Task` constructor. But there are few more interesting ones are lefts so let's examine them in turn:

- `name`: You can optionally give a name to a task up to maximum of 500 characters containing letters, numbers, hyphens and underscores. The task name must be unique within a queue and if a task with the same name already exists, the call to add the task to the queue will fail. As we'll see later, you can delete tasks as well and if you do so, the name of the task will be unavailable for seven days even though it has been deleted. If you don't specify a name as we have been doing so far, Google App Engine would automatically generate one for us.

- `countdown`: Number of seconds to wait before executing this task. This is handy if you don't want to execute the task immediately but want to wait for a certain period of time such as 10 minutes. In that case, specify the countdown as 600 seconds and it won't be executed before 10 minutes.

- eta: Instead of the number of seconds to wait, this is a proper Python datetime object indicating the time before which this task should not be executed. This eta and countdown are mutually exclusive; you can only provide either eta or countdown. ETA usually means a countdown to something as you might have noticed while downloading some large file or performing some other such long time taking operation on your machine. But here, the Google App Engine team has picked somewhat wrong nomenclature as this isn't a countdown but a time in the future before which the task should not be executed.

- retry_options: We have discussed retry options while examining the queue definitions. Those settings apply to the whole queue but you might want to have more granular control on a Task level. So you can specify that here too. It is just an instance of the class TaskRetryOptions from google.appengine.api.taskqueue module and has the same properties (min_backoff_seconds, max_backoff_seconds, max_doublings, task_retry_limit, task_age_limit) as in queue.yaml except specifying them here would be applicable to just that task.

- target: We briefly mentioned the target directive when we talked about queue.yaml in the previous section. That is applicable to the whole queue but you can specify the target on per task basis as well and that's the way to do it – specify it under the target keyword argument. What actually is the target? We'll examine it in detail later in this book.

Please note that all these arguments are applicable to the taskqueue.add() method as well as to the constructor of the Task class. Now that we know how to define queues and add tasks, it is time to talk about how to process them.

Processing tasks

The tasks from the queues are delivered to you as HTTP requests so you need to have a handler for them and return an HTTP status code from 200 to 290 to indicate a success; everything else is considered a failure. Recall from *Chapter 2, Handling Web Requests* that you have to respond to each HTTP request within 60 seconds. But when the HTTP request is from a task queue, this time limit is up to 10 minutes. You can go beyond that too if you want to but that would require use of modules and mentioning an appropriate module in the target parameter. We will examine modules in last chapter when talking about deployment and scaling options.

Now that's what happens to various things that you submitted while creating
the task:

- `params`: In this the dictionary these will end up as either GET or POST request
  parameters. How you access them varies by the web framework you are
  using but we'll show how to access them using `webapp2`, the framework
  shipped with Google App Engine.

- `headers`: These would end up as request headers if supplied.

- `payload`: This would end up as the request body if supplied.

So here's how you will write such a handler:

```
import webapp2

class TaskWorker(webapp2.RequestHandler):

    def post(self):
        # All this would be printed to the
        # development server console.
        print "params: ", self.request.params
        print "headers: ", self.request.headers
        # This is payload. Not every task has them.
        print "body: "self.request.body

        # Not required at all to generate a response.
        self.response.write('All well')


app = webapp2.WSGIApplication([
    ('/tasks', TaskWorker),
], debug=True)
```

Add this handler in `main.py` of a new app. Open up the admin console at
`http://localhost:8000/console` and enter the following code:

```
from google.appengine.api import taskqueue

headers = {'a-header': 'with value'}
params = {'filename': 'horizon.png', 'type': 'png', 'size': 34345}
taskqueue.add(url='/tasks', headers=headers, params=params)
```

Execute it in the interactive console. Now in the terminal window that is running
the development server, you will see the output, the headers and all the params
will be printed.

Almost all the web frameworks automatically set the HTTP status code to 200 and therefore this task would be considered successfully executed. But what if you want to indicate that the task failed and it should be tried again? You simply return an HTTP status code outside the 200 to 299 range. In the context of web frameworks, raising an unhandled exception would do the trick because almost all web frameworks return an an HTTP status 500 if you raise an exception:

```
raise Exception('Task failed')
```

Or you can simply do that:

```
self.response.status = 500
```

So that's it about failure. We mentioned that the time limit for the default type of machine instances (there are many configurations around that as we will see later in this book) is for 10 minutes. What happens when the time expires? Well before that, Google App Engine would throw DeadlineExceededError exception from google.appengine.runtime module. You can catch that like this:

```
from google.appengine.runtime import DeadlineExceededError

# Rest of the request handler code

try:
    # Your work here
except DeadlineExceededError:
    # Save the state of work
    # Log about it
    # If need to retry this, set status code to >= 300
```

While catching the exception, you can save the state of your work and log any messages for later inspecting what went wrong or where the handler was while processing the task. Furthermore, you may want to retry the task again for which you would have to either raise yet another exception or even better set the HTTP status code on the response object beyond the 200–299 range.

An important note here is that Google App Engine tries its level best to make sure that every task is executed only once but it might happen that a task is dispatched to your task handlers more than once. In that case, you should write your code in such a way that it is idempotent. By idempotent we mean that repeated execution of the same handler does not have any side effects.

The other related important note while processing tasks is that although we have been calling them queue and by queue you would be rightfully assuming **First In, First Out (FIFO)** behavior. But that's not the case; you should never assume or rely on the fact that the tasks would be handed over to your application in order once you have added them to the queue. Although Google App Engine makes the best possible attempt to deliver the tasks in the order they are added to the queue but there are no guarantees of that whatsoever hence your code shouldn't assume such an ordering.

As you can see that the task processing just consists of a simple request handler. And just because of that, it would be accessible to the outside world as well. So anyone can just point the browser to your URLs and might trigger the task computation, which might be expensive or might have other side effects. How should you guard against that?

First thing is that all the requests that are initiated by Google App Engine will always be from IP address `0.1.0.2` so you can always check for that and reject processing otherwise:

```
if self.request.remotemote_addr != '0.1.0.2':
    # Set to status code to 403 Forbidden.
    self.request.status = 403
    return # Halt further processing
```

Besides that, Google App Engine also adds custom headers to the request when it is dispatched to your task handler. You might have already noticed them in the console output on the terminal if you have tried the previous code example. Here are the headers that a request from Google App Engine's task queue would have:

- Name of the queue from which task is coming `X-AppEngine-QueueName`
- Name of the task `X-AppEngine-TaskName`
- Number of times this task has been retried `X-AppEngine-TaskRetryCount`
- Number of times the task has failed `X-AppEngine-TaskExecutionCount`
- The ETA time if any set while adding the task would be in `X-AppEngine-TaskETA`

If the request contains any of the above headers, you can be sure that it is coming from Google App Engine and not anywhere else. If any external request contains these headers, they are stripped by Google App Engine before the request reaches your code except in case you have logged in as an administrator (we'll examine that later in the book) or you are running the local development server. In those two cases, this allows you manually simulate an incoming request to debug your tasks.

Putting it all together

That's enough theory on queue definitions and processing the tasks. Now let's put it all together. We are going to write a simple web application that accepts a URL and downloads the page, compresses it and stores it in the datastore. It's pretty simple.

But the catch is that instead of doing it all at once in the request handler, we divide this into two tasks:

- Downloading the page
- Compressing and storing the page

The page download task has its own queue named downloads and the compression has its own queue called zip-files. Here's the queue.yaml:

```
queue:
- name: downloads
  rate: 10/s
  retry_parameters:
    task_retry_limit: 7
# This last one for processing zip files.
- name: zip-files
  rate: 10/s
```

For the downloads queue, if a URL is failing because the server is down or the page is inaccessible, the task would fail and we do not want to keep trying infinitely therefore we have set task_retry_limit to seven so we shall try a maximum of just seven times and never more.

The config.py file contains various constants and variables that we will refer to later on:

```
import os
import jinja2

APP_ENGINE_QUEUE_IP = '0.1.0.2'
DOWNLOAD_QUEUE_URL = '/tasks/download'
DOWNLOAD_QUEUE = 'downloads'

ZIP_QUEUE_URL = '/tasks/compress'
ZIP_QUEUE = 'zip-files'


CURRENT_DIRECTORY = os.path.dirname(__file__)
TEMPLATES_DIRECTORY = os.path.join(CURRENT_DIRECTORY, 'templates')
    JINJA_ENV = jinja2.Environment(loader=jinja2.FileSystemLoader
        (TEMPLATES_DIRECTORY))
```

So we have defined the URL and name of each of the queue: DOWNLOAD_QUEUE_URL, DOWNLOAD_QUEUE for downloads queue and ZIP_QUEUE_URL, ZIP_QUEUE for the zip-files queue.

We have already showed how to use jinja2 templates on Google App Engine in *Chapter 2, Handling Web Requests*. Because we are using jinja2 templates here as you can see, the import would fail so that's why we will have to add it into our app.yaml. Here's the complete file:

```
application: push-downloader
version: 1
runtime: python27
api_version: 1
threadsafe: true

handlers:
- url: /.*
  script: main.app

libraries:
- name: jinja2
  version: "2.6"
```

This will let us use jinja2 templating system without shipping it with our application. More about the list of available libraries can be seen here: https://cloud.google.com/appengine/docs/python/tools/libraries27. Our config.py initializes the jinja2 environment as well as previously discussed.

All the HTML pages are stored in the datastore for which the models.py file contains this:

```
from google.appengine.ext import ndb

class HTMLPage(ndb.Model):
    """
    Stores a compressed HTML page.
    """
    url = ndb.StringProperty(indexed=False)
    content = ndb.BlobProperty(indexed=False)
    original_size = ndb.IntegerProperty(indexed=False)
    compressed_size = ndb.IntegerProperty(indexed=False)

    @property
    def compression_ratio(self):
        return float(self.original_size) / float(self.compressed_size)
```

We store the page content, page `url`, original size, and compressed size. Contents are always stored after compression. Note that we are using `BlobProperty` because our data is binary after compression and not text. Because we do not want to execute any datastore queries at all, we have set the `indexed=False` for all the properties. That way, not only will we save space but writing operations will be fast as well because no indexes will have to be updated on each write operation. We have a property `compression_ratio` that is computed on the fly.

Next, we have some utility functions in `utils.py` that will be used later. Let's take a look:

```python
import logging
import bz2
import hashlib

from google.appengine.api import taskqueue, urlfetch

import config
from models import HTMLPage

def get_page(sha1):
    """
    Gets the page
    """
    page = HTMLPage.get_by_id(sha1)

    if not page:
        return "404 - Page not found!"

    return bz2.decompress(page.content)


def download_page(url):
    """
    Downloads the page from given URL
    """
    result = urlfetch.fetch(url)

    # If failed, return.
    if result.status_code != 200:
        logging.error("Failed to download page %s" % url)
        raise Exception("Failed to download page.")
```

```
    params = {'content': result.content, 'url': url}

    kwargs = {
    'queue_name': config.ZIP_QUEUE,
    'url': config.ZIP_QUEUE_URL,
    'params': params
    }

    taskqueue.add(**kwargs)

    return result.content

def compress_and_save(url, content):
    """
    Compresses and saves the page to datastore.
    """

    content = content.encode('utf-8')
    sha1 = hashlib.sha1(content).hexdigest()

    # Logic to check if already exists.
    if HTMLPage.get_by_id(sha1):
        logging.info("Page already exists.")
        return

    # Compress
    compressed = bz2.compress(content)
    size = len(content)
    compressed_size = len(compressed)

    # Save.
    page = HTMLPage(id=sha1)
    page.url = url
    page.content = compressed
    page.original_size = size
    page.compressed_size = compressed_size
    page.put()
```

After the imports, this basically defines three functions, which will be used later by various request handlers:

- `download_url()`: This will download the page given the URL. Once downloaded, a new task in the `zip-files` queue will be added along with the page contents as `params` so that it can be later compressed and saved.

- `compress_and_save()`: This takes a URL and content. First, it calculates its SHA1 hash and will look into the datastore if a page with identical content already exists. If so, the compression and writing to the datastore would be skipped altogether. Otherwise, we compress the data using `bz2` compression, and write to the datastore with all properties. Note that we do not let the datastore generate ID for the `HTMLPage` entities; rather, we use SHA1 as the ID. This allows us to check later if similar page exists.

- `get_page()`: This will fetch an `HTMLPage` entity from the datastore, decompress its contents and will return given its SHA1 hash. This will be later used by the request handler to render page contents as we will see.

Now comes the actual request handling stuff, which includes both types of handlers: request handlers that process requests from the users and serve them a user interface and handlers that process tasks from the request queue.

So here's our `main.py`:

```python
import logging
import webapp2

from google.appengine.api import taskqueue
from google.appengine.runtime import DeadlineExceededError

import config
import utils
from models import HTMLPage


class AppEngineTaskHandler(webapp2.RequestHandler):
    """
    The base class for task handlers. Ensures that
    unauthorized access for task handlers is forbidden.
    """
    def dispatch(self):
        """
        Checks for the requester's IP. If not originated
        from Google App Engine's behalf, simply reject
        further processing.
```

```
    """
    # Ensure that request really is coming from Google App
        Engine
    if self.request.remote_addr != config.APP_ENGINE_QUEUE_IP:
        self.response.status = 403
        logging.warn("Someone tried to access task handlers
            from %s" %
            self.request.remote_addr)
        self.response.write("Access denied. Your IP is
            recorded!")
        return
    try:
        return super(AppEngineTaskHandler, self).dispatch()
    except DeadlineExceededError:
        # We failed, log it to investigate later.
        message = "Task {task} from queue {queue} timed out." \
            + \
                "It was tried {tries}, executed {times}
        before."
        task = self.request.headers['X-AppEngine-TaskName']
        queue = self.request.headers['X-AppEngine-QueueName']
        tries = self.request.headers['X-AppEngine-
            TaskRetryCount']
        times = self.request.headers['X-AppEngine-
            TaskExecutionCount']
        logging.warn(message.format(task=task, queue=queue,
            tries=tries, times=times))
        # So that it gets retried again.
        self.response.status = 500


class DownloadHandler(AppEngineTaskHandler):
    """
    Downloads the file.
    """
    def post(self):
        url = self.request.params.get('url')

        # Silently ignore.
        if not url:
            return
        utils.download_page(url)


class ZipHandler(AppEngineTaskHandler):
    """
    Compresses the file.
```

```
    """
    def post(self):
        url = self.request.params.get('url')
        content = self.request.params.get('content')
        utils.compress_and_save(url, content)


class MainPage(webapp2.RequestHandler):
    """
    The main page.
    """
    def get(self):

        sha1 = self.request.params.get('id')

        if sha1:
            self.response.write(utils.get_page(sha1))
            return

        # List all the pages.
        # Or a single page.
        main_template = config.JINJA_ENV.get_template
            ("index.html")
        pages = HTMLPage.query()


        self.response.write(main_template.render({'pages':
            pages}))

    def post(self):
        """
        Creates a download task.
        """

        url = self.request.params.get('url')

        kwargs = {
        'url': config.DOWNLOAD_QUEUE_URL,
        'queue_name': config.DOWNLOAD_QUEUE,
        'params': {'url': url},
        }

        taskqueue.add(**kwargs)
        message = 'Page <a href="{url}">{url}</a> would be
            downloaded. <a href="/">Go back</a>'
```

```
            self.response.write(message.format(url=url))

app = webapp2.WSGIApplication([
    (config.DOWNLOAD_QUEUE_URL, DownloadHandler),
    (config.ZIP_QUEUE_URL, ZipHandler),
    ('/?', MainPage)
], debug=True)
```

Let's look at the user facing handler. In the `get()` method, if an `id` parameter
is given, we simply call the `get_page()` method and render its contents. The
`get_page()` method has already been discussed. But if the ID parameter is missing
in the request, we fetch `HTMLPage` entities and render the `templates/index.html`
and pass it the entities that are rendered in a table.

```
            main_template =
                config.JINJA_ENV.get_template("index.html")
            pages = HTMLPage.query()
            self.response.write(main_template.render({'pages':
                pages}))
```

The template contains an HTML form as well so that users may submit a URL.
Here's the `index.html`:

```
<!doctype html>
<html>
<head>
    <title>Download a page</title>
</head>
<body>
    <h1>Download and store any HTML Page</h1>
    <form method="post">
        <input type="text" name="url" placeholder="Enter a page URL">
        <input type="submit" value="Download">
    </form>

    <h2>List of pages:</h2>
    <table>
        <tr>
            <th>
                URL
            </th>
            <th>
                Compression ratio
            </th>
        </tr>
        {% for page in pages %}
```

```
            <tr>
                <td><a href="/?id={{page.key.id()}}" target="_
blank">{{page.url}}</a></td>
                <td>{{page.compression_ratio|round(precision=2)}}
times</td>
            </tr>
        {% endfor %}
    </table>
</body>
</html>
```

Now comes to the two handlers that execute the tasks. First is the `DownloadHandler`, its `post()` method simply reads the `url` from request parameters and executes the `download_page()` method from `utils`. This `download_page()` would add a compression task in `zip-files` queue.

The other handler is `ZipHandler` that would just read the contents of the downloaded file and would call the `compress_and_save()` method which we already have seen. But there's one thing common to both the methods: instead of being inherited from `webapp2.RequestHandler`, we have our own custom class `AppEngineTaskHandler` that is parent to both and implements `dispatch()` method.

Why is that so? We'll examine that but before that, let's talk about something which is specific to the web framework we use. This `weapp2` calls the method based on HTTP method so for HTTP GET, `get()` would be executed and for HTTP POST, `post()` would be executed. But before these methods are executed, the base class `webapp2.RequestHandler` executes its own `dispatch()` method, which is the first method to be called before any HTTP specific method. This means that if there's some code that should be executed before actual request handler code runs, we can override `dispatch()` and put our magic/validation there.

Because both `ZipHandler` and `DownloadHandler` require some validation before the code executes, we have placed the common code in a base class instead of repeating it twice. What's that common thing that we want in both handlers?

Recall that the request handlers for requests are just URLs that are accessible to the public and we would not want anyone to hit them. How do we validate that? We check that the IP address like this in `dispatch()`:

```
if self.request.remote_addr != config.APP_ENGINE_QUEUE_IP:
        self.response.status = 403
        logging.warn("Someone tried to access task handlers
            from %s" %
            self.request.remote_addr)
        self.response.write("Access denied. Your IP is
            recorded!")
        return
```

So if the IP is not `0.1.0.2`, we simply set the response code to `403 HTTP Forbidden`, log the IP address and warn the user. Because `dispatch()` would run before `get()` or `put()`, this would ensure our task specific code never runs and because this class is parent to both task handler classes, it would be executed for both.

> This was just to illustrate the internals of task queues. But the better and simpler way to protect your task handing URLs to list them separately in `app.yaml` and put the `login` directive like this:
>
> ```
> handlers:
> - url: /tasks/download
>   login: admin
>   script: main.app
> ```
>
> This way, you do not need to do any IP or request headers validation in your code as that will be already done by Google App Engine.

Now that we have validated the IP, we go ahead and let water takes it course by calling the `dispatch()` from the base class (`webapp2.RequestHandler`), which in turn would execute the `post()` methods containing the actual task processing code:

```
return super(AppEngineTaskHandler, self).dispatch()
```

But this execution of the `post()` method that would happen by calling the `dispatch()` above might take some time. Recall the that maximum amount of time executing a task is to be 10 minutes and just before the time slot expires, Google Engine throws a `DeadlineExceededError` exception at you. We can take advantage of the fact and catch this exception, record the task name, and the queue name from the request headers like this:

```
try:
    return super(AppEngineTaskHandler, self).dispatch()
except DeadlineExceededError:
    # We failed, log it to investigate later.
    message = "Task {task} from queue {queue} timed out." \
        + \
            "It was tried {tries}, executed {times}
        before."
    task = self.request.headers['X-AppEngine-TaskName']
    queue = self.request.headers['X-AppEngine-QueueName']
    tries = self.request.headers['X-AppEngine-
        TaskRetryCount']
    times = self.request.headers['X-AppEngine-
        TaskExecutionCount']
```

```
logging.warn(message.format(task=task, queue=queue,
    tries=tries, times=times))
# So that it gets retried again.
self.response.status = 500
```

We already have discussed the custom HTTP headers that accompany the request when it is initiated by Google App Engine from a task queue. Just that we are reading them here and so that we may investigate things later.

To summarize, `config.py` contains the queue names and URLs, `queue.yaml` we know well. The `app.yaml` contains additional configuration for libraries. Our utility functions are in `utils.py` and `models.py` contains model. Finally, `main.py` has all the request handlers relying on the utility functions.

So that completes our discussion of push queues except one important improvement that shall make the whole thing much easier.

Using a deferred library

If you look at the previous example, there's lot of plumbing code that has to be around the utility functions that are to be included. For example, executing the `download_page()` means:

- We have to have request handlers for the task.
- We have to validate if the request is coming from Google App Engine.
- The request parameters are to be read from the request in the handler.
- The new task is to be created by supplying all the required parameters.

This might not seem very complicated but will start to turn into a mess when you have many small tasks that are to be executed because they will require handlers for each and all the plumbing code.

Fortunately, Google App Engine has a library that can turn all this into a very simple call like this:

```
from google.appengine.ext import deferred

deferred.defer(download_page, url)
```

And that's it. This will be taken care of, and would be added into default queue. If you want to change the queue, you supply `_queue` parameter like this:

```
deferred.defer(utils.download_page, url,
    _queue=config.DOWNLOAD_QUEUE)
```

So this shall put the task into `downloads` queue instead of default one. In fact, all the keyword arguments that the `Task` constructor or `taskqueue.add()` method takes can be supplied here by prefixing an _ to them like this:

```
deferred.defer(utils.download_page, url,
    _queue=config.DOWNLOAD_QUEUE), _method='GET')
```

But where are the handlers that actually process these tasks? They are built right into Google App Engine but you have to enable them in your `app.yaml`:

```
builtins:
- deferred: on
```

You can read more about the built-in request handlers that perform various tasks here in the reference documentation: `https://cloud.google.com/appengine/docs/python/config/appconfig#Python_app_yaml_Builtin_handlers`

So that just enables them – where are the actual handlers? You have to specify that too in your `app.yaml` like this:

```
handlers:
- url: /.*
  script: main.app
- url: /_ah/queue/deferred
  script: google.appengine.ext.deferred.deferred.application
```

To put this all in practice, we will change our earlier example to use a deferred approach. The rest of the code stays the same; we only list the files that change. First, is the `app.yaml` file:

```
application: deferred-downloader
version: 1
runtime: python27
api_version: 1
threadsafe: true

builtins:
- deferred: on

handlers:
- url: /.*
  script: main.app
- url: /_ah/queue/deferred
  script: google.appengine.ext.deferred.deferred.application
  login: admin

libraries:
- name: jinja2
  version: "2.6"
```

This is just as before, except that built-ins are enabled and we have added a new built-in request handler as highlighted. The `login: admin` directive would ensure that the built-in handler is only accessible internally. More can be read about it in the `app.yaml` documentation here: `https://cloud.google.com/appengine/docs/python/config/appconfig#Python_app_yaml_Requiring_login_or_administrator_status`

Next, in our `utils.py` everything else stays the same except the `download_page()` method:

```
def download_page(url):
    """
    Downloads the page from given URL
    """
    result = urlfetch.fetch(url)

    # If failed, return.
    if result.status_code != 200:
        logging.error("Failed to download page %s" % url)
        raise Exception("Failed to download page.")

    deferred.defer(compress_and_save, url, result.content, _
queue=config.ZIP_QUEUE)
    return result.content
```

So that the code that was adding tasks to the queue for compressing the file instead calls the `deferred.defer`. Much simpler.

Finally, our request handlers are all gone because we do not need to implement them. So, two request handlers for the tasks and their base class are all gone. The `main.py` file turns up much simpler and is like this:

```
class MainPage(webapp2.RequestHandler):
    """
    The main page.
    """
    def get(self):
        pass # Same as before, skipped for readability.

    def post(self):
        """
        Creates a download task.
        """
```

```
        url = self.request.params.get('url')

        deferred.defer(utils.download_page, url,
            _queue=config.DOWNLOAD_QUEUE)

        message = 'Page <a href="{url}">{url}</a> would be
            downloaded. <a href="/">Go back</a>'
        self.response.write(message.format(url=url))


app = webapp2.WSGIApplication([
    ('/?', MainPage)
], debug=True)
```

And as you can see, things are much simpler except it is the user facing request handler that uses the deferred library. The rest is taken care of.

With this, we come to an end of our discussion on push queues. To summarize, you can have one more task queue with configurable task execution and task retry parameters. Each task is just a URL with optionally having parameters, headers, or payload. To handle the tasks you have to write request handlers as they are dispatched to your code as HTTP calls.

Note that the push queues cannot be used outside of Google App Engine because the URLs for each task must be within your app. But what if that's not what you want and you want to do something outside in some other cloud machine such as Rackspace or Amazon or even on your local machine? Pull queues are the answer, which we are going to examine next.

Now you might be wondering when to use the deferred library and when to use the task queue web hooks as we demonstrated earlier. You should use the deferred library if you have lots of different tasks for which writing lots of request handles would be cumbersome or that the arguments for the tasks are complex that they need some sort of serialization. In such cases, you should be using a deferred library as otherwise you will not only be having lots of request handlers but serialization/ deserialization logic as well. The deferred library can also be useful when you have existing code in forms of functions and you want to reuse it without resorting to request handlers.

On the other hand, you would use the task queue API when you want more control over task executions and you prefer web hooks over the RPC model or where the overhead of the deferred library is significant enough not to use it.

Pull queues

Besides push queues you have pull queues as well. The main differences between push and pull queues are summarized below:

- In push queues, tasks are thrown to your application, in pull queues, you would have to fetch tasks yourself.

- Because tasks are pushed to your application, Google App Engine takes care of scaling as well. New machine instances will be started when there's more load than a single instance can handle. And all that happens automatically. In case of pull queues, you are responsible for the scaling part yourself.

- When a task gets successfully executed in a push queue, it is automatically deleted by Google App Engine with no effort at your end. In case of pull queues, you have to do that yourself as well.

- In push queues, you are limited to the Google App Engine environment as your task handling code must be mapped to URLs within your application. In contrast, in the case of pull queues, because the tasks are pulled they can be pulled from anywhere such as a machine in Rackspace or Amazon cloud or even your humble or mighty laptop.

Defining pull queues is simple too. There are only two things that you need to do:

- In `queue.yaml`, specify `mode` as `pull`, which if not specified, defaults to `push`.
- When you're adding tasks specify the method parameter with value `PULL`.

And you are good to go. So a simple pull queue definition will look like this:

```
queue:
- name: zip-files
  mode: pull
  rate: 10/s
```

Now, because tasks won't be supplied to you, how do you get them? It's pretty simple. You instantiate a `Queue` object, and call the `least_tasks()` method like this:

```
q = Queue('zip-files')
tasks = q.lease_tasks(3600, 10)
# Now process them.
# When done, deleting them is also your responsibility
q.delete_tasks(tasks)
```

The process is pretty simple. You first get the tasks; you do your work as tasks and finally delete them. When you lease a task, you also specify something called a lease time in seconds. The first argument to `lease_tasks()` is just that. You are supposed to finish and delete the task within this time frame. If you fail to do so, the task is considered to have failed and would be leased again to some other caller. The second argument is the number of tasks to be retrieved. It is better if you get them in batches; here we are getting 10 tasks with care returned as a list of `Task` objects.

It is appropriate to note that the `Queue` class has a `purge()` method as well, which would delete all the tasks. No matter what the size of the queue, the purging operation will take about 20 seconds during which time the tasks in execution would continue to execute and existing tasks in queue would be dispatched as well until the Google App Engine runtime recognizes that the queue has been purged.

Please note that the above code will only work in the Google App Engine environment because the `Queue` class is provided by the Google App Engine runtime libraries. If your code is running outside the Google App Engine, you will have to use the REST API for the queues, which is documented here:

```
https://cloud.google.com/appengine/docs/python/taskqueue/rest/
```

But because consuming raw REST API might be cumbersome for you, there are many client libraries as well for Java, C#, PHP, and Python. For Python, you can download from here: `https://developers.google.com/api-client-library/python/`

We talked about queue configurations in great detail in this chapter. But when it comes to pull queues, the following options aren't applicable to pull queues:

- `bucket_size`: This is because there are no buckets for the pull queues as tasks are not pushed to your application.
- `max_concurrent_requests`: This is because you pull the tasks so that's meaningless.
- `rate`: This is meaningless because you're in charge of pulling the tasks at whatever rate.
- `retry_parameters`: Most of its sub directives (`task_age_limit`, `min_backoff_seconds`, `max_backoff_seconds`, `max_doublings`) are not applicable except `task_retry_limit`, which if specified means the maximum number of times you can lease this task over and over in case you fail to delete it within the lease time frame.
- `target`: we will talk about this in detail later in this book but target is not applicable because it is your choice what machine you want to pull and process the tasks.

To summarize, pull queues aren't very different but you are responsible for fetching and processing tasks and deleting them along with any scalability issues. The main advantage is that you can process your tasks outside Google App Engine as well using the REST API or the client libraries.

This concludes our discussion on pull queues and queues in general on Google App Engine.

Summary

We stared our discussion from the need to perform the tasks in the background and from there, we introduced the queue paradigm of processing tasks that store messages that are processed by worker nodes. Then we focused our attention on the queue model as implemented by Google App Engine. Next, we took a very detailed look into how to configure queues using `queue.yaml` file. We learned that we can have multiple queues with different task processing rates and retry parameters. Next, we focused on how to add tasks to the queue and how to add information using headers, parameters, and payload. Finally, we did put all this into practice by a URL downloader application that downloads the HTML pages and compresses them.

Once comfortable with push queues, we learned about a helpful library deferred that can remove lots of boilerplate code. So we wrote our earlier application using the aforementioned library and found out that newer version of our code became much simpler.

Finally, we turned our attention towards pull queues, how to get tasks, process them and delete them once we are done. We also learned that when a task is fetched from a pull queue, it is leased for a specific time frame within which it has to be deleted. Failing to delete the task within the specified time frame would be considered as a failure.

With that, we concluded our discussion on task queues. Next, we are going to make contact with the outside world. So stay tuned!

8
Reaching out, Sending E-mails

All the things that we have done so far were internal. Even when we contacted the outside world in the previous chapter, we just fetched pages into our app and compressed and saved them. But often there's information that needs to go out as well, not just on the interface but also through other mediums. This chapter is all about sending e-mails.

In this chapter, we'll learn the following:

- The history of e-mail and SMTP
- Sending e-mails
- Receiving e-mails
- Handling bounce notifications

Before we start exploring the aforementioned topics, let's have a glimpse at how e-mail works and what it is all about.

About e-mails

E-mails have been with us for a very long time now. E-mail might seem complex under the hood, but it is not; the working principle is pretty simple. The first thing that we need to know about is the SMTP server. So, why the SMTP server and not the Godzilla server? We call it the SMTP server because it speaks **Simple Mail Transfer Protocol (SMTP)**.

SMTP is just a plain text protocol like the HTTP protocol that you may be familiar with. Your browser sends HTTP requests (which is nothing but plain text) over TCP, and the HTTP servers respond as per the request. The same is the case with the SMTP servers.

The SMTP servers historically listened on port 25, which is deprecated and now port 587 is standard these days. When you want to send an e-mail, you open your e-mail client (a desktop application such as Outlook, Thunderbird, or any Android or iOS mobile application) and type in your message that you want to send across.

This e-mail is formatted as SMTP text commands, and a connection to the SMTP server (such as `smtp.gmail.com`) is opened, which is is something that your e-mail client knows about from its configurations. The e-mail client comes preconfigured if you are using a mobile app or a web client such as Gmail or the web mail of Yahoo!. Otherwise, you will have to configure it when you set up your e-mail client.

Now that your mail is transferred from your mail client to the SMTP server, it is stored on the disk in your outbox. Either of two possible scenarios will happen now. If the recipient of the mail has an e-mail account on the same domain, the mail is just copied to the recipient's inbox. For instance, a mail sent from `peter@gmail.com` to `john@gmail.com` is a case where the SMTP server will discover that it is the same server and the e-mail just has to be copied.

However, consider a situation where a mail is sent from `peter@gmail.com` to `alice@yahoo.com`. This situation is different because, as you can judge from the domain names in the e-mail address, the users reside on different e-mail servers operated by different companies. In such a situation, the SMTP server at `smtp.gmail.com` will split the receiver's e-mail address at the `@` character and examine the domain part, which is `yahoo.com`. Then, it will contact the DNS service to find a mail server called `yahoo.com`. Note that there's a website at `http://www.yahoo.com` as well. How can `yahoo.com` be an IP address for a website and an IP address for an SMTP server at the same time? The answer to this question is that there's a separate record type for mail servers of the MX type. You can read more about DNS record types by visiting `https://en.wikipedia.org/wiki/List_of_DNS_record_types`.

The DNS server returns the IP address of the machine that runs the SMTP server of `yahoo.com`. Now, the SMTP server at Gmail (`smtp.gmail.com`) will connect to this server, this time as an e-mail client, and hand over your message. Now, the SMTP server at `yahoo.com` will copy this message to the inbox of the recipient of the mail. This is a very simple way of landing in an inbox, and this used to be the case before the spamming mafia came into existence.

Nowadays, before the message lands in the inbox, there are tons of filters that are applied on it to check whether this really is a message that is intended for you and not spam. In fact, a major part of the e-mail service provider's infrastructure these days is dedicated to spam detection and techniques such as machine learning, or sophisticated techniques such as neural networks are used for spam detection.

Once in the receiving user's account, `alice@yahoo.com` in this case, the message would remain there till the user connects to the SMTP server (`smtp.yahoo.com`) by using their client, which will pull the message to their local machine, be it a mobile- or web-based client. To pull messages from the SMTP servers, there are two different protocols — **Post Office Protocol (POP)** and **Internet Mail Access Protocol (IMAP)**. Either of the two protocols can be used to fetch e-mails to the local machine.

 You can read more about the SMTP server and client interaction at `https://en.wikipedia.org/wiki/Simple_Mail_Transfer_Protocol#SMTP_transport_example`.

In today's connected world with push notifications and mobile devices, it might seem that e-mail is a push technology that gets pushed to you, whereas in reality this is not the case. All mobile apps have a task running in the background to fetch your e-mail at fixed intervals. There are some optimizations to this process but they are specific not to the SMTP protocol, but rather to the mobile platform itself, such as sending a push notification that is not visible to the user and which indicates that the mobile device should now fetch the e-mail. This will make it look like e-mail and SMTP work as a push technology.

Now that we have some knowledge about how e-mail works under the hood, let's take a look at how e-mails are sent.

Sending e-mails

Sending e-mails in Google App Engine is pretty simple. We have two options if we want to send e-mails:

- Use the `send_mail()` function from `google.appengine.api.mail`
- Use `EmailMessage` from the same module

While sending an e-mail you need some information, such as the recipient of the e-mail, the subject of the e-mail, the contents of the message, and so on. All of this can be supplied via keyword arguments.

The following keyword arguments can be supplied while calling the `send_mail()` function and are equally applicable for the `EmailMessage` class's constructor:

- `sender`: This is the `From` field. There are some restrictions on it. We'll take a look at this later.

- `to`: This is the address of the recipient of the e-mail. This can be a Python list of e-mail addresses as well.

- `cc`: This is the address of the recipient who gets a copy of the e-mail. It can be a string or a list of strings for multiple e-mail addresses. It is an abbreviation for **carbon copy**.

- `bcc`: This is the address of those who should receive a copy, but each receiver won't get to know who else this e-mail was sent to. This is an abbreviation for **blind carbon copy**.

- `reply_to`: This is used when a user clicks to reply in their (web or desktop) e-mail client: where should the e-mail be sent to? That is the e-mail address of the recipient. It defaults to the sender if not specified.

- `subject`: This is again well-known. This is what should go in the subject line.

- `body`: This contains the message that you want to send.

- `html`: This helps you send an HTML version of the preceding message so that clients that are able to render rich content will present this version instead.

- `attachments`: This is a list of tuples. Each tuple contains the name of the file as the first element, and the data as the second one. There's a restriction on the kind of content that you can send; we'll talk about this in a later section.

- `headers`: This comprises additional e-mail headers that you would like to send. We'll talk about this later.

Now, before we examine the functions and methods that accept these parameters, let's discuss who can send an e-mail. The following are few restrictions regarding the e-mail address that you specify as the `sender` in your e-mail messages:

- This e-mail address should be any of the administrators of the Google App Engine application. As you know by now, to deploy a Google App Engine app, you need a Google account and hence, a Gmail address. So, that address can be the one sending out the e-mails. If you do not want to use that e-mail address, your options include creating another Gmail address and adding it as your application's' administrator from the `Application` settings. For this, visit `https://console.developers.google.com/project/<YOUR-APP-ID>/permissions`.

- This e-mail ID can be that of the user who has signed in. We will talk more about signing in and signing out users in the next chapter.

- This can be an e-mail address that can receive e-mails for the application. We will talk more about ways to receive e-mails later in this chapter.

Now, all the aforementioned arguments can be specified to the `send_mail()` function. The following is a basic example:

```
from google.appengine.api import mail

content = "<html><head><title>Page!</title></head><body>Simple page!</body>"
mail.send_mail(sender="mohsinhijazee@gmail.com",
        to="john@hotmail.com",
        cc = ["merry@yahoo.com", "tom@gmail.com"],
        subject="Hello world!",
        body="Got the email? Reply me!",
        html="Got the email? <b>Reply me!</b>",
        attachments = [("simple.html", content)],
        reply_to="support@xyz.com")
```

Now, this is pretty simple. We sent an e-mail from mohsinhijazee@gmail.com to john@hotmail.com, merry@yahoo.com and tom@gmail.com are on CC, and if anyone replies to this e-mail, the response will go to support@xyz.com.

The subject and body are pretty simple as well, just plain text. Beside the body, we sent the HTML version of the same message as well.

An interesting thing to note is the way we are sending the attachments. Because an e-mail might have multiple attachments, we have a list. Each list element is a tuple representing an attachment. The first element is the name of the file as it would appear to the user receiving the e-mail. The second element is the actual data. The data that we are sending is just a hard-coded string variable, but you can populate it from anywhere, such as a disk, network, or a datastore.

Now, if you run the development server and paste the following code in the interactive console, as we have been doing till now, and execute it, an e-mail won't be sent. Instead, you will see the following output on the development console:

```
From: mohsinhijazee@gmail.com
To: john@hotmail.com
Cc: merry@yahoo.com
Cc: tom@gmail.com
Reply-to: support@xyz.com
```

```
Subject: Hello world!
Body:
   Content-type: text/plain
   Data length: 24
Body:
   Content-type: text/html
   Data length: 31
Attachment:
   File name: simple.html
   Data length: 64
```

Note that `Body` appears twice because we have specified the body once under the `body` keyword argument and again under `html`. So, both have different `Content-type`. The e-mail is not actually sent. The content is just printed on the terminal. We will learn how to configure the local development server to actually send an e-mail later in the chapter.

The object-oriented API

Besides the `send_mail()` function that we just saw, you can send an e-mail by using the `EmailMessage` class as well. This class is under the same `google.appengine.api.mail` package, and its constructor takes exactly the same keyword arguments that you would have supplied to `send_mail()`. But there are a few more methods as well:

- `initialize()`: This method and the constructor take the same arguments (which means the same as the `send_mail()` accepts), and you can initialize an `EmailMessage` instance by using this method.

- `check_initialized()`: This will check whether the `EmailMessage` instance has been initialized properly. If it has not been initialized properly, an exception will be raised.

- The `is_initialized()` method is the same as `check_initialized()` except that it will not raise an exception. It will return `True` if the `EmailMessage` instance has been initialized properly. Otherwise, it will return `False`.

- Finally, the `send()` message will simply send the e-mail message.

You can create a single `EmailMessage` instance and reuse it multiple times by calling the `initialize()` method with different values and then calling the `send()` method to send it. Internally, the `send_mail()` function also uses the `EmailMessage` class, and an instance is created to send the e-mail.

You may recall that for the `attachments` parameter in `send_mail()`, we passed a tuple of two elements per attachment. The first element is the name of the file that you'd like the receiving user to see, and the second element is the actual file data. But now you have an object-oriented drop-in replacement for the attachment (that was passed as a tuple earlier) in the form of the `Attachment` class in the `google.appengine.api.mail` package. The constructor of this class takes two arguments, which are the filename and payload, as follows:

```
from google.appengine.api.mail import Attachment
attachment = Attachment('index.html', content)
```

This is the same as having a tuple. Now, in light of the preceding lines, our first example can be written in the following way:

```
from google.appengine.api.mail import EmailMessage, Attachment

content = "<html><head><title>Page!</title></head><body>Simple page!</
body>"
email   = EmailMessage(sender="mohsinhijazee@gmail.com",
          to="john@hotmail.com",
          cc = ["merry@yahoo.com", "tom@gmail.com"],
          subject="Hello world!",
          body="Got the email? Reply me!",
          html="Got the email? <b>Reply me!</b>",
          attachments = [Attachment("simple.html", content)],
          reply_to="support@xyz.com")

if email.is_intialized():
    email.send()
```

As you can see, instead of calling the `send_mail()` function, we have instantiated an `EmailMessage` instance and populated it with keyword arguments to the constructor. The `attachments` variable has an `Attachment` instance instead of a tuple, although nothing can stop you from having a tuple here instead. Finally, we check whether the e-mail is initialized with the `is_initialized()` method. If it has been initialized, we send it by calling the `send()` method.

E-mail on the development console

As we saw previously, whenever an e-mail is sent from our code on the development server, it appears on the terminal in the log output. But you might want to send a real e-mail instead while developing your app. How do you do that? There are two ways. The first one is that if your local system has `sendmail` configured, you can use it. This route will require a working `sendmail` installation. We will skip it because that's outside the scope of this book.

The other way is that if you have an SMTP server of your own, you can mention this sever while running the local development server. So, the e-mail from your code will be handed over to the SMTP server and the rest will be handled and dispatched from the server. Fortunately, Gmail works as an SMTP server as well. So, we can use it to send our e-mails while developing them locally.

However, before you can do this, you need to enable a setting from your Gmail account's security settings at `http://myaccount.google.com/security` and allow less secure apps to use your account. You can enable it temporarily for development and later switch it off. This is what it looks like:

Once done with this, you just need to run your development server with the following options:

```
/path/to/sdk/dev_appserver.py --smtp_host smtp.gmail.com --smtp_port
587 --smtp_user youre-your-gmail-address-here@gmail.com --smtp_
password 'password' --smtp_allow_tls True /path/to/app/direcotory/
```

At the highlighted places, you will have to fill in your own credentials, and your e-mails will be sent using this Gmail account.

Headers

We talked about how you can send additional e-mail headers under the `headers` keyword argument to either the `send_email()` function or to the constructor of the `EmailMessage` class, but we didn't talk about how to actually do this.

The `headers` are provided as a dictionary, where each key is the name of the header and `value` is the value for the header that you would want to send. So, this is what it looks like:

```
from google.appengine.api import mail

mail.send_mail(sender="mohsinhijazee@gmail.com",
        to="john@hotmail.com",
        subject="Hello world!",
        body="Got the email? Reply me!",
        headers={'Resent-To': 'merry@yahoo.com'}
  )
```

You can learn more about e-mail headers in RFC 4021 at `https://tools.ietf.org/html/rfc4021`, but from all of these headers, Google App Engine allows only the following headers for security reasons:

- `In-Reply-To`
- `List-Id`
- `List-Unsubscribe`
- `On-Behalf-Of`
- `References`
- `Resent-Date`
- `Resent-From`
- `Resent-To`

A discussion of these headers is beyond the scope of this book. In case you are interested, RFC 4021 is the way to go.

Now that we know about how to send e-mails, the arguments that are accepted, how to send attachments, and how to supply custom headers, let's talk about how to receive e-mails.

Receiving e-mails

Receiving e-mails is pretty much a simple thing in Google App Engine. First, you have to enable the incoming e-mails for your app. This can only be done in your `app.yaml` file (as there's nothing on the application settings when deployed). To do this, you add the following line to `app.yaml`:

```
inbound_services:
- mail
```

Now, how are the e-mails delivered to your app? Can you pull them on your own? The answer is that the e-mails are delivered to your application as HTTP POST requests. So, which URL do they hit? That's actually `/_ah/mail/address`, where `address` is the e-mail address to which the e-mail is sent.

The e-mail address should be of the following form:

`account@appid.appspotmail.com`

Here, `account` can be anything that you like, and `appid` is your application ID from `app.yaml`. To handle the incoming requests at `sales@myapp.appspotmail.com`, you can have the following handler:

```
- url: /_ah/mail/sales@myapp\.appspotmail\.com
script: my_email_handler.app
login: admin
```

Let's look at the preceding definition in detail. The URL pattern contains some \ characters to escape the . characters. Basically, the URL patterns are regular expressions and a . character in a regular expression means match any character, and that's not what we want. We want to actually match the . character. Therefore, we escaped it by writing it as \. so that it does not have a different meaning in the context of regular expressions.

Next, we have the `script` directive, which indicates the Python script that will handle these types of requests. This is up to you, to either handle everything from a single Python file, or split them up as you want. Note that we don't say `my_email_handler.py`. Instead, we say `my_email_handler.app`, where `app` is the WSGI application function. You can review our discussion of CGI and WSGI from *Chapter 2, Handling Web Requests*.

Lastly, the `login` directive ensures that this URL pattern is only accessible either to the admin users that are authenticated as administrators, or internally from Google App Engine to the other Google App Engine components and services. We will learn more about users in Google App Engine in the next chapter.

So, once the preceding plumbing is done, what's next? Of course you need to add a Python handler to your code, as follows:

```
class EmailHandler(webapp2.RequestHandler):

    def post(self):
        # Request body contains email.
        print self.request.body

app = webapp2.WSGIApplication([
    ('/_ah/mail/.+', EmailHandler),
], debug=True)
```

Nothing fancy here, just an HTTP handler that handles the HTTP POST requests, as seen in the `post()` method. We just printed the request body that contains the e-mail message in textual form because essentially, SMTP is just a text-based protocol. Note that we have `/_ah/mail/.+` as the regular expression while mapping. This will handle all the e-mail requests for all e-mail accounts, but we can be more specific as well if we want to. Our `app.yaml` would contain the following:

```
- url: /_ah/mail/.+
  script: my_email_handler.app
  login: admin
```

So with this, all e-mail requests are directed to `my_email_handler.py` and inside `my_email_handler.py`, each e-mail account can have their own HTTP handling class with different mappings, as follows:

```
app = webapp2.WSGIApplication([
    (r'/_ah/mail/support@myapp.appspot.com', SupportEmailsHandler),
    (r'/_ah/mail/sales@myapp.appspot.com', SalesEmailsHandler),
    (r'/_ah/mail/info@myapp.appspot.com', InfoEmailsHandler),
], debug=True)
```

As you can see, each e-mail account has its own HTTP handler. This is just a matter of personal preference and how you'd like to arrange and organize your code.

You can actually simulate sending an e-mail to your app on your local development server by visiting `http://localhost:8000/mail` (accessible from **Inbound Mail** to the left of the development sever) and filling in the form fields. Consider a situation where you have an e-mail handler, as shown in the preceding code, which just prints the request body with the following command:

```
print self.request.body
```

If you send an e-mail from the preceding form, you'll see something like the following:

```
Content-Type: multipart/alternative;
 boundary="===============0489308295320330388=="
MIME-Version: 1.0
To: reply@mgae-01.appspot.com
From: mohsinhijazee@gmail.com
Cc:
Subject: A message for you!
Date: Thu, 11 Jun 2015 10:26:34 -0000

--===============0489308295320330388==
Content-Type: text/plain; charset="utf-8"
MIME-Version: 1.0
Content-Transfer-Encoding: base64

VGhpcyBpcyB0aGUgbWVzc2FnZSB0aGF0IH
lvdSB3aWxsIGdldCCwgaXQgaXMgdXAgdG8geW91IHRv
IGRlY29kZSBpdCBhbmQgZG8gcmVzdCBvZiB0aGUgdGh
pbmdzIHdpdGggaXQuIEp1c3QgcGFpbnRl
ZCBoZXJlLCBwcm9jZXNzWQgYnkgZHJpdmVycyBhbmQgYWxsLg==

--===============0489308295320330388==
Content-Type: text/html; charset="utf-8"
MIME-Version: 1.0
Content-Transfer-Encoding: base64

VGhpcyBpcyB0aGUgbWVzc2FnZSB0aGF0IHl
vdSB3aWxsIGdldCCwgaXQgaXMgdXAgdG8geW91IHRv
IGRlY29kZSBpdCBhbmQgZG8gcmVzdCBvZiB0aGUgdGhp
bmdzIHdpdGggaXQuIEp1c3QgcGFpbnRl
ZCBoZXJlLCBwcm9jZXNzWQgYnkgZHJpdmVycyBhbmQgYWxsLg==

--===============0489308295320330388==--
```

So, that seems pretty raw and doesn't make sense. We will have to parse it using the e-mail module that ships with the Python standard library, as follows:

```
import email
class EmailHandler(webapp2.RequestHandler):

    def post(self):
        # Returns Message object from email.message
        message = email.message_from_string(self.request.body)
```

The preceding code will return an instance of the `Message` class from an `e-mail.message` package in Python's standard library. You will have access to the e-mail headers and everything about which you can read more in the official documentation at `https://docs.python.org/2/library/email.message.html#email.message.Message`, but this is a longer route.

There's a better way to do it on Google App Engine. The webapp framework available on Google App Engine contains a built-in handler called `InboundMailHandler`, which can be imported, as follows:

```
from google.appengine.ext.webapp.mail_handlers import
InboundMailHandler
```

Now, if you base your handler on this `InboundMailHandler`, all you need to do is implement a method called `receive()`, as follows:

```
class FeedbackHandler(InboundMailHandler):

    def receive(self, email):
        """
        Recieves the email.
        """

        body = list(email.bodies('text/plain'))[0]
        _, body = body
        body = body.decode()
```

This method is handed over to an instance of the `InboundEmailMessage` class from the `google.appengine.api.mail` package. This is actually a base class of the `EmailMessage` class that we saw earlier. Therefore, it has all of its properties. One aspect of this is that this class can contain multiple bodies, such as one for text, another for HTML, and so on. The `bodies()` method returns an iterator that will let you iterate all the bodies. But if you supply the MIME type of the body that you want to get, only the iterator for that type of body will be returned.

As you can see in the preceding code, we supply `text/plain` as an argument. So, we only get the text body. We converted the iterator into a list, which will be a single element list if there's only one text body, which sometimes is the case. Now, each element in the list is a tuple. The first element of the tuple is the MIME type, the other is the raw body. That's exactly what we are dealing with:

```
_, body = body
```

Because `body` on the right is a tuple, both values are unpacked and assigned to each variable in order on the left. We do not need the MIME type. So, we just name the variable as _ and `body` now contains the raw body. Because it is raw, the data won't make sense unless we decode it, and that's why we called the `decode()` method on the returned `body` parameter, which finally returns plain text that can be processed.

As you can see, processing e-mails becomes far simpler this way. Now that we know how to send and receive e-mails, let's learn how to get bouncing e-mail notifications if our outgoing e-mails fail.

Handling bounce notifications

If you are sending e-mail messages, delivery might fail for multiple reasons, for instance, the account does not exist, the inbox of the receiving party is full, and anything in between. The bounce notifications are also delivered to your application as HTTP POST requests if you have enabled them. So first, you have to enable them by adding this to your `app.yaml`, as follows:

```
inbound_services:
- mail
- mail_bounce
```

As you can see, we added `mail_bounce` to the inbound services. So, this enables the bounce notifications for our application that are delivered as HTTP POST requests. All bounce notifications are always delivered to the `/_ah/bounce` URL. So, you need to have a request handler for that as well, as follows:

```
handlers:
- url: /_ah/bounce
  script: bounce1_handler.app
  login: admin
```

You can take the raw route of handling these bounce notifications by having an HTTP request handler in your code, just as we saw in the previous section on receiving e-mails.

However, things can be much simpler if you use a built-in
`BounceNotificationHandler` handler from the same `google.appengine.`
`ext.webapp.mail_handlers` module. Just like we saw in the previous section,
this handler too has a `receive()` method that you can override in your own
class by inheriting from it. This method is handed over to an instance of
`BounceNotification` from the same module. This instance has the
following properties:

- `original`: This is a dictionary that contains the `to`, `from`, `subject` and `text`
  keys. These are actually the values from the original mail that we tried to
  send but failed.

- `notification`: This again is a dictionary that contains the `to`, `from`, `subject`
  and `text` keys. This actually describes the bounce notification itself. The *from*
  will usually be `mailer-daemon@google.com`, whereas `text` will contain a
  detailed error message that informs you why the message delivery failed.

- `original_raw_message`: This is the original e-mail that we were trying to
  send. This will be plain pure text that can be parsed using the Python e-mail
  module, as discussed when exploring the topic of receiving e-mails.

So, this is what a bounce handler will look like:

```
class BounceHandler(BounceNotificationHandler):
    """
    Handles email bounce backs.
    """

    def receive(self, bounce_message):
        logging.info('Received bounce post ... [%s]', str(self.
request))
        logging.info('Bounce original: %s' + str(bounce_message.
original))
        logging.info('Bounce notification: %s' + str(bounce_message.
notification))
```

This can be used to keep track of the bounced messages and record them for later
reference. Now, what you do with the bounce notifications is up to you. You might
want to send e-mails again or keep track of the number of attempts and give up on
sending e-mail messages.

Putting it all together

Now that we are done exploring everything about e-mails on Google App Engine, it is time to put it all together. We are going to develop an app that is similar to what we did in the last chapter. You give it a URL and an e-mail address. The page is downloaded, compressed, and stored in the datastore like before. But besides that, we also e-mail that page to the given e-mail address. In case the sending of the e-mail fails, we handle the bounce notifications and record this information in logs.

In case the user replies to the e-mail, we parse the incoming e-mails and record the feedback as well. Let's go through everything file by file. The first one is app.yaml:

```
application: your-app-id
version: 1
runtime: python27
api_version: 1
threadsafe: true

inbound_services:
- mail
- mail_bounce

handlers:
# Emails
- url: /_ah/mail/.+
  script: email_handler.app
  login: admin
# Bounce backs
- url: /_ah/bounce
  script: email_handler.app
  login: admin
# Normal URLs
- url: /.*
  script: main.app

libraries:
- name: jinja2
  version: "2.6"
```

As you can see, we enabled two inbound services—mail and mail_bounce. This is so that the incoming e-mails and bounce notifications are delivered to us as HTTP POST requests.

The next important thing is in handlers. We are handling `/_ah/mail.+`, and `email_handlers.py` is the file that will handle all the incoming e-mails. We are also handling `/_ah/bounce` as well, and that too is in `email_handler.py`. Both the URL handlers are guarded by setting the `login: admin` directive so that they are not accessible to the outside world. Lastly, everything else goes to `main.py`.

The order of these URLs is very important here. If you list the `/.*` pattern first and the other e-mail handler patterns below it, all the URLs will be matched by the `/.*` expression because that's very broad. The way Google App Engine's request processing works, the first match is found in the URL patterns that are listed in the `app.yaml` file, the request is handed over to the script, and the search halts right there. That's what we don't want here. So, we have listed some more specific URL patterns first and then added `/.*` towards the end.

Next comes the `config.py` file, which contains some constants and a few other things:

```python
import os
import re
import jinja2

ID_PATTERN = re.compile(r'<ID:([a-z0-9]{4,40})>')

# On Sat, Jun 13, 1846 at 11:12 AM kind of timestamp
GMAIL_TIMESTAMP = re.compile(r'On \w+, \w+ \d{2}, \d{4} at \d{2}:\d{2} (AM|PM)')

FROM_EMAIL = "mohsinhijazee@gmail.com"

REPLY_TO = "feedback@mgae-01.appspotmail.com"

CURRENT_DIRECTORY = os.path.dirname(__file__)

TEMPLATES_DIRECTORY = os.path.join(CURRENT_DIRECTORY, 'templates')

JINJA_ENV = jinja2.Environment(loader=jinja2.
FileSystemLoader(TEMPLATES_DIRECTORY))
```

It is pretty much the same `config.py` that we saw in the last chapter except for the two new regular expressions and an e-mail address. The first is the `ID_PATTERN` expression. When we send a downloaded page as an e-mail, we mention its `sha1` hash in the e-mail message. This regular expression lets us parse and extract that hash later in case someone replies to that e-mail.

In case we receive a response from someone who got the HTML page, we have another pattern to split the response body into the quoted text and their reply. Almost all e-mail clients have timestamps such as `On Sat, Jun 13, 1846 at 11:12 AM <peter@hotmail.com> wrote:`. So, we have an expression to search for it, split the message on that boundary, and extract the reply of the sender. We'll see more when we examine our e-mail receiving code later.

Lastly, we added a new `REPLY_TO` value, which is `feedback@your-app-id.appspotmail.com`, which is the e-mail address to which all the replies would be sent.

Our `utils.py` file stays almost the same except that the existing methods no longer put the tasks in queues: rather, they execute them right there. Additionally, we have a simple `send_email()` method that, given the `sha1`, URL, and the contents of a page, sends it to the given e-mail address. Here's the full code for `utils.py`:

```python
import logging
import bz2
import hashlib

from google.appengine.api import urlfetch
from google.appengine.ext import deferred
from google.appengine.api import mail

import config

from models import HTMLPage

def get_page(sha1):
    """
    Gets the page
    """
    page = HTMLPage.get_by_id(sha1)

    if not page:
        return ""

    return bz2.decompress(page.content)


def download_page(url):
    """
```

```
    Downloads the page from given URL
    """

    result = urlfetch.fetch(url)

    # If failed, return.
    if result.status_code != 200:
        logging.error("Failed to download page %s" % url)
        raise Exception("Failed to download page.")


    return result.content

def compress_and_save(url, content, email):
    """
    Compresses and saves the page to datastore.
    """


    sha1 = hashlib.sha1(content).hexdigest()

    page = HTMLPage.get_by_id(sha1)
    # Logic to check if already exists.
    if page:
        page.url = url
        page.sent_to = email
        page.replied = False
        page.reply = ''
        page.put() # Just update attributes, content is new so it is
not sent.
        logging.info("Page already exists, has been updated! %s" %
email)
        return sha1


    # Compress
    compressed = bz2.compress(content)
    size = len(content)
    compressed_size = len(compressed)

    # Save.
    page = HTMLPage(id=sha1)
    page.url = url
    page.content = compressed
    page.original_size = size
```

```
page.compressed_size = compressed_size
page.sent_to = email
page.replied = False
page.put()
return sha1

def send_email(key, url, content, email):
    """
    Sends the content as attachemtn to
    the given email. URL is included in
    message body.
    """
    subject = "Article: {key}".format(key=key)
    body = "Someone sent {url} <ID:{key}> for you to read. See
attachment".format(url=url, key=key)

    filename = url.split('/')[-1] + ".html"
    mail.send_mail(sender=config.FROM_EMAIL,
        to=email,
        subject=subject,
        body=body,
        attachments = [(filename, content)],
        reply_to=config.REPLY_TO)
```

As you can see, `send_email()` is using the `send_mail()` function from the `google.appengine.api.mail` package. We split the URL on the / character and picked up the last piece to use as the filename. The content is in the `content` variable. So, the extracted `filename` function from `url` and `content` together form the attachment. Also note that we are sending the `sha1` hash in the body of the e-mail. We will extract this hash from the e-mail body later to load the associated datastore entity and store the e-mail response there.

Our `main.py` file contains all the user-facing handlers. It is pretty simple:

```
import logging
import webapp2
import jinja2

import config
import utils
from models import HTMLPage
```

```python
class MainPage(webapp2.RequestHandler):
    """
    The main page.
    """
    def get(self):

        sha1 = self.request.params.get('id')

        if sha1:
            self.response.write(utils.get_page(sha1))
            return

        # List all the pages.
        # Or a single page.
        main_template = config.JINJA_ENV.get_template("index.html")
        pages = HTMLPage.query()

        self.response.write(main_template.render({'pages': pages}))

    def post(self):
        """
        Downloads the page.
        """

        url = self.request.params.get('url')
        email = self.request.params.get('email')

        attachment = utils.download_page(url)
        key = utils.compress_and_save(url, attachment, email)
        utils.send_email(key, url, attachment, email)
        message = 'Page <a href="{url}">{url}</a> downloaded. <a
href="/">Go back</a>'
        self.response.write(message.format(url=url))


app = webapp2.WSGIApplication([
    ('/?', MainPage),

], debug=True)
```

As you can see, all the magic happens in the post() method, where we call the download_page() utility methods to download the page, compress_and_save() to save it to the datastore, and finally, send_email() to send it as an attachment to the user.

Our `templates/index.html` page also stays the same, although we show the e-mail response from the user except for the compression ratios, as we did in the previous chapter:

```html
<!doctype html>
<html>
<head>
    <title>Download a page</title>
</head>
<body>
    <h1>Download and store any HTML Page</h1>
    <form method="post">
        <input type="text" name="url" placeholder="Enter a page
URL"><br>
        <input type="text" name="email" placeholder="Email to send
this to"><br>
        <input type="submit" value="Download">
    </form>

    <h2>List of pages:</h2>
    <table>
        <tr>
            <th>URL</th>
            <th>Sent to</th>
            <th>Reply</th>
        </tr>
        {% for page in pages %}
            <tr>
                <td><a href="/?id={{page.key.id()}}" target="_
blank">{{page.url}}</a></td>
                <td><a href="mailto:{{page.sent_to}}">{{page.sent_
to}}</a></td>
                <td>{{page.reply}}</td>
            </tr>
        {% endfor %}
    </table>
</body>
</html>
```

Now comes the part for receiving the e-mails. This is our `email_handlers.py` file. Let's look at the code and discuss it in detail:

```python
import logging
import webapp2
import jinja2
import email

from google.appengine.ext.webapp.mail_handlers import
InboundMailHandler
from google.appengine.ext.webapp.mail_handlers import
BounceNotificationHandler

import config
import utils
from models import HTMLPage


class FeedbackHandler(InboundMailHandler):

    def receive(self, email):
        """
        Recieves the email.
        """

        body = list(email.bodies('text/plain'))[0]
        _, body = body
        body = body.decode()

        print "And the body is ", email.body

        match = config.ID_PATTERN.search(body)

        logging.debug("Email body: %s" % body)

        if not match:
            logging.debug("Couldn't find pattern %s" % config.ID_
PATTERN.pattern)
            return

        sha1 = match.groups()[0]
```

```
        page = HTMLPage.get_by_id(sha1)

        if not page:
            logging.error("Could not find page with ID %s" % sha1)
            return

        # Split on timestamp, just pick the reply
        body = config.MAIL_TIMESTAMP.split(body)[0]

        page.replied = True
        page.reply = body
        page.put()

class BounceHandler(BounceNotificationHandler):
    """
    Handles email bounce backs.
    """

    def receive(self, bounce_message):
        logging.info('Received bounce post ... [%s]', str(self.
request))
        logging.info('Bounce original: %s' + str(bounce_message.
original))
        logging.info('Bounce notification: %s' + str(bounce_message.
notification))

app = webapp2.WSGIApplication([
    (r'/_ah/mail/%s' % config.REPLY_TO.replace(".", "\."),
FeedbackHandler),
    (r'/_ah/bounce', BounceHandler)
], debug=True)
```

As you can see, we have two separate handlers. The first is the FeedbackHandler derived from InboundMailHandler. We override the receive() method in it and perform some processing.

The first step is obtaining the plain e-mail text from the InboundEmailMessage instance, which is done in the following way:

```
body = list(email.bodies('text/plain'))[0]
_, body = body
body = body.decode()
```

We already discussed the fact that the `bodies()` method returns an iterator to all the bodies of the e-mail message. You can pass it as a MIME type (such as `text/plain` and `text/html`) to get the iterator only for that type of body. We are interested in plain text. So, that's why we have `text/plain` as an argument to this method. But the return value is not just the body, but also a tuple. The first element contains the MIME type, and the second contains the raw e-mail body. That's why we have the `_, body = body` statement. Lastly, we have to decode it, so we call the `decode()` method. Finally, we have the plain text response from the user who sent us the e-mail.

Because we sent the `sha1` hash of the downloaded page in the e-mail's body, we try to extract it by using the regular expression defined in `config.py`:

```
match = config.ID_PATTERN.search(body)
```

If there is no match, we abort the processing and log this fact. Otherwise, we load the `HTML Page` from the datastore:

```
sha1 = match.groups()[0]
page = HTMLPage.get_by_id(sha1)
```

Now, we have the page for which we got a feedback e-mail. We already extracted the plain text body of the feedback e-mail, but this might contain the original e-mail message as a quote, and we need to discard this. To do this we split the e-mail body on the timestamp boundaries, which is defined as a regular expression in `config.py`:

```
MAIL_TIMESTAMP = re.compile(r'On \w+, \w+ \d{2}, \d{4} at \d{2}:\d{2}
(AM|PM) ')
```

Just a simple regular expression. Read it as it is. Regular expressions themselves might require a whole chapter of their own, and there are a lot of books on them as well. The topic is not very large, but it is beyond the scope of this book. So, we will just give a brief explanation of the above expression: — \w means any character, and \w+ would mean one or more character. The \d means any digit, and \d{number} means any digit exactly `number` times. AM|PM means either AM or PM. But if you are still curious about regular expressions, there are good online interactive tutorials at `http://regexone.com/` and `http://tryregex.com/` for you to learn.

So, we split our feedback e-mail's body on this boundary and pick the first part after splitting, because that is the reply from the user who got the e-mail:

```
body = config.MAIL_TIMESTAMP.split(body)[0]
```

The next code is pretty simple; we just update the datastore entity with an e-mail response and set the `replied` flag to `True`:

```
page.replied = True
page.reply = body
page.put()
```

We are done! For this to work, you will have to deploy it. Make sure that you mention the correct application ID in `app.yaml`, which means that the application exists on Google App Engine. If it does not, you will have to create a new application, or you can deploy it to an existing one if you want. To deploy the application, change to the directory of the application where `app.yaml` is, and execute the following command:

```
$ /path/to/gae/sdk/appcfg.py --oauth2 update .
```

This will open up a browser for you, where you will have to enter the credentials for your Gmail account, and the application will be deployed. You can play with it on `http://your-app-id.appspot.com`. Send a link to your self as an e-mail, reply to it, and you'll see that your response will be listed on the main page when you refresh it.

Summary

In this chapter, we looked at how e-mails work at a very high level. We saw that SMTP is a text-based protocol and the SMTP servers listen on `port 587` for the e-mail clients to access them. E-mails, if on the same server, are just copied to the destined user's inbox. If they are on a different server, a DNS lookup is performed to find out the IP of the SMTP server and the e-mail is handed over to that server.

Next, we saw how to send e-mails. We saw that `send_email()` is the function that we can use. We also saw that `EmailMessage` is a class whose instance can be created and used to send an e-mail. We learned that both the function and the `EmailMessage` class's constructor take the same keyword arguments. We also learned how to send attachments with our e-mails.

After that, we learned how to send e-mail headers. We examined the available headers that are allowed in Google App Engine.

Once done with all aspects of sending e-mails, we focused our attention on receiving e-mails. We learned that the e-mail has to be enabled in `app.yaml`, and any e-mail account of the `account@your-app-id.appspotmail.com` form can receive e-mail. All the e-mails are sent as an HTTP POST request to the `/_ah/mail/address` URL. These are raw and need to be parsed, where `address` is the e-mail address to which the e-mails are being sent. We studied built-in e-mail handlers that do all the heavy lifting for us.

Once equipped with this, we learned how to handle bounce notifications. We learned that if a sent e-mail bounces, that too is delivered as an HTTP POST request to `/_ah/bounce`. But for that to work, we have to enable bounce mail under inbound services in `app.yaml`. We also examined built-in handlers that are similar to those that we saw while experimenting with e-mail receipts that do all the heavy lifting of parsing the e-mail for us.

Finally, we assembled this together to write a web application that, given a URL and an e-mail, downloads the page and sends an attachment to the given e-mail. If the receiving user replies to that e-mail, the reply is recorded as well in the datastore.

With this, we are done with e-mails. In the next chapter, we will examine some more useful services that are at our disposal to get the best out of Google App Engine.

Working with the Google App Engine Services

We have worked with various services that are provided by Google App Engine such as datastore, task queues, and e-mail, but these are not the only services that are offered by the platform. Google App Engine provides a wide variety of services that are at your disposal and which can be integrated into your application.

We will examine some of the most important services that are required by almost all web applications in one way or the other. In this chapter, we will examine the following services:

- **Memcache**: Used to cache and speed up performance
- **Multi-tenancy**: Used to have multiple logical compartments in your application
- **Users**: Used for authentication and various operations
- **Blobs and Cloud storage**: Used for storage and to serve large files
- **Images**: Used to process and transform images

Memcache

If you have some experience in developing web applications, you will know that in order to generate a dynamic response as HTML to the end users, there's certain computational and I/O overhead involved. For instance, a blogging website's main page will contain the latest blog entries. To generate this main page, you need to do the following:

- Fetch the blog entries from the database. This involves computational overhead because you will be filtering blog posts by user, and the database engine will also perform a sort by date. Once this is done, this involves I/O overhead as well because the collected records, after filtering and sorting, are to be returned over the socket connection, as almost all communication with all the major database engines happens over network sockets.

- Once you have a list of blog posts, you have to generate an HTML page for which you can either use plain string concatenation, or rely on a templating engine, where the HTML page will have placeholders and some control statements, for the repetition of items. The end result of the rendering process will be the text generated by combining the template and the values that you supplied. All this certainly consumes computational time.

This seems pretty simple, but let's assume that the first step of fetching items from the database takes 850 milliseconds and it takes about 150 milliseconds to render the template into text. This amounts to 1000 milliseconds, or one second, to generate a page for one user. You may recall our discussion on scalability (from *Chapter 1, Understanding the Runtime Environment*) as regards how important it is to reduce computational times and its impact on scalability.

Here's a recap of that discussion. Assuming that you can only serve one user at a time (that is, no concurrency) and your one request to the homepage takes about one second, you will only be able to serve 60 users in a minute. The 61st user will face a delay until the system gets done with the processing request for some other user. But the 120th user in the same minute will face a huge delay of about 1 minute (60 seconds to wait till the other 60 users get served, to the point where the machine is free to serve them) and yet, a timeout may also occur.

Now, we know that spending time with computations is important. But how do we reduce this time? things will certainly take the time they need to; we cannot do anything about it. What we can certainly do is perform such computations only once and store their results somewhere. The next time we need to perform such a computational, we simply use the results that we stored earlier, and the whole process sees a boost in performance.

That is exactly the idea behind Memcache. It is just a distributed key-value store written for LiveJournal. The initial version was written in Perl and later, it was rewritten in C. When we refer to key-value store, you can just assume that it is like a Python directory, which has keys and values. But there are two additional things to remember with the values. The size of the key and the value combined cannot be more then 1 MB. The other additional thing is that you can specify a lifetime for a key's value. That is, you can say that the value that you are setting against a key should be retained for an hour, a day, a week, or whatever your requirement is. After this time, it will be deleted and the memory will be freed. So, memory you say? Yes, everything is kept in memory and nothing is on the disk.

The other thing is that—the keyword in Memcache is distributed. By the term "distributed", we mean that more than one machine is used to store key-value pairs. This not only increases the overall capacity of the system in terms of memory, but also the load gets distributed across multiple machines because the key-value pairs are also distributed based on hashing algorithms across the machines in the cluster.

Now, let's take a closer look at the Memcache operations.

The Memcache operations

Let's look at the operations that are available to us. There are only three basic operations that you can perform. That's all:

- We can set a key and its value. If the key already exists, it will be overwritten. The key and the value both combined should be at the most 1 MB in size. Optionally, you can specify an expiry time in seconds or as a date after which, the item will be automatically removed from Memcache and will be no longer available. Whatever you provide as a value gets serialized by using Python's pickle module. We'll discuss this in more detail later.

- Given a key, you can get its value. If a value exists, it will be desterilized back to the Python equivalent by using the pickle module.

- Given a key, you can delete it. Once deleted, subsequent attempts to get it will return nothing.

So as you can see, it's pretty simple. But there are additional operations that are just variations of the preceding ones.

- You can **add** a key. It is just like the set operation but with the difference being that the key and the value will only be stored if they do not already exist.

- You can **replace** a key's value. That is, you can provide a key and a value. The value will be placed if, and only if, the key already exists.

- You can **increment** a key's value. This actually means getting the key and setting a new value after the increment. You can specify the amount of increment, which if not specified, defaults to 1. You can specify an initial value as well, which will be used in case the key doesn't already exist, so that it will be created with the given initial value. If you don't give an initial value and the key doesn't exist, nothing will be done.

- Similarly, you can **decrement** a value as well. The rest of the semantics remain the same as they are used to increment a value described above.

- Finally, you can **flush all** the keys. This will remove everything in Memcache.

So, these are all the operations that are available to us. One aspect that we'd like to revisit is, for how long does a key-value pair remain in Memcache if no expiry time is specified while adding key-value pair? The answer is that Memcache tries to retain a key-value pair as long as possible and as long as memory is available. Memcache keeps track of each key-value pair, and of how many times it has been accessed. If new key-value pairs are being submitted by clients and the system is low on memory, the least recently used key-value pairs are evicted from Memcache to make room for newer ones.

Now, this raises the question, how much memory is available to you when using Memcache? The answer is—it depends. When you are using the free version of Memcache, you are actually using a shared hosted version where there are no guarantees about the available memory or the number of operations per second that can be performed. The service will try its level best to retain the keys as much as it can. But in case you are using the paid version, you can get guaranteed capacity ranging from 1 GB to 100 GB along with 10,000 operations per second per GB for items that are less than 1 KB in size. For more details on configuration, visit `https://cloud.google.com/appengine/docs/python/memcache/#Python_Configuring_memcache`.

In general, your application should never assume the presence of a key-value pair in Memcache and should be able to function gracefully if a key it is looking for doesn't exist and possibly place it in such case.

Now, let's look at how Memcache is available in Google App Engine.

Memcache in Google App Engine

Memcache is not specific to Google App Engine in any way; it is a distributed key-value store that can be deployed on its own as well, and that's how most deployments are made. But that comes at the cost of you managing all the configuration and deployment issues.

Because Google App Engine is a **Platform as a Service (PaaS)**, Memcache is also provided as a service. The same Python Memcache API that you would otherwise use in case of normal self-hosted Memcache servers, is the one that you will use here.

For free apps in Google App Engine you have shared Memcache, which is shared among many applications. But if you want to, you can have a dedicated Memcache, managed and hosted by Google on your behalf. This is billed according to GB per hour, and it currently has a rate of $0.06. So, if you have 1 GB of data cached for one hour, you'll end up paying $0.06. This is just a figure that might change, and the billing model itself might change as well. So, it's better to consult the online pricing page at `https://cloud.google.com/appengine/pricing`.

The Memcache client

No matter what kind of Memcache you are using, the API stays the same. The following functions are at your disposal from the `google.appengine.api.memcache` module:

- `get(key)`: This returns the value for the given key where `key` is a string. If the key doesn't exist, this function returns `None`.

- `get_multi(keys, key_prefix)`: This gets the values for all the given keys, where `keys` is a list of strings. This is actually batching multiple `get()` calls for efficiency so that there are no additional server round trips. The return value is a dictionary that `contains` keys and their corresponding values. If all the keys have some common prefix, you can specify that it is a `key_prefix` argument. The return value is a dictionary that contains the keys that were asked for. Note that the keys don't contain `key_prefix` in them even if you have supplied `key_prefix` in the arguments, as we'll see shortly.

- `set(key, value, time=0)`: This will set a key-value pair in Memcache. By default, it won't ever expire, but it might be evicted if the memory is under pressure. In such a case, the least recently used key-value pairs are evicted from the memory. You also have the option to specify an expiry time in seconds after which, the key-value pair will be automatically deleted. The maximum expiration time can be a month, so the maximum value for this will be 86,400 seconds a day times 30 days, which is 2,592,000. If the key-value pair was successfully placed, this function returns `True`. Otherwise, it returns `False`.

- `set_multi(mappings, key_prefix, time=0)`: This is the same as `get_multi()`; it just batches the calls to set multiple keys in one go. The mapping is a dictionary of keys and their values that are to be set. The return value is a list of keys that were not set, because they failed for some reason.

- `add(key, value, time=0)`: This is the same as `set()`, but we will add the key only if the key doesn't already exist. The `time` function is the expiration time in seconds, just like that of the `set()` function.

- `add_multi(mappings, key_prefix, time=0)`: This is just the batch version of `add()`. It returns a list of keys for which the values were not set, because they already existed.

- `delete(key, seconds=0)`: This simply removes the value at the given `key` function. The return value is interesting. It is an integer; if it is `0`, it means that a network error occurred. If it is `1`, it means that the key-value pair that was requested for deletion doesn't exist. Finally, a value of `2` means that it was removed successfully. Mostly, you won't care if a key doesn't exist, and you asked for its deletion. So, if the return value is greater than zero, you can assume all went well. The optional `seconds` argument is interesting too. What this means is that the deleted key will be unavailable for that amount of time. So, if you specified `seconds` as `60`, the subsequent calls to `add()` will fail because the key, even if deleted, will be considered available. The same goes for the `replace()` function, which only sets the value against a key if it already exists, unlike `set()`, which will set the key regardless of whether it already exists.

- `delete_multi(keys, key_prefix, seconds=0)`: This is just the batch version of `delete()` for efficiency. The `keys` function is just a list of keys, and `key_prefix` is the same as what we've examined in the other calls. It returns `True` if all the keys were deleted. Otherwise, it returns `False` even if it failed to delete a single key.

- `replace(key, value)`: This is the same as the `set()` function except that it will only place the key-value pair in the memory if the value with that key already exists in the memory.

- `replace_multi(mappings)`: This works just like the preceding `replace()` function except that it batches the call for multiple key-value pairs that are present in `mappings`, which is a dictionary.

- `incr(key, delta=1)`: This increases the value of a `key` by the `delta` amount, which defaults to `1` if not specified.

- `decr(key, delta=1)`: This decreases the value of a `key` by the `delta` amount, which defaults to `1` if not specified.

- `offset_multi(mappings, key_prefix)`: This is the batch version for both the `incr()` and `decr()` functions. `mappings` is a dictionary of keys to their intended offsets. The offsets can be positive or negative.

- `flush_all()`: This deletes all the keys in a single operation. The return value is always `True` irrespective of whether there are any keys in the cache or not. `False` is returned in case the underlying RPC call fails altogether.

So, that's a list of all the functions that are available to you so that you can interact with Memcache. You can launch the local development server and play with Memcache in the interactive console. Here's one such session:

```
from google.appengine.api import memcache

# Set a single value. Expire after 1 hour.
memcache.set('name', 'Mohsin', time=3600)

# Set multiple values with prefix
memcache.set_multi({'id': 45, 'age': 93}, key_prefix='user_')

# Get a single key
print memcache.get('name')

# Get multiple keys with prefix
print memcache.get_multi(['id', 'age'], key_prefix='user_')

# Increment a key, returns new value 45 to 47.
# Delta if not given, defaults to 1
print memcache.incr('user_id', delta=2)
# Decrement a key, returns new value 93 to 91
print memcache.decr('user_age', delta=2)

# Add 3 to user_id, subtract -11 from user_age
print memcache.offset_multi({'id': 3, 'age': -11},key_prefix='user_')

# Will do nothing because key already exists.
memcache.add('name', 'Peter')

# Only user_country would be set because that exists
print memcache.add_multi({'id': 7894, 'country': 'Canada'}, key_
prefix='user_')

# Replace the name
```

```
memcache.replace('name', 'Uknown')

# Only id would be replaced to 700
memcache.replace({'id':700, 'group':'C'}, key_prefix='user_')
```

The preceding interaction should give you a very good idea of how to use the Memcache API.

The object-oriented client

Besides the preceding functions that have been listed, there's an object-oriented interface to Memcache as well. You can define it like this:

```
from google.apengine.api.memcache import Client
mc = Client()
mc.set('price', 17)
mc.set_multi({'quantity': 55, 'weight': 3, 'unit': 'kg'})
```

This client has all the methods with the same name as we saw in the preceding section. An additional thing is that for some of the methods, there are asynchronous versions. This means that you can call them and move on to other stuff. Once you're done, you can collect the result. For example, we want to get multiple keys. So, this is how we'll do it:

```
result = mc.get_multi_async(('price', 'quantity'))
# Do other expensive stuff that you wanted to do.
# Once done, call the get_result(), this is a blocking call!
print result.get_result()
```

Not every method has an asynchronous version, but the following is the list of all the asynchronous methods that are at your disposal:

- `set_multi_async()`
- `get_multi_async()`
- `add_multi_async()`
- `replace_multi_async()`
- `incr_async()`
- `decr_async()`
- `offset_multi_async()`
- `delete_multi_async()`
- `flush_all_async()`

All of these methods return an instance of `UserRPC` that has the `get_result()` method, which is a blocking call. The rest of the functionality stays the same. You can invoke any of these functions, and an instance of the `UserRPC` class will be returned. Whenever you have time, you can call the `get_results()` function to get the results.

Multi-tenancy

Imagine that you are building an invoicing application and you intend to adopt the **Software as a Service (SaaS)** model. Your application will certainly have products and clients who will order those products. You'll have to keep a record of this. So all in all, in such a minimal application, you will store clients, products, and orders.

However, there's no point if there's only one business or establishment that can use your system. You can't hope to make any profits that way, and you'd want more and more businesses to sign up and pay for it. In that case, every business will have a different set of products and clients and the orders that they will get.

The typical way around that situation is to have another table or model in your system with a name, organization, company or business. Every product, customer, or order that you create will have a reference to their corresponding organization. When someone signs up, you create a company/organization record and a user for them and assign that company to the user record as well. When someone signs in, you check which company or organization they belong to and from that point onwards, all the read, update, and create operations will use that company by default for filtering or while creating new records.

This feature is actually the style of a software architecture called **multi-tenancy** because a single application can serve multiple organizations as compared to cases where one business application is developed with a single organization using it. Multi-tenancy is a great feature that brings lots of economic returns and gains, but is of course something that is to be considered while programming your application right from the schema all the way up to the read, write, and update operations.

This is actually almost equal to creating compartments where the data of each organization doesn't mix with the data of other organizations, and this of course requires a mention of the organization when writing or updating the data. It also requires filtering by the organization in question while reading the data for presentation to the user.

Google App Engine provides this feature out of the box with very little effort on your part. No scheme changes are required. The idea is that at the very outset of your request processing, you set a namespace, which is just a unique string such as the unique identifier of a user or an organization. All the subsequent interactions with the App Engine APIs now happen in this context. All the namespace-related functions (four of them actually) are in the `google.appengine.api.namespace_manager` module. To set a namespace, you just have to do this:

```
# Import the function
from google.appengine.api.namespace_manager, import set_namespace
# Set name space
set_namespace('wallmart.com')
```

This `set_namespace()` method only takes a single string argument, the name of the namespace. Namespace names should only contain numbers, letters, or the _ or - character, and can have a maximum length of 100 characters. They should also not start with an _ character, as it is reserved for Google App Engine's internal usage. When in doubt whether the string you want to use as the namespace is valid, you can use the `validate_namespace()` method, which will return `True` or throw a `BadValueError` exception.

Now, after this call to `set_namespace()`, the current namespace will be set to `wallmart.com` and the following four APIs will respect that:

- Datastore
- Memcache
- Task queues
- Search

By respect, we mean that if you set the namespace to `wallmart.com`, write anything into the preceding four services, set the namespace to `amazon.com`, and try to read it back, you won't find it, and will be as if it had never been created at all in that namespace. Only when you switch the namespace back to `wallmart.com` will you see what you stored earlier. So, this is the kind of compartmentalization that we are talking about here.

As you can guess, there's a corresponding `get_namespace()` method that returns the current namespace.

Internally, these methods set an `HTTP_X_APPENGINE_CURRENT_NAMESPACE` environment variable, which of course shouldn't be touched directly. Instead, you should go through the namespace API.

As you may know, you can get a business Gmail account for which you won't have `yourname@gmail.com`; rather you can have a `yourname@yourdomain.com` kind of email address. In such a case, you might want to get the domain name associated with the current user. You can simply call `google_apps_namespace()`, and this will return the associated domain with it. So in this way, for both the `john@wallmarkt.com` and `harry@wallmart.com` users, this method will return `wallmart.com`, which can be set as the namespace, effectively creating a compartmentalization for that particular organization.

Automatically setting the namespace

As you saw, we have to call the `set_namespace()` method ourselves. If we somehow forget this, we might be writing and reading from someone else's namespace, thus causing a data leakage, which defeats the whole purpose of compartmentalization. How do we avoid this? There's a mechanism for this. We'll review it yet again in the next chapter. All that you have to do is create a file named `appengine_config.py` at the root directory of your package and define a function in it of the name `namespace_manager_default_namespace_for_request()`, which will return the namespace that you'd want to use for the request. How you determine which namespace to use for the request is up to you, but the point here is that it is the only place that you have for it, and nowhere in your application code are you bound to call functions to set the namespace or worry about it. So, this is how it looks:

```
# appengine_config.py at root directory of your project
from google.appengine.api.namespace_manager import google_apps_
namespace

def namespace_manager_default_namespace_for_request():
    # Return the associated google apps namespace for current logged
in user.
    return google_apps_namespace()
```

So, what did we do here? We created a file named `appengine_config.py` and defined a `namespace_manager_default_namespace_for_request()` function, which returned the Google apps domain associated with the logged in user. This function will be called by Google App Engine before the request is handed over to the request handler scripts in your application. So, by the time the execution reaches your request handling code, the stage is already set.

We told you about namespaces and how simple it is to achieve compartmentalization with it. It is now up to you to write the next killer business application on top of Google App Engine for small to medium businesses, or even for an enterprise if you wish!

The API-specific notes

Setting the namespace once, globally affects all the functions and methods of the aforementioned APIs, but you can override this, as all the methods accept an optional `namespace` parameter. With this, you can override the globally set namespace and locally change it for one particular function call that you are making.

Now that we know what namespaces are and their advantages, let's review some API-specific notes.

The Datastore

You might recall that we mentioned the `namespace` keyword argument and how it plays a role in key formation while creating the `ndb.Key` instances. That's the main mechanism by which datastore achieves compartmentalization. Both the `ndb.Key` and `ndb.Query` classes accept a `namespace` keyword argument in all of their methods (where it makes sense and is applicable of course) and defaults to the current namespace if it is not specified. But you can of course override this by providing it yourself.

Memcache

It is worth mentioning that Memcache is not a solution that is specific to or originating from Google. It is independent software, just like MySQL or Apache HTTP Server. In reality, Memcache has no notion of namespaces at all of any sorts, and everything falls into a single flat space. However, Google App Engine emulates namespaces in Memcache by prefixing the current namespace when you set the keys in Memcache and stripping this prefix when you ask for the keys that you set, thus making it transparent for you. This impacts your key length, which will be larger because it will have the current namespace as well. So, if you have a `my_key` key of six characters and the current namespace is `wallmart.com`, the total key length in reality will be the character length of both the key and the current namespace. As you already know, the total size of a key-value pair value must not exceed 1 MB, including the key as well, and this namespace takes a toll due to the key part of the equation.

Task queues

Task queues work just fine with namespaces just as you'd expect, except for the fact that the task names aren't specific to any namespace. This means that they have to be unique across all your namespaces anyway. That's the only catch, which of course isn't going to be a big hindrance.

Search

The search indexes of each namespace are kept separate, and all the calls will respect the globally set namespace, just as for the other APIs.

Blobstore

Blobstore doesn't come under the APIs that are namespace-aware, and everything falls under a single namespace. There's no compartmentalization. But as long as your `blob` keys are stored in datastore, Memcache, search indexes, or task queues, you'll be fine because these APIs themselves are namespace-aware. Hence, they will only return the objects, records, or entities associated with the current namespace and by virtue of the same, you'll usually not access blobs from other namespaces. However, unlike the other four namespace APIs that we talked about, you can still read blobs from anyone's namespace regardless of what the current namespace is set to.

Blobs

While discussing datastore, we mentioned that you can store binary objects in `ndb. BlobProperty`, but there's a better way to do this. The `ndb.BlobProperty` directly stores uninterpreted bytes in datastore. One of the criteria for datastore pricing is the amount of data that goes out of datastore. So, if you have stored large blobs in datastore, it will become expensive while reading out your entities.

However, you can avoid this by using GQL (or projection via API) and only selecting a few properties, and this might save you some bandwidth. But the real problem still exists. You may recall that all the entity properties are stored in a single column in the underlying BigTable. So, even if you select only a few properties, this might save you the internal bandwidth, but the performance penalty will still be there.

So, a better option is Blobstore which can handle very large binary objects, be it images or large high-quality video files. When you hand over a file to Blobstore, you get a unique string, called a blob key, against it. This is the reference to your file. So, you can read it again, serve it to the users, or delete it. So, it is basically a kind of key-value store. You can think of Blobstore as Amazon S3 but with no buckets, access policies, and CDN.

There is a limitation to Blobstore. The files cannot be created from your code. They can only be uploaded via HTTP requests to a given URL. However, you can read an existing file as you like and process it, and you can of course delete an existing file, but what you cannot do is create a file from your code. They always have to be uploaded.

We'll now learn how to upload a file to Blobstore, serve a file, and read an existing file.

Uploads

Uploads are pretty simple. You can create an HTML file with as many file upload files as as you'd like, one, two, three, or more. The only difficulty is that the URL to which your form is posted doesn't belong to your application. This URL is of a Blobstore service, and when a user posts a form, all the data will be posted there.

So, what about the other fields that you might have? Where will those go? Nothing to worry about. Once the Blobstore service is done receiving the files, it will redirect you to your application with all the form values. Okay, so where do you get the URL from? This is how we get it:

```
from google.appengine.ext import blobstore
upload_url = blobstore.create_upload_url('/upload')
```

The /upload is the URL where Blobstore will redirect once the files are uploaded. Technically, it won't be redirected, but an HTTP POST request will be made with all the form fields.

So, if you have a form like the following, you will have to set the action property of the form to the preceding URL that was generated:

```
<form action="{{upload_url}}" method="post" enctype="multipart/
form-data">
    <input type="text" name="title" placeholder="Enter title"><br>
    <input type="file" name="photo"> <br>
    <input type="submit" value="Upload">
</form>
```

Now, if you have a request handler at /upload, this will receive an HTTP POST request, and you'll have all your form fields available.

But where's the file? Did Blobstore post it along with the request body? No, it didn't. Not directly actually. There's a mechanism in the HTTP protocol where, instead of including the request body along with request, you can specify that the request body exists somewhere else, and the receiving party should obtain it from there.

For example, consider a case where you have files in Dropbox and you want to send a file to some endpoint via an HTTP request. One obvious way for you to do this is to download the Dropbox file, read it into the request body, and send it. Now, at the receiving end, the whole file will travel across the network. So, as you can see, the file data had to be first downloaded from Dropbox, uploaded back as a part of your request, and yet again downloaded at the receiving end. This is three times the actual work.

This is where the HTTP external request body mechanism comes in handy. Now, instead of downloading the whole file from Dropbox and sending it along with the request body, you can just send a reference to the file in a `Content-Type` header, like this:

```
Content-Type: message/external-body; access-type="dropbox;
file="mohsin/got.mp4";
```

So, instead of sending the file, we are setting the `Content-Type` to `message/external-body`. The other two key-value pairs that are separated by `;` are file set to `mohsin/got.mp4` and `access_type` is set to `Dropbox`. Note that only the `Content-Type: message/external-body` and `access-type` are a part of the HTTP standard. It is up to you to decide and interpret the value of the `access-type` and any other additional values. So, in our case, we are indicating that the file has to be accessed from Dropbox, whereas the file is `mohsin/got.mp4`.

Now, the receiving end will know how to construct a URL to download the request body by `http://dropbox.com/mohsin/got.mp4`. You can have another `access-type: github` with `file=mohsin/mycoolrepo/myfile.zip`, and it is up to the client to interpret this and act in accordance.

The point is that the HTTP requests can have external bodies residing elsewhere and in such cases, they are mentioned by setting `Content-Type` to `message/external-body` and indicating `access-type` as how it can be accessed.

This is exactly the mechanism that Blobstore uses to send you the uploaded files when it makes an HTTP POST request to your provided URL. The uploaded files are included as an external request body like this:

```
Content-Type: message/external-body; blob-key="Y3-nzo3Nmr7VG_
Bac12pcA=="; access-type="X-AppEngine-BlobKey"
```

As you can see, the `Content-Type` is set to `message/external-body` and `access-type` is set to `X-AppEngine-BlobKey`. Now, at the receiving end (which itself is a part of App Engine and runs before the request is handed over to your URL), it knows that it has to fetch the blob from Blobstore with the `Y3-nzo3Nmr7VG_Bac12pcA==` key mentioned under `blob-key`.

When the request is posted to us, it has all the form values as request parameters. Now, the way to access the request parameters varies of course from web framework to web framework. Everyone has their own ideas on how things should work, but in our case, we have been using the built-in webapp2 framework for which, this form of processing boils down to the following:

```
class UploadHandler(webapp2.RequestHandler):

    def post(self):
        """
        Handles photo upload
        """
        title = self.requestt.params('title')
        photo = self.request.params.get('photo')
```

We obtained the title and photo from the request parameters, whereas the title is just a string. But the photo is even more interesting. What is it now? Is it text or a file? None of these. This is basically an instance of the cgi.FieldStorage class, which comes from the standard python library. From the standard documentation.

This class provides the naming, typing, files stored on the disk, and more. Among others, this class has the following attributes:

- name: This is the name that was given on the HTML form. In our case, it will be photo.
- filename: This is the original file name as it was uploaded.
- type: This is the content type of the file. It is just the MIME type that you are familiar with. For example, in the case of PNG images, it will be image/png.
- type_options: This is a dictionary that contains all the extra key-value pairs that were specified with the Content-Type header. So, because Blobstore sent an HTTP POST request with the external body, the blob-key and access-type are what interest us. The blob-key is actually the unique string ID of the blob that we uploaded.
- file: This is the file-like object that you can iterate and read in if you want to. Because Blobstore just sent us the blob key as an external request body, the App Engine downloads and reads the content into this property while instantiating this cgi.FieldStorage instance.

To summarize what we know by now about uploads, we point the HTML forms to a Blobstore URL, which takes the uploaded files, stores them, generates a unique string ID, and then makes an HTTP POST request (with an external request body, as discussed in detail) that contains the blob key. App Engine, before handing over this request to us, parses it and initializes all the form fields. File fields are instantiated with the files that are read into the file object, as discussed before.

Getting BlobInfo

So, before your given request handler gets hit, the file is already uploaded on Blobstore. There's one last thing that's done in the background. A datastore entity is created to keep the information about the uploaded files. This contains things such as the filename, file size, content type, and an MD5 hash. The kind name of this entity is __BlobInfo__, and it is represented by a model-like BlobInfo class from the google.appengine.ext.blobstore module.

So, we can actually get the associated BlobInfo entity like this:

```
from google.appengine.ext import ndb

class UploadHandler(webapp2.RequestHandler):

    def post(self):
        photo = self.request.params.get('photo')

    # get Blob key
        blob_key = photo.type_options.get('blob-key')
        # Construct a datastore key
        key = ndb.Key(blobstore.BlobInfo.kind(), blob_key).to_old_
key()

        # Now perform a GQL query
        blobinfo = blobstore.BlobInfo.gql("WHERE __key__ = :1", key)
    [0]

        # Do something with blob, may be store its
        # key into some other entity.
        return "All well!"
```

Okay, now this looks scary, but it is not. Let's break it down. First, we just got the photo (which is a cgi.FieldStorage instance) from the request parameters, like this:

```
photo = self.request.params.get('photo')
```

Simple. Next, we get the blob-key from type_options. We already explained what type_options are and how the blob-key actually gets there and where it comes from:

```
blob_key = photo.type_options.get('blob-key')
```

Okay, now we have the blob key, which is a string. Now, we need to obtain the datastore entity corresponding to this. Now, when the `BlobInfo` entity is stored for a `blob` in datastore, the unique string ID generated by Blobstore is used as its key. So, all that we have to do is query by key:

```
blobinfo = blobstore.BlobInfo.gql("WHERE __key__ = :1", key)[0]
```

What is a key? We cannot use the raw `blob-key` here. It has to be `db.Key` and not `ndb.Key`. But we only know about `ndb` and we didn't touch `db`, as that's the old way of doing things. But we can certainly create an `ndb.Key` instance like this:

```
ndb.Key(kind_name, key)
```

The key is the `blob-key`, but what is `kind_name`? It is just the name of the model class or the value returned by the `kind()` method of a model class if it doesn't want its class name to be the kind name. So for `BlobInfo`, we can use the following code:

```
ndb.Key(BlobInfo,kind(), blob_key)
```

As we mentioned, this is an `ndb.Key()` instance, but the `gql()` method on `BlobInfo` expects a `db.Key` instance. Fortunately, that's easy. So, we can do this by calling the `to_old_key()` method:

```
key = ndb.Key(BlobInfo,kind(), blob_key).to_old_key
```

Now, you can easily query datastore for the `BlobInfo`. So, let's summarize the whole thing in steps:

```
# Step 1: Get the file field from request
photo = self.request.params.get('photo')
# Step 2: Get Blob key
blob_key = photo.type_options.get('blob-key')
# Step 3: Construct a datastore key
key = ndb.Key(blobstore.BlobInfo.kind(), blob_key).to_old_key()
# Step 4: Now perform a GQL query
blobinfo = blobstore.BlobInfo.gql("WHERE __key__ = :1", key)[0]
```

What the heck, you may say. Pretty complicated. Well, you can use the `BlobInfo.get()` method if you have the `blob_key` from the request. So, the whole thing boils down to the following:

```
photo = self.request.params.get('photo')
blob_key = photo.type_options.get('blob-key')
blobinfo = blobstore.BlobInfo.get(blob_key)
```

You can make the last line even shorter by calling the `get()` utility method from the `blobstore` module, like this:

```
blobinfo = blobstore.get(blob_key)
```

The longer explanation was just to show you how things work under the hood and there's no magic involved. It uploads the file to Blobstore, which makes an HTTP POST request to the URL that you specified. Before your request handler gets executed, a BlobInfo that contains meta data of the uploaded file is already created. It has the same datastore key as the blobstore key.

Let's take a closer look at the BlobInfo object.

More BlobInfo methods

Each BlobInfo has the following properties:

- filename: This is the name of the file.
- size: This is the size of the file in bytes.
- content_type: This is the content type of the uploaded file.
- creation: This is the time when it was uploaded. It is a datetime object.
- md5_hash: This is the MD5 hash of the file.

There are two interesting methods as well:

- open(): This will return a BlobReader instance, which acts like a file object. It is useful if you want to read and process the uploaded files. We'll have a look at this in more detail later.
- delete(): This will delete both the file from the Blobstore and the BlobInfo entity. In your request handler, which handles the HTTP POST request from Blobstore, if you are not satisfied with some of the values that the users provided, this is your chance to delete the file right there by just calling the delete() method on it.

We mentioned that BlobInfo is a model-like class. So, it has two more interesting methods. One is the all() method:

```
allfiles = BlobInfo.all()
```

This will return all the uploaded files for your application. Then there's just the gql() method that we saw earlier. You can query files based on different criteria, as follows:

```
from google.appengine.ext.blobstore import BlobInfo
# Any specific file
panda = BlobInfo.gql("WHERE filename = :1", 'panda.jpg')
# For certain mime types, all the PNG images:
```

```
pngs = BlobInfo.gql("WHERE content_type = :1", 'image/png')

# All JPEG images greater then 500 kb:
jpgs = BlobInfo.gql("WHERE content_type = :1 AND size >= ", 'image/
jpg', 500 * 1024)
```

The main idea is that `BlobInfo` is just a model class representing entities in datastore, and you can leverage this fact and query whatever you want.

Serving

Now that you have a blob in Blobstore, you'd want it to be accessible to the users. Serving a blob is pretty simple. All you need is just one thing—the blob key. Once you have it, just simply set it on the response headers under the `X-AppEngine-BlobKey` key, and you're done. Google App Engine will make sure that the blob is read and sent to the requesting client:

```
class ImageHandler(webapp2.RequestHandler):
    def get(self):
        # It is just a string
        blob_key = self.request.params.get('blob-key')
        self.response.headers['X-AppEngine-BlobKey'] = str(blob_key)
```

That's all. This will appear in the browser like this:

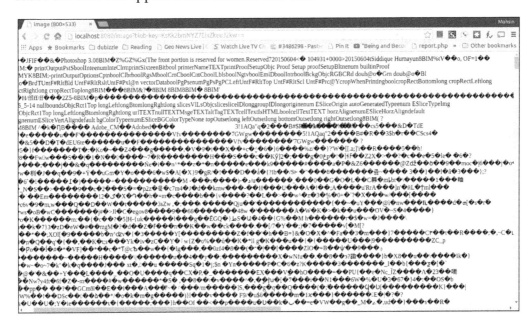

Why did this happen? This happened because the HTTP response that we sent gives out all the bytes that the file contained, but it contains no information as to what those bytes mean. Are they a PDF document, a PNG image, or an MP3 audio file? Yes, that's right. You need to send the MIME type as well if you want it to work flawlessly. How do we get the MIME type? That's why, you'll now see that `BlobInfo` is useful, as it records metadata about each blob stored in Blobstore. So, we can just fetch the `BlobInfo` and set the content type as well, like this:

```
class ImageHandler(webapp2.RequestHandler):

    def get(self):

        blob_key = self.request.params.get('blob-key')
        # Get the BlobINnfo from the key
        blob = blobstore.get(blob_key)
        # Converting strings to unicode
        self.response.headers['Content-Type'] = str(blob.content_type)
        self.response.headers['X-AppEngine-BlobKey'] = str(blob_key)
```

Note the call to the built-in `str()` function. This is used to convert the strings to normal Python strings instead of the Unicode ones because that's what the web framework expects them to be. If you want the user's browser to download and store the file on the disk instead of showing it right away in the browser, you can set the content disposition header like this:

```
        content_disposition = 'attachment; filename="{filename}"'
    .format(filename=blob.filename)
        self.response.headers['Content-Disposition'] = str(content_
    disposition)
```

Now, the user will see the file downloaded on your disk or a dialog prompting them about where to save the file depending on their browser.

The preceding solution might work very well for smaller files within a range of 1 MB or so, but for larger files, this might not be a stable solution for a few reasons. In the preceding solution, if the download stops in the middle, it will have to start from the beginning, which can be cumbersome for larger files. There's a solution in HTTP for this called a partial response. In a partial response, you can only send a portion of a larger file. For instance, for a 550 MB file, you can send just the first 10 Mbs by setting the `X-AppEngine-BlobRange` header like this:

```
self.response.headers['X-AppEngine-BlobRange'] = '0-%d' %
(1024*1024*10)
```

It will first send 10 MB of data. Now, in the next request, the client will include a Range header like this:

```
Range: bytes=10485760- 20971520
```

Now, what this means is that this time, the client wants the data from the 10th MB to the 20th MB. Both the starting and ending values are in bytes and are separated by the – character. In fact, that's how you can set the values for the Range header, as follows:

- 0-100 means the first 100 bytes
- 100- means bytes starting from the byte number 101 until the end
- -100 means the last 100 bytes

This is useful in case the client has downloaded a certain number of bytes and some error occurs. The client can inform the server in a subsequent HTTP request the byte from which it needs to get the data, and the server will return data appropriately. This is what's called a **resumable download**.

However, you can simplify these things by using a built-in HTTP handler for Blobstore that comes with the webapp framework. Your subclass from webapp.blob_handlers.BlobstoreDownloadHandler will look like this:

```python
from gogole.appengine.ext.webapp import blob_handlers
from google.appengine.ext import blobstore

class ImageServer(blob_handlers.BlobstoreDownloadHandler):

    def get(self):
        blob_key = self.request.params.get('blob-key')

    # Just a safety check,if blob doesn't exist, send HTTP 404
        if not blobstore.get(blob-key):
            self.error(404)
            return

        self.send_blob(blob_key)
```

The send_blob takes care of everything, including the parsing of the incoming byte range headers in the HTTP requests and the sending of appropriate chunks from the blob. This takes a blob key, which can be either a string, or a BlobKey or BlobInfo instance. You can supply save_as to True so that the user will get a dialog box that asks them to save the file, whereas the filename will be picked from the BlobInfo.

But if you want to override this, simply specify a filename such as `save_as`, and it will be used instead:

```
# Picks the file name from BlobInfo
self.send_blob(blob_key, save_as=True)
# Or you can override and give a name yourself.
self.send_blob(blob_key, save_as='song.mp4')
```

So, that's all about serving blobs. You might want to read the blobs sometimes yourself instead of serving them. That's what we'll look at next.

Reading

Reading a blob is pretty simple. The `BlobReader` function from `google.appengine.ext.blobstore` is your friend. This takes a blob key and returns a file-like object that you can treat like a read-only file:

```
blob = BlobReader(blob_key)
```

To optimize for performance, you can specify a buffer size so that the data is pulled in locally to fill in the buffer like this:

```
# 5 MB buffer size
blob = BlobReader(blob_key, buffer_size=1024*1024*5)
```

The blob is just a file-like object with the `seek()` and `tell()` methods. So, if it is a large binary file, you might want to start reading from some specific position instead, which is possible too:

```
# Start reading after 10th MB
blob = BlobReader(blob_key, position=1024*1024*10)
```

This completes our discussion of the Blobstore. You can use it for large file uploads and serve them later. Pretty useful.

Users

It is often the case that there are certain parts of your web application that you don't want to be accessible to everyone, especially in the case of SaaS applications. That's where you need to guard certain functionalities or the entire application behind some sort of user management.

Google App Engine provides you with some really solid and strong user management out of the box. The process is pretty simple. The API is defined in the google.appengine.api.users package. The whole package contains a total of four functions and a single User class, which are as follows, and that's how the process works:

- get_current_user(): This returns the current logged in user. This is an instance of the User class, which we'll examine in a while. If this function returns None, this means that nobody is logged in.

- Now, in a case where nobody has logged in, we will have to serve them a login form. How do we do this? There's nothing that you have to do at your end. You just call create_login_url(), which will return a URL. Now, place the URL as a link on your page and let the user click on it. When a user clicks on this URL, they are taken to a login form that is generated and hosted by Google. Once a user logs in, it will be redirected to the URL that you can pass to the create_login_url() function as an argument while getting a URL for the login form.

- Now that you have a logged in user, you might want to determine whether a person is an admin user. An admin user is the one who is allowed to access the Google App Engine application's dashboard and console and is authorized to deploy or update new versions. So, if it is your application that you deployed and logged in, you're an admin user. This can be handy if you wish to develop admin-specific functionalities that are not visible to normal users.

- Finally, you'd want the users to log out as well. For this, we have create_logout_url(destination_url) that generates a logout URL. Once the user clicks on it, the user will be logged out and will be redirected to the destination_url.

So, this is how this looks like in practice:

```
import webapp2
from google.appengine.api import users

class LoginHandler(webapp2.RequestHandler):

    def get(self):

        # Step 1: Get current user
```

```
user = users.get_current_user()

# If user, means someone logged in.
if user:
    message = 'Hello %s! <a href="%s">Logout</a>'
    username = user.nickname()
    login_logout_url = users.create_logout_url('/')
# else, create a login URL
else:
    message = 'Hello %s. Wanna <a href="%s">login?</a>'
    username = 'stranger'
    login_logout_url = users.create_login_url('/')
self.response.write(message % (username,
    login_logout_url))
```

That's all about user management. It's pretty simple. Now, you might be wondering, there's a `login` and a `logout`, but where's the `registration` in all this? Who can log in? The answer to this is below. Here are the following types of users that can sign in:

- A user with a Google account such as `mohsinhijazee@gmail.com`, `john@gmail.com`, and so on

- A Google Apps user who is tied to a specific domain such as `mohsin.hijazee@olx.com`

- Anyone with Open ID

The support for Open ID is experimental. So, its support might be withdrawn altogether or it might change significantly. Therefore, we will skip our discussion on this.

Note that the aforementioned options are mutually exclusive and are set when you create the application. Once you have decided to allow only users from a certain Google Apps domain, you cannot change it back for normal Google users or Open ID. Similarly, if you opted for Google users, you can only switch between Open ID and the Google account users and cannot later restrict them to a certain Google Apps domain.

Like the HTTP protocol itself, Google App Engine also has no notion about sessions. This has an impact if you want to build your own user management system instead of relying on the Users service provided by Google App Engine. In the initial days of Google App Engine, this meant that you either had to implement your own session management code using Memcache or datastore to store session data or rely on the web framework's support. But almost no web framework had this kind of support for Google App Engine out of the box. Things have changed now. You can use webapp2.extras.sessions to create a session store that is backed up on either just the HTTP cookies, Memcache, or datastore, like this:

```
import webapp2
from webapp2_extras import sessions

class BaseHandler(webapp2.RequestHandler):
    """
    Base class for all handlers.
    """
    def dispatch(self):
        """
        This method gets called before get(), put(),
post()
        """

        # Create the session store. It is just a store,
nothing
        # is specified how it would store the session
        # data
        self.session_store = sessions.get_
store(request=self.request)

        try:
            # Now let the things happen
            webapp2.RequestHandler.dispatch(self)
        finally:
            # And then save session store
```

```
            self.session_store.save_sessions(self.
response)

    def session(self):
        # Backend can be any of datastore, memcache,
and securecookie
        # which is default.
        return self.session_store.get_
session(backend='memcache')
```

Now, you can access the session like this:

```
self.session['price'] = 70
# And get it back later:
self.session['price']
```

You can do and build whatever you want on top of session management, as just shown.

Now, coming back to the User class. What is it? There are a total of five methods on it, two of which are related to OpenID. As we're not discussing OpenID here, this all that you've got:

- user_id(): This returns a string, which is a unique user ID. This stays the same forever, even if a user's email changes later.

- email(): This returns the email of the user.

- nickname(): This returns the user's nickname, which is usually the first part in their email address, such as john if the email address is john@gmail.com.

That's all. It's as simple as advertised.

Storing users in datastore

If you want to store references to a certain user, always store the value from user_id(), as that's guaranteed not to change ever. So for example, if we have an Album model and you'd like to associate it to the currently logged in user, this is how you'll do it:

```
from google.appengine.ext import ndb
from google.appengine.api import users

class Album(ndb.Model):
```

```
        name = ndb.StringProperty()
        user = ndb.StringProperty()

    user = users.get_current_user()

    # If the user is not logged in.
    if not user:
        # log the error, abort execution etc.
        print "User is not logged in, can't create album."
        return

    holidays = Album(name="Holidays in Holland")
    # user_id() returns a string.
    holidays.user = user.user_id()
    album.put()
```

Images

Just because it is useful to some extent, we are going to talk about the image processing capabilities that are available to you on Google App Engine. They might not be as sophisticated as you'd expect from other image processing libraries in other languages, but they are still good enough for most common cases in web applications.

The entire functionality resides in the google.appengine.api.images module. The main class here is Image, which can be initialized with raw binary data like this:

```
    image = Image(image_data=data)
    where data can be from a file or from request like this:
    class ImageResize(webapp2.RequestHandler):
        def post(self):
            # photo is an <input type='file'> from HTML request
            photo = self.request.params.get('photo')
            # photo is FieldStorage class which has file attribute
                which is like a file object.
            image = images.Image(image_data=photo.file.read())
```

The Image class can also be initialized from Blobstore if you have a blob key as a string or a BlobKey or a BlobInfo object. You can initialize the image instance like this:

```
    image = images.Image(blob_key=blob)
```

Your image will be ready for further processing. Now, the mode of operation is that you apply whatever transformations you want to, on this image object, which can be one of the following:

- `image.horizontal_flip()`: This flips the image horizontally.

- `image.vertical_flip()`: This flips the image vertically.

- `image.rotate(degrees)`: This rotates the image by the given degrees. The `degree` must be an integer and must be a multiple of 90.

- `image.resize(width=0, height=0, allow_stretch)`: This resizes the image, as follows:
  - If only `height` or `width` are specified, the image is resized to that height or width, whereas the second dimension is resized while maintaining the aspect ratio.
  - If both `width` and `height` are specified and `allowed_stretch` is set to `True`, the image is stretched to fit in the specified dimensions and in such a case, the aspect ratio won't be maintained anymore.

- `image.crop(left, top, right, bottom)`: This crops the image according to the given dimension. This basically defines a cropping box. Each of the number is a `float` in the range of `0` to `1.0`. You can think of it as a percentage of the image that needs to be cropped. So, a value of `0.1` for `left` and `top` means that 10 percent of the image width from the left should be cropped and `10` percent of the image height should be cropped from the top. Now, if you specify `0.9` for `bottom` and `right`, this will actually define a bounding box that will crop the image by 10 percent from each side.

- `image.im_feeling_lucky()`: This just automatically adjusts the contrasts and colors of the image. This is something that is very specific to Google, as you can guess from the method name.

Now, the following is a simple handler that performs many operations on the uploaded file:

```
class ImageResize(webapp2.RequestHandler):

    def post(self):
        photo = self.request.params.get('photo')
        image = images.Image(image_data=photo.file.read())

        image.crop(0.1, 0.1, 0.9, 0.9)
        image.resize(width=128)
```

```
        image.horizontal_flip()
        image.vertical_flip()
        image.rotate(90)
        image.im_feeling_lucky()

        new_image = image.execute_transforms()

        self.response.headers['Content-Type'] = 'image/png'
        self.response.write(new_image)
```

As you can see, we read the file data from the request and applied some transformations. Finally, we executed the `execute_transforms()` method on the image object, which returns the newly transformed image data as `str` (a Python string), which we simply write to the response along with the content type.

This is useful, but if you only want to resize the image from Blobstore and serve it as a thumbnail, as is usually the case with web applications, you're better off using the `get_serving_url()` method like this:

```
url = get_serving_url(blob_key, size=64)
```

This will return a URL that will be directly served by the highly optimized Google's image serving URL. This won't cost you instance hours, because your request handlers won't serve this image as we've been doing so far.

Putting it all together

Now that we had a look at the various services that are available to us on Google App Engine, it is time to put these things together. We are going to develop a very simple application that lets users log in and log out. Once logged in, users can upload pictures with a title and description. The uploaded pictures are listed on the page along with previews. Each user of course has their own collection when they log in and can't see photos from another user. We use users, namespace, Memcache, Blobstore, and the images API to implement this. Let's go through the code file by file.

First, we have `config.py`, which contains a few definitions:

```
import os
import jinja2
# Used as key to store rendered photo templates in memcache
PHOTOS_CACHE_KEY = 'photos'
CURRENT_DIRECTORY = os.path.dirname(__file__)
TEMPLATES_DIRECTORY = os.path.join(CURRENT_DIRECTORY, 'templates')
JINJA_ENV = jinja2.Environment(loader=jinja2.
FileSystemLoader(TEMPLATES_DIRECTORY))
```

The next in logical order that is close to the `config.py` is `appengine_config.py`.
The functions in this file are executed on every incoming request before our request
handlers. This is how it looks like:

```
from google.appengine.api import users

def namespace_manager_default_namespace_for_request():
    user = users.get_current_user()

    # If no logged in user, return the default namespace.
    if not user:
        return ""

    return user.user_id()
```

The `namespace_manager_default_namespace_for_request()` method is
invoked by Google App Engine's runtime every time a request comes in. This in
turn gets the currently logged in user and sets its user ID as the current namespace.
That way, data will be automatically partitioned for each user separately. If no user
has logged in, we return an empty string, which denotes the default namespace.

Next, we have `models.py`, which defines a simple model to store the photos that
are uploaded by a user:

```
from google.appengine.ext import ndb

class Photo(ndb.Model):
    """
    Stores a compressed HTML page.
    """
    title = ndb.StringProperty()
    description = ndb.TextProperty()
    picture = ndb.BlobKeyProperty()
```

The rest is business as usual except for the following two things:

- The picture property is of the `ndb.BlobKeyProperty()` type. So, the value
  it expects is an instance of `BlobKey`, which can be obtained by calling the
  `BlobInfo.key()` function. As discussed in detail, `BlobInfo` is a model-like
  object and is stored in datastore. Similarly, the instances of `BlobKey` are keys
  except that it is a different class name. This is a somewhat unfortunate design
  decision by App Engine's design team. The underlying objects really are a
  datastore entity and a key, but they are artificially made not to look like a
  datastore entity on the API level. However internally, they actually are.

- We promised that each user will have their own photos and they won't be able to see each other's uploaded photos. But here in the model, we don't see any user attribute on which we may filter the stored photos. How does this work then? It works by using namespaces. Whenever a user logs in, we set the namespace to the currently logged in user's user ID, as we just saw.

> Because we are using the user ID, which is always unique, this is not going to happen. But in case we choose something that is not unique across users (such as the first name or something like that), then of course things will be mixed together for the users sharing a common namespace name. This situation is known as data leakage and to avoid it, you should ensure that the strings that you use for namespace are unique across your users or whatever base of compartmentalization you're aiming for.

Now, let's look at the utility functions in `utils.py`:

```python
import logging

import config
from google.appengine.api import images
from google.appengine.api import memcache
from google.appengine.api import users

from models import Photo


def get_photos():
    """
    Gets photos and renders the template
    """

    rendered_template = memcache.get(config.PHOTOS_CACHE_KEY)

    if rendered_template:
        return rendered_template

    photos_template = config.JINJA_ENV.get_template("photos.html")
    photos_template.globals['images'] = images
    photos = Photo.query()

    rendered_template = photos_template.render({'photos': photos})
```

```
        memcache.set(config.PHOTOS_CACHE_KEY, rendered_template)

        return rendered_template

def create_photo(request):
    """
    Creates the photo from request.
    """
    photo = request.params.get('photo')
    title = request.params.get('title')
    description = request.params.get('description')
    blob_key = photo.type_options.get('blob-key')
    blob_info = blobstore.get(blob_key)

    photo = Photo()
    photo.title = title
    photo.description = description
    photo.picture = blob_info.key()
    photo.put()

    # And most importantly, invalidate the cache.
    memcache.delete(config.PHOTOS_CACHE_KEY)

def get_login_logout_urls():

    # Get the currently logged in user
    user = users.get_current_user()

    login_url = logout_url = ''

    if user:
        logged_in = True
        logout_url = users.create_logout_url('/')
    else:
        logged_in = False
        login_url = users.create_login_url('/')

    return {
            'login_url': login_url,
            'logout_url': logout_url,
            'logged_in': logged_in
            }
```

As you can see, there are just three functions defined here:

- `get_photos()`: This first checks in Memcache whether something exists in Memcache under `config.PHOTOS_CACHE_KEY`, and if something does exist in it, it is returned. But in case nothing exists in Memcache, it gets all the `Photo` entities from datastore. Next, it obtains a template from `templates/photos.html` and passes the list of the `Photo` entities to it. But before that, it makes sure that the `google.appengine.api.images` module is available within the template by putting it in the `template.globals` dictionary like this:

```
photos_template.globals['images'] = images
```

We'll see later how this is used. Now finally, the template is rendered and the resulting string is set in Memcache so that we don't have to fetch entities again and render the template if it is asked for again.

- `create_photo()`: This takes a request object and extracts request parameters out of it, creates a datastore entity, and stores it. Take note of the place where we obtain the `blob-key` from the request, obtain the `Blob_Info` object for it, and assign its key (the `BlobKey` instance) to the new `Photo` entity. These three steps look like this:

```
blob_key = photo.type_options.get('blob-key')
blob_info = blobstore.get(blob_key)
photo = Photo()
photo.picture = blob_info.key()
```

- As you can see, we assigned the `BlobKey` instance by calling the `BlobInfo.key()` method to the `Photo` entity's picture property. Note that because a new `Photo` entity is created, the already rendered `photos.html` template in Memcache, if any, is obsolete now and shall be rendered again. Therefore, we delete the key from Memcache, which will render it again in a subsequent call to the `get_photos()` function.

- `get_login_logout_urls()`: This simply returns three things in a dictionary—whether a user is logged in or not and the login and logout URLs.

Now, let's take a look at the `templates/photos.html` template that we just talked about:

```
<table>
        <tr>
            <th>Title</th>
            <th>Description</th>
            <th>Preview</th>
            <th>Download link</th>
        </tr>
```

```
{% for photo in photos %}
<tr>
    <td>{{photo.title}}</td>
    <td>{{photo.description}}</td>
    <td><img src="{{images.get_serving_url(photo.picture,
        size=64)}}"></td>
    <td><a href="/images/download?blob-key=
        {{photo.picture}}">Download</a></td>
</tr>
{% endfor %}
</table>
```

This is a pretty simple template. There's nothing new in it except for the highlighted code. You may recall that we passed the reference to the google.appengine.api. images module to the template under globals so that it can be accessed within the template. Now, for each stored blob, we are generating a smaller URL with a size of 64 pixels. The other interesting thing is the download URL that we are generating. It is simply /images/download?blob-key=key, and we will handle it in the section on request handlers.

Next is the main template, which is templates/index.html. It looks like this:

```
<!doctype html>
<html>
<head>
    <title>Photo Album</title>
</head>
<body>
{% if logged_in %}
    <h2>Album in cloud!</h2>
    <p>
    You can upload a picture along with its title and description.
        Its on us to retain it
    in the cloud for you. Simple, easy, free! You can <a
        href="{{logout_url}}">logout here</a> if you're done with
            your
    album management.
    </p>
    <form action="{{upload_url}}" method="post"
        enctype="multipart/form-data">
        <input type="text" name="title" placeholder="Enter
            title"><br>
        <textarea name="description" placeholder="More description
            for photo"></textarea><br>
        <input type="file" name="photo">
        <input type="submit" value="Upload">
```

```
   </form>
   <h2>Your photos</h2>
   {{photos}}
{% else %}
<h2>Album in cloud!</h2>
   <p>
   This simple application lets you maintain your pictures in an
album stored in cloud. But to use it, you will have to login. Please
<a href="{{login_url}}">click here</a> to login.
   </p>
{% endif %}
</body>
</html>
```

Now, at the very outset, we have a condition based on the value of the `logged_in` variable. This variable is passed from the request handler to the template, where it actually comes from the `get_login_logout_urls()` function. If the user is not logged in, we simply output a message with a link to the login URL. In case the user is logged in, we render a form with three fields—`title`, `description`, and `photo`. Note that the form `action` attribute is set to `upload_url`, which was obtained by calling `blobstore.create_upload_url()`. The logout URL is also shown in case the user wants to log out. As regards photos, you can see that the `photos` variable is rendered in the output as is. This too is passed from the request handler, where it is obtained by the `get_photos()` functions that we just examined in `utils.py`.

Now comes the last bit—the orchestration stuff. The `main.py` contains all the request handlers:

```
import logging
import webapp2
import jinja2

from google.appengine.ext import blobstore
from google.appengine.api.namespace_manager import get_namespace
import config
import utils


class MainPage(webapp2.RequestHandler):
    """
    The main page.
    """
    def get(self):

        # Get login, log out URLs. This returns a dict.
```

```
        values = utils.get_login_logout_urls()

        # Add form upload URL
        values['upload_url'] = blobstore.create_upload_url('/')
        # This returns rendered photos template from
            templates/photos.html.
        # Rendered separately so that we can cache it.
        values['photos'] = utils.get_photos()

        logging.info("Current namespace: %s" % get_namespace())

        main_template =
            config.JINJA_ENV.get_template("index.html")
        self.response.write(main_template.render(values))

    def post(self):
        """
        Handles photo upload
        """

        # Create the photo from request.
        utils.create_photo(self.request)
        return self.redirect('/')

class ImageDownloadHandler(webapp2.RequestHandler):
    """
    Handles the image serving.
    """
    def get(self):

        blob_key = self.request.params.get('blob-key')

        content_disposition = 'attachment; filename="{filename}"'
        blob = blobstore.get(blob_key)
        self.response.headers['Content-Type'] =
            str(blob.content_type)
        self.response.headers['X-AppEngine-BlobKey'] = str(blob_key)
        self.response.headers['Content-Disposition'] = str(content_
disposition.format(filename=blob.filename))

app = webapp2.WSGIApplication([
    ('/?', MainPage),
    ('/images/download/?', ImageDownloadHandler)

], debug=True)
```

At the very end, this file contains the following two request handlers:

- `MainPage`: This will render a template in the case of an HTTP GET request. It simply calls the utility functions, which we already discussed. In case of an HTTP POST, we create the photo by calling the `create_photo()` function, which we discussed under `utils.py`.

- `ImageDownloadHandler`: This handles image downloads. It reads the `blobkey` from the HTTP request and gets the BlobInfo object by calling the `blobstore.get()` method so that we can set an appropriate file name and MIME type. Finally, it sets the `blob-key` to the `X-AppEngine-BlobKey` response header, which makes Google App Engine read the `blob` from Blobstore and serve it to the user. Note that we set the `Content-Disposition` header so that instead of the image being shown with the browser, it prompts for a **Save** dialog box, which of course varies from browser to browser.

- Finally, to top it off and bind it together, we have the `app.yaml`, which is very simple this time:

```
application: album
version: 2
runtime: python27
api_version: 1
threadsafe: true


handlers:
- url: /.*
  script: main.app

libraries:
- name: jinja2
  version: "2.6"
```

You can run this application locally as well given that you have `pillow` installed. To install `pillow` in a virtual environment, here's how you'd do it:

```
$ pip install pillow
```

However, if you do not have a virtual environment and want it across the system, you'll have to execute it with `sudo`, like this:

```
$ sudo pip install pillow
```

Now, run the application, as follows:

```
$ /path/to/appengine/sdk/dev_appserver /path/to/album/app
```

Point your browser to `http://localhost:8080` and click on **login**. For the local development server, you can enter any e-mail address without a password, and you'll be logged in as that user. But of course, when deployed on production, this will not be the case. Try logging in with some user, upload a few pictures, log out, and then log in as a different user. You'll find that the latter user has no uploaded photos. Upload a few photos for this user too, log out, and log in as the previous user. You'll find that both the users have different sets of photos. This is the compartmentalization that namespaces offer us without us attributing each uploaded user with its use.

Summary

We covered a lot of ground in this chapter. We saw that sometimes, storing the computed results can be useful for performance. So, we introduced Memcache, and that is how we can add and delete keys. Then, we turned our attention towards multi-tenancy. We saw that we can use namespace features for the compartmentalization of our app, thus letting multiple users, or organizations use our application without getting into the complicated logic at our end. Next, we looked at services provided for the user and how to create the login and logout URLs. We learned how to log in and how to log users out.

From that point, we focused on how to upload files using Blobstore. We learned that uploads are handled by Blobstore and once the uploads are done, our application receives an HTTP POST request. Each uploaded file has a corresponding entity of the `__BlobInfo__` kind, which is represented by the `BlobInfo` class. We explored how Blobstore works internally by using HTTP external request bodies. We also examined how to serve stored blobs and use partial HTTP responses to send partial files.

After that, we looked into the images API and the available operations. Finally, we put this all into practice by implementing a sample application, which allowed users to sign in and upload images.

Now that we know some of the useful services that are available to us, we're getting closer towards the construction and deployment of a useful application. In the next chapter, we will take a closer look at how to deploy applications in production.

10
Application Deployment

Developing an application is an exciting thing in that you can bring your idea to life, solve interesting problems, and see how the whole thing comes to life. But nothing is as exciting as floating your application out in the wild for users to use. That's right, launching or deploying an application into production is what we are talking about. This chapter is all about deployment.

We will study the following topics in this chapter:

- Deployment configurations, versions, and scaling options
- Dividing applications into modules
- Crons, logs, and admin pages
- Profiling and remotely accessing an application environment

So, that's a tall but interesting order. Let's get started.

Deployment configurations

Let's review the various configuration files that are part of an application:

- `app.yaml`: This is the main configuration file that contains information about request handlers, libraries, and other things.
- `index.yaml`: This is automatically generated by the development server. It is required to build indexes for a datastore. We have discussed this in detail.
- `queue.yaml`: This defines queues and the related configuration. We've covered this as well.
- `cron.yaml`: This defines tasks that should be executed repeatedly. We'll learn about that in this chapter.

- `dos.yaml`: This is used to blacklist certain requesting IP addresses to prevent Denial of Service attacks (**DoS**). You can read more about this at `https://cloud.google.com/appengine/docs/python/config/dos`.

- `dispatch.yaml`: This is used with modules. We'll explore modules in this chapter and this file as well.

We will examine the newer files in detail later in this chapter, but let's focus on how to deploy applications for now.

Deployment revisited

Before we start exploring various deployment configurations, let's revise how to deploy an application. The most basic command that can be used to deploy the application is this:

```
$ /path/to/gae/sdk/appcfg.py update /path/to/app/dir/containing/app.yaml
```

Instead of writing `/path/to/gae/sdk/appcfg.py`, we will just write `appcfg.py`. You should assume the rest. Also, instead of `/path/to/app/dir/containing/app.yaml`, we will just write `app/dir`, and you should assume that it is either absolute or relative to the application directory that contains `app.yaml`.

In the older versions of the SDK, you were asked for your e-mail and password to deploy the application. Now this has changed, and OAuth 2 is the way to go. In future versions, the e-mail and password approach might be discontinued and this could be the default authentication mechanism, but for now you have to specify the `--oauth2` flag for OAuth based authentication, like this:

```
$ appcfg.py update --oauth2 app/dir
```

This will open up a browser where you have to enter your e-mail and password. You'll be authenticated and the application will be deployed. In case you don't have access to a browser in cases where you have no UI (as in a server environment), you can pass in the `--noauth_local_webserver` flag, like this:

```
$ appcfg.py update --oauth2 --noauth_local_webserver app/dir
```

Now this command, instead of opening a browser, will print a link for you that can be copied and opened up in some other browser (maybe on your mobile or another laptop) and you can enter your credentials. Once done with this, you'll be given a verification code that has to be pasted back on the prompt.

If you authenticated using the password-based approach, a cookie is stored in your home directory under the `.appcfg_cookie` filename, and if you opted for an `Oauth 2` based approach, the access token is stored in the JSON format in a file named `.appcfgy_oauth2_tokens`. This is important if you are doing this on a machine that is not yours. In this case, you should remove these files once you're done.

When you deploy an application like this, all the configuration files (`index.yaml`, `cron.yaml`, `queues.yaml`, and `dos.yaml`) get updated automatically.

Add individual component updates, download source code, and download logs.

Versions

A Google App Engine application, when deployed, can have many versions. A version is specified in `app.yaml` like this:

```
version: first-launch
```

The version number can contain numbers, letters, and hyphens, and can have a maximum length of 63 characters. However, you can use as version names neither the `default` or the `latest`, nor any string that starts with `ah` because many internal URLs start with `ah`. The rest is up to you to decide what you want to name the version.

Note that the `version` is optional in `app.yaml`, and if not specified, it can be specified on the command line to `appcfg.py` like this:

```
$ appcfg.py update –version my-version app/dir
```

In case the version is specified in `app.yaml` and is given on the command line as well, the command line version takes precedence.

When an application is deployed and there's an already a version of the same name as specified in `app.yaml` (or on the command line), then it is overwritten by the files on the disk. But if the version of the given name doesn't exist, a new version is created and files are copied from the disk to Google App Engine.

Each Google App Engine application can have a maximum of 10 versions. This means that Google App Engine actually has 10 copies of your application code. If you upload another version when you already have 10 versions, you'll get an error.

So, this means that an application can have many versions. But which version will serve the incoming traffic when a user hits a URL? The answer is that every application has a default version, which can be selected from the admin console. When uploading a new version, it is automatically made the default version.

Now, the other issue is that when we hit the application URL, we are served with the default version automatically. Is there any way for us to get served by an older version of the application instead of the default one? The answer is yes. Basically, if your application ID is `myapp`, then its URL will be `http://myapp.appspot.com`, which will be served by the default version. But you can address and get served by any application version by using the `http://<version>.myapp.appspot.com` scheme. So, if your application has a version called `search-fixes`, which is not the default version, you can access it by using `http://search-fixes.myapp.appspot.com`.

This brings us to the following general URL scheme:

`http://[version].[application_id].appspot.com`

Just keep in mind that this general URL scheme will have two more components. We'll explore them when we learn more about our deployment options.

The instance classes

The question is, what is running your code? These are actually the virtual machine's instances that are running. Can we configure the type of machine that runs our code? We certainly can. The following are the types of instances that are available to us:

- F1 with 128 MB RAM and 600 MHz processor

- F2 with 256 MB RAM and 1.2 GHz processor

- F4 with 512 MB RAM and 2.4 GHz processor

- F4_1G with 1024 MB RAM and 2.4 GHz processor

These are the instance types that are available for automatic scaling.

 So, it turns out that there are various types of scaling when it comes to Google App Engine. Yes, there are basically three types of scaling modes—**Manual scaling**, **Basic scaling**, and **Automatic scaling**. We will explore each of these modes in detail shortly.

In case we have manual or basic scaling, the following are the types of available instances:

- B1 with 128 MB RAM and 600 MHz processor
- B2 with 256 MB RAM and 1.2 GHz processor
- B4 with 512 MB RAM and 2.4 GHz processor
- B4_1G with 1024 MB RAM and 2.4 GHz processor
- B8 with 1024 MB RAM and 4.8 GHz processor

> We have been using the phrase virtual machines here. Technically speaking, and as is apparent from the time it takes to boot new instances in Google App Engine, these are not virtual machines. Rather, they are Linux containers, such as Docker. Starting a virtual machine's instance is a very slow process as it involves memory allocations and it actually boots up the whole guest operating system.

By default, all applications have automatic scaling. So, your choices in this case are limited to the F series of instances. Let's suppose that we want our code to run on a 2.4 GHz machine with 1 GB RAM. We will specify the type of instance that we want to use in `app.yaml` by using an `instance_class` directive like this:

```
instance_class: F4_1G
```

Now, let's divert our attention to how we can access individual instances.

Instance addressability

An application can have many versions, as we know by now. An application version runs on one or more instances, depending on the traffic or scaling configurations, as we will see when we look at the scaling options. Each virtual machine instance, when created, gets a unique ID, and of course a version can have many instances running to serve requests.

> It is pertinent to note that it is not necessary that an application version (even the default one) always has an instance running for it, and this largely depends on the scaling configurations that we'll explore shortly. But one such interesting case is where you have an old version of your application and someone accesses it via a URL after a very long time. In this case, there will be no instance to serve the request. So, one virtual machine instance will be booted to serve the request. A side effect of this is that this first request will have some delay because of this VM instantiation process.

So, the question is, can we also make our request be served by a specific running instance out of many? The answer is yes. This `http://00c61b117c2d8ea3916d6263` `1c6e7fea12d3d626.downloader.mgae-01.appspot.com/` request not only targets a specific version (downloader) of the application `mgae-01`, but also a specific instance with the ID as `00c61b117c2d8ea3916d62631c6e7fea12d3d626`.

So now, our updated URL scheme turns out to be `http://[instance-id].` `[version].[application-id].appspot.com`.

The only catch is that this only works for basic or manual scaling and doesn't work for automatic scaling, which is the default mode.

In summary, an application can have many versions, and a version can have many running instances to serve requests. We can target our requests to both a specific version or a specific running instance.

Scaling types

Now that we know about the various types of virtual machine instances that are available to us and how we can specify that in `app.yaml` using the `instance_class` directive, let's take a look at the scaling options that we have in Google App Engine. There are basically three types of scaling at our disposal:

- Manual scaling
- Basic scaling
- Automatic scaling

Automatic scaling is the default type of scaling at work when you don't specify one. Let's take a look at each of these types of scaling.

Manual scaling

When you opt for manual scaling for your application, these instances will run continuously forever until you shut them down yourself from the admin console. You have only one configuration parameter when specifying manual scaling, and that is the number of instances that you want to run. To specify manual scaling, use the following in the `app.yaml` (or in the other configuration files, as we'll explore when going through modules) like this:

```
instance_class: B4
manual_scaling:
    instances: 5
```

Chapter 10

Now here `manual_scaling` specifies that we are opting for manual scaling. The instances directive is the only applicable directive, and we supplied a value of `5`, which means that five instances will be running. No matter how much traffic your application gets, just a single request in the entire day or thousands of requests per minute, five instances are all that you've got running.

 The `instance_class` is not part of the scaling options, and we have seen this directive already.

There are a few noteworthy things about manual scaling, which are as follows:

- You may recall that request handlers have a deadline of 60 seconds to produce a response and 10 minutes to process a task. This is not the case with manual scaling. To handle a request, instances with manual scaling have an indefinite amount of time to respond. In contrast, for the task requests from task queues, instances with manual scaling have 24 hours to run.

- Once started, these instances remain in memory (in memory because these are the virtual machines or docker containers; they are in the main memory of the host OS).

- You may also recall that we cannot create background threads in request handlers. This is not the case with instances that have manual scaling. You can create threads and do things in the background.

- When an instance is started, it gets a `/_ah/start` request. Your code can handle this request and start something lengthy without ever returning an HTTP response. This is useful if you want to initialize and kick off something.

- When an instance is stopped (either from the admin console, or for some other reason), it gets a `/_ah/stop` request. Your code can handle this to perform any shutdown and cleanup. Note that if you handle this, your code has a maximum of 30 seconds to perform whatever it wants to. We'll talk about when and how instances are started and stopped in detail.

- The instances that have manual scaling are addressable, just as we discussed earlier. We will revisit the instance addressability in detail in a while.

So, that's all about manual scaling. It is very simple. You just define the number of instances you need, and they will keep on running all the time. However, when they are started, they get a /_ah/start request. If you respond to this request with a code range of 200 to 299 or an HTTP 404, all goes well. Otherwise, the instance will be terminated and another one will be created. As far as stopping is concerned, these types of instance will receive a /_ah/stop request that, you have to process and clean up within 30 seconds.

Now, let's take a look at the next mode of scaling.

Basic scaling

In basic scaling, Google App Engine scales the application for you, but only up to the limits that you define. You can define the following two parameters:

- You can define the maximum number of instances Google App Engine can start for you.

- Optionally, you can define the time after which the instances will be shut down if they don't receive any request. If you don't specify this, it defaults to 5 minutes.

This is how you define it in app.yaml:

```
basic_scaling:
    max_instances: 20
    idle_timeout: 10m
```

So here, what we are telling Google App Engine is that it should handle scaling for our application as the incoming traffic increases, but it should boot a maximum of 20 instances and no more. Further, if an instance doesn't get a request for 10 minutes, shut it down. Pretty simple.

Now, the following are a few notable things about basic scaling:

- The deadlines for request execution are the same as those for manual scaling. The requests can run indefinitely, and for task queue requests, you have 24 hours as the deadline before timeout. Instances, when started, get a /_ah/start request, and when stopped, get a /_ah/stop request as well, just as in manual scaling.
- Threading is allowed just as in manual scaling.
- Individual instances are addressable just as in manual scaling.

The only difference between basic and manual scaling is that in manual scaling, instances are created for you up to your specified maximum limit and are turned down only after a certain amount of idle time.

Now, let's take a look at the last and most advanced scaling mode.

Automatic scaling

This is the default scaling mode when you specify nothing. It scales your application to whatever number of instances are is required to serve the traffic, but you get a chance to configure it according to your particular needs. You may recall from our discussion on how Google App Engine applications scale (in *Chapter 1, Understanding the Runtime Environment*) that there's a queue called the **request queue**. All the incoming requests are enqueued in the queue and handed over to an available instance. Now, with this in mind, you can tweak the following parameters:

- `min_idle_instances`: This is the minimum number of idle instances that run all the time. If this is a high number, you will have many instances running all the time regardless of the amount of incoming traffic. This will of course cost more, as the instances will be running all the time. On the other hand, a lower number will cost less but the requests might face a delay if all the idle instances are busy and Google App Engine has to spin new instances.

- `max_idle_instances`: This is the maximum number of idle instances that run all the time. If this number is high, Google App Engine will scale down gradually and more slowly after it has served a spike of incoming traffic. For instance, we set the maximum number of idle instances to 25 and currently, there are only five instances running. Now, an incoming spike comes in and the system has to boot many instances, say up to 50 instances. Now, because 25 is quite a high number, the system will bring the whole fleet down much more slowly and gradually to 25 running instances compared to a situation where it was set to a lower value, such as five maximum idle instances.

- `min_pending_latency`: This is the minimum amount of time an incoming request should wait in queue before Google App Engine spins a new instance to handle it. A low number would mean the requests will spend less time in a queue, and Google App Engine will spin an instance to handle it. This will result in more instances and will cost more. On the other hand, if this value is high, Google App Engine will make the request wait in the queue longer and users will face a slight delay if all the existing instances are busy serving requests.

- `max_pending_latency`: This is the maximum amount of time a request should wait in queue before starting a new instance. After this time, if there's no available instance, Google App Engine will start a new instance even when there's no available instance to handle the request.

- `max_concurrent_requests`: This is the maximum concurrent requests an instance should be handling at a time. This defaults to 8 requests if you don't specify. Now, if you set it to a higher number, each instance will handle more requests and hence you'll need fewer of instances. It mainly depends on what kind of things you are doing in your request handlers and how much compute-intensive they are. Furthermore, if your code is not doing much, you can safely increase this number. But you should experiment and tweak this number very carefully so that the instances are not overburdened. It is interesting to note that the maximum value that you can specify as the number of requests that an instance can handle concurrently is 80.

We talked about the minimum number of instances in the preceding session. This means that a reserved army of instances is used to serve the incoming requests. Shouldn't it then be prepared for this like some sort of initialization, like the `/_ah/start` requests for instances with manual and basic scaling? Instances with automatic scaling don't get a `/_ah/start` request. Instead, they get a warm-up request, which has to be enabled in `app.yaml` under `inbound services`, like this:

```
inbound_services:
- warmup
```

Now, when Google App Engine spins new instances, they get an HTTP GET request to `/_ah/warmup`, which can be handled, and you can do whatever required initialization is specific to your application. These requests will only be dispatched by Google App Engine if you set the `min_idle_instances` to something other then `auto`.

Now, lets' take a look at the sample configuration in `app.yaml`:

```
automatic_scaling:
  min_idle_instances: 5
  max_idle_instances: 25  # default value is automatic.
  min_pending_latency: 30ms  # default value is automatic
  max_pending_latency: automatic
  max_concurrent_requests: 50
```

Each incoming request has a maximum of 60 seconds to generate a response, and after that, an exception of the DeadlineExceededError type is raised, which can be handled, and you can quickly take note of things. For the requests coming from the task queues and the cron entries, a maximum of 10 minutes is allowed.

Some of the characteristics of the automatic scaling are:

- No threading is allowed at all.
- Instances are to be of the F1, F2, F4, or F4_1G types.
- Individual instances aren't addressable, as you can with manual and basic scaling types.

So, with this, we are done with the scalability options and configurations that are available to us in Google App Engine. It's time to see what we can do with the different types of scalability options.

Modules

Now that we know about scaling types, we seem to have one limitation. We can only opt for a single type of scaling in our application. Either we can opt for manual scaling, in which case we will have a fixed number of instances with no scalability at all, or we can go for either of the basic or automatic scaling. This is not very useful, because we might have different scaling requirements for different things in our application. For example, for a mobile request, we'd like to have automatic scalability with the minimum possible latency, whereas for any long-running tasks or compute-intensive things such as image processing, we might want to have a certain number of instances running all the time.

But the issue is that in our app.yaml file, we can opt for only one type of scaling. How do we work around that? Is there any solution for this problem?

Definitely yes! Each Google App Engine application can have one or more modules, and each module can have its own scaling type along with other options, including script handers. We can define a number of modules to handle different types of requests. Each yaml file looks just like app.yaml, but it has an additional directive called **module** that gives a name to the module.

Let's take a practical example. Let's suppose that our application has grown pretty popular. We are not only serving requests to users from the Web, but also have mobile users who use our API. Besides this, there are certain time-consuming tasks that we do in the background.

Now, in such a situation, a monolithic approach to deployment wouldn't be the most optimal, as an application needs to serve different things differently. That's where the modules come in. Each module is defined by a yaml file that indicates the type of scaling required (and optionally, different script handlers) and the rest is just the same.

Let's examine a very simple application and refactor it into modules to understand the whole thing better. This is the app.yaml file, which is very simple:

```
application: mgae-01
version: 1
runtime: python27
api_version: 1
threadsafe: true

handlers:
- url: .*
  script: main.application
```

We know everything here by now. A WSGI application object defined in main.py on the root directory of the project is handling everything. Now, let's examine the main.py file:

```
import webapp2
from google.appengine.api import modules

def get_code_info():
    values = {
        'module': modules.get_current_module_name(),
        'version': modules.get_current_version_name(),
        'instance': modules.get_current_instance_id(),
        }

    message = "\n\nRunning version {version} of module {module}
        on instance {instance}"

    return message.format(**values)
        class MainPage(webapp2.RequestHandler):

    def get(self):
        self.response.write('This is the web request.')
        self.response.write(get_code_info())

class APIHandler(webapp2.RequestHandler):
    def get(self):
        self.response.write('This is the API handler')
```

```
        self.response.write(get_code_info())

class BackendHandler(webapp2.RequestHandler):

    def get(self):
        self.response.write('Backend requests would be
            perfomed here.')
        self.response.write(get_code_info())

application = webapp2.WSGIApplication([
    ('/', MainPage),
    ('/api/?.*', APIHandler),
    ('/backend/?.*', BackendHandler)
], debug=True)
```

Nothing fancy here. There are just three request handlers:

- `MainPage` handles the / and is intended to serve web requests
- `APIHandler` responds to all the /api/ requests
- `BackendHandler` responds to all the /backend/ requests

The only thing is that we have a get_code_info() function that lets us know what version of what module is running on what instance that is responding to this request. We are using the functions from the Modules API to get the name of the current module, version, and the instance ID and print them out to the response.

Now, let's break into independent modules. So first, let's examine the app.yaml file itself:

```
application: mgae-01
version: 1
module: default # Not required, you can skip this
runtime: python27
api_version: 1
threadsafe: true

instance_class: F2 #Optional element, not required.

# Automatic scaling is not required, if omitted it is default.
# But in case you want to tweak some parameters:
automatic_scaling:
    min_idle_instances: 2
    max_idle_instances: automatic # Or you can set a maximum
    min_pending_latency: 30ms
    max_pending_latency: automatic # Or you can set a maximum
```

```
    max_concurrent_requests: 50

handlers:
- url: .*
  script: main.application
```

This is pretty much the standard `app.yaml`, whereas the newer elements are highlighted:

- A `module` directive tells the application that it is the `default` module. This directive is not required and defaults to `default`, but it is just added here to show that we can be explicit about it. A default module is the one that handles requests if they are not directed to any particular module. We'll come to requests and modules in a while.

- Next, we define the `instance_class`. This is optional too, but it is just included here to demonstrate its usage.

- Next, we have some automatic scaling parameters that we already discussed.

- Lastly, we are saying that all the URLs are handled by the application WSGI object in `main.py` in the root application directory. Nothing new here either. We've done this many times before.

Now, let's define another module to handle the API requests. For this, we will create another configuration `api.yaml` file, which contains following:

```
application: mgae-01
version: 1
module: api
runtime: python27
api_version: 1
threadsafe: true

instance_class: B4
basic_scaling:
    max_instances: 20
    idle_timeout: 15m

handlers:
- url: .*
  script: main.application
```

Now here, we defined another module named `api`. This module has basic scaling. The maximum number of instances allowed is 20. However, if an instance is idle for 15 minutes (didn't handle any request in the last 15 minutes) then it will be shut down. We already discussed the basic scaling in detail. So, we won't repeat all those details here.

Now, the interesting part is the handler directive. This also points to `main.py`'s `application` object. This module will have the same code as the first one, but there's nothing stopping you from putting your code for each module separately in different Python modules or packages.

Now, we'll come to the last module. This is supposed to handle any long running tasks, so it has to be running all the time. Here's the file for `backend.yaml`:

```
application: mgae-01
version: 1
module: backend
runtime: python27
api_version: 1
threadsafe: true

instance_class: B8

manual_scaling:
    instances: 10

handlers:
- url: .*
  script: main.application
```

As you can see, the rest is all the same except that we set the module name using the `module` directive to `backend`. Besides this, we also set the scaling type to `manual scaling` and set 10 instances at work of the `B8` class. In script handling, everything, yet again, is directed to the `application` object in `main.py`.

The factoring application

Here, we have three modules, but all point to the same Python file, which in turn has request handlers for different URL patterns. For larger applications, this might be very cumbersome. We can factor out an application pretty neatly. For instance, we can have three separate Python files, `main.py`, `api.py`, and `backend.py`. Now, in each of the yaml files for the modules, reference your respective Python files containing the WSGI application object. You can even have Python packages for each of the modules in directories while having the yaml module files in the application root directory. It is up to you to decide how to organize your code.

Now, to deploy this application, run the following command:

```
$ appcfg update app.yaml api.yaml backend.yaml --oauth2
```

You may have noticed that this deployment command is different from what we have been doing earlier. When you deploy modules, you have to supply the `yaml` file that needs to be deployed for each on the command line, and that's exactly what we're doing here.

If you want to run it locally, you will have to supply the the module configuration files on the command line too, like this:

```
$ dev_appserver app.yaml api.yaml backend.yaml
```

This will start all the module instances, which can be examined from the administrator console at `http://localhost:8000/`, where each instance will run on a separate port.

Now that we have factored the application into three different modules and deployed them, how do we access them? Let's learn about that.

Accessing the modules

So, when you have deployed your application, how do you access each module? Let's build our knowledge bit by bit:

- When you visit `http://mgae-01.appspot.com`, this will be served by the default module's default version, by any instance that's available to serve the request

- When you access `http://api.mgae-01.appspot.com`, this will be served by the `api` module's default version of the `mgae-01` application, with whichever instance is available

- When you visit `http://v2.api.mgae-01.appspot.com`, this will be served by the `v2` version of the `api` module of the `mgae-01` application, by any available instance

- Finally, if you visit `http://00c61b117c2d.v2.api.mgae-01.appspot.com`, this will be served by the `v2` version of the `api` module of the `mgae-01` application, running on the instance with an ID of `00c61b117c2d`

Note that you can only address individual instances if the scaling type of the module is set to either basic or manual scaling. Individual instances won't be accessible in this manner for modules that have automatic scaling. We already discussed about this while talking about instance addressability.

Now, to generalize, the following is the URL form:

```
http://instance-id.version.module.app-id.appspot.com
```

When using these services, you can use these URL forms to be specific about which application's, which module, which version should be served the request.

The dispatch.yaml file

So, we now know how to factor an application into modules and how to access each module. But what if we want certain URL paths to be handled by certain modules instead of relying on the host name / path scheme?

We can do this. The trick is a file called the dispatch.yaml file that contains the URL patterns and the modules that are supposed to handle them. This is what it looks like:

```
dispatch:
    - url: "*/api*"
      module: api
    - url: "*/backend*"
      module: backend
```

This file basically contains two path entries that map to two different modules. The first one is */api*, which means anything containing api in it should be handled by the api module. The second one means that anything starting with backend should be handled by the backend module.

 These are unfortunately not regular expressions. These are globing characters. Also note that the patterns are in quote due to the yaml syntax. Each such path entry is limited to only 100 characters and dispatch.yaml can contain a maximum of 10 entries. So use this wisely!

Now, to deploy this configuration, we execute the following:

```
$ appcfg.py update app.yaml api.yaml backend.yaml --oauth2
```

This will deploy all the modules. This will deploy the dispatch.yaml file as well, but in case you make changes to dispatch.yaml and want to deploy just that, you can do that too, as follows:

```
$ appcfg.py update_dispatch
```

After this, the URL patterns, as listed in the file, will start redirecting requests to the appropriate modules.

To run and test this locally, we will have to include the dispatch.yaml file in the list of arguments to dev_appserver.py as well, like this:

```
$ dev_appserver.py app.yaml api.yaml backend.yaml dispatch.yaml
```

Now, this will start a dispatcher on port `8080`. Run the application locally and access `http://localhost:8080/` and note what module, version, and instance information you get in response. Next, try with `http://localhost:8080/api/` and `http://localhost:8080/backend/` respectively. Note that with `dispatch.yaml` in place, these URLs are being handled by the respective modules, as configured. If you remove `dispatch.yaml` and try again, everything will go to the `default` module.

Enough of modules and requests. Let's focus on doing something else. Specifically, let's concentrate on doing things repeatedly over certain intervals.

Scheduled tasks

There are certain things that we want to do regularly over fixed intervals, such as processing some items, downloading new data from some source, or something on those lines. The typical way to do that in Unix/Linux systems is called **cron job**. In a cron job, you indicate a program or a script and a schedule on which it is supposed to run. Just like a timer or an alarm clock, this will be regularly executed for you at the specified intervals.

This kind of feature is also available in Google App Engine and is called **Scheduled tasks**. However, the processing model is slightly different in the Unix/Linux `cron` jobs, including the format of how we define a schedule. These definitions are specified in a file called `cron.yaml` in the root directory of your application, and it gets automatically uploaded with each application deployment.

In `cron.yaml`, you can define multiple `cron` entries. Each entry must define at least the following things:

- `url`: Instead of a program or a script, you define a URL. This URL will get an HTTP GET request. The receiving handler has 10 minutes to process it (but it can have more, as we'll see later), and it is supposed to return an HTTP status code in the range of 200 to 299.

- `schedule`: You can define the schedule on which the above URL should be invoked by Google App Engine. The syntax is not the same as that for the Linux/Unix `cron` entries, and it is much more readable, as we'll see in a while.

Besides these things, you can optionally define the following configuration parameters as well:

- `description`: This is a readable description of the `cron` entry. This will appear in the admin console on the local development server as well as when you deploy it in production.

- `timezone`: This is optional too. If not specified, UTC is assumed to be the time zone. But if that's not what you want, you can specify your own time zone. The value can be anything from the `tzdatabase`. Just for reference, you can visit `https://en.wikipedia.org/wiki/List_of_tz_database_time_zones`, and the values in the `TZ` column are the values that you can use.

- `target`: This is usually the hostname. This is basically used to direct the scheduled tasks to a specific module of your application. We already discussed the application modules in detail.

So, that's just two of the entries in `cron.yaml` as a sample:

```
cron:
  - description: Sends emails
    url: /jobs/emails
    schedule: every 30 minutes

  - description: Fetches feeds
    url: /jobs/feeds
    schedule: every 1 hours from 09:00 to 18:00
    timezone: Asia/Karachi
    target: downloaders
```

Here, we are actually defining two `cron` entries. The first one is supposed to send e-mails every 30 minutes. So every 30 minutes, Google App Engine will send an HTTP `GET` request to `/jobs/emails`. Your application will handle this and return an HTTP status code between 200-299 within 10 minutes. Otherwise, the `cron` invocation will be considered a failure.

> If you want to delete all the `cron` entries, just edit the `cron.yaml` file and set it to the following:
>
> ```
> cron:
> ```
>
> Deploy your application. All the existing `cron` entries will be deleted. You can only deploy the `cron.yaml` file with the following command:
>
> ```
> $ appcfg.py update_cron ./path/to/app/dir
> ```

The next entry is also just a cron job that gets executed every 1 hour but only between 9 am to 6 pm. We will look at the schedule format in detail in a while. But there are two additional things here. The first is that the timezone is set to `Asia/Karachi`. So, this means that instead of UTC, it will invoke this job every 1 hour between 9 am to 6 pm in Karachi. You can specify your own time zone as per your requirements. The valid values for the time zone are listed on the Wikipedia page mentioned earlier.

Besides all this, the `cron` entry specifies that this processing should be handled by the `downloaders` module instead of the default one.

So by now, we have a pretty good idea of how to define cron jobs on Google App Engine. However, there are two things that we need to look at in more detail, the schedule format and the protection of the URLs that handle cron.

The Scheduled tasks format

The scheduler format is pretty simple:

```
every number (minutes|hours)
```

Here, `number` is an integer, and you can choose the minutes or hours, as follows:

```
every 10 minutes
every 3 hours
```

It could be the case that you want to do something every hour but only during certain timings. A business case could be that you are pulling some data from some clients who use your system to publish their data. Now, you'd like to pull feeds every hour, but only during the business hours of 9 to 5 and not beyond that, because that's when most offices are closed and there would be almost no updates. So, it is not important to pull changes after those hours. So, this format has a restriction to it:

```
every number (minutes|hours) from start_time to end_time
```

You know the first part already. The second part specifies two time boundaries, the starting and ending time. Both are in the 24-hour `HH:MM` format. The following will execute the cron job every 30 minutes, but only from 9 am to 5 pm:

```
every 30 minutes from 09:00 to 17:00
```

This 9 am to 5 pm is in UTC time. If you want it to be in your local time, then either convert your local time into UTC and specify it here, or use the time zone directive to specify your time zone, as discussed earlier.

For cron jobs without any `from` clause restrictions, if the last invocation is still processing and the time to execute it again has come, the Google App Engine scheduler won't run it again until the last one has finished.

In contrast, when you specify a time restriction using the `from` clause, as shown in the preceding code, each job gets started, whether its last invocation has finished processing or not.

So, what if you want something to always run every 30 minutes regardless of whether its last invocation is still processing or not? We can use this clever trick:

```
every 30 minutes from 00:00 to 23:59
```

So, this means that there's a restriction round the clock. Because of the `from` clause, the job will be executed when the time comes, regardless of whether the last one has finished processing yet or not. The same can be written like this:

```
every 30 minutes synchronized
```

The `synchronized` function is just the same as saying from `00:00` to `23:59` and has the same effect—a new job will be executed regardless of whether the last one finished or not.

So now you know about how to schedule your jobs. There's another syntax that is much more powerful and expressive than this. You can say something like this:

```
every day time
```

Here, `day` can be anything such as `sunday` and `monday`, and you can specify a comma to separate the list of days as well. However, `time` has the same time format that we just saw—`HH:MM` in the 24-hour format. So for instance, this will run the job every Sunday morning at 08:00 am:

```
every sunday 08:00
```

However, you might want to run it during the weekend. So, you can do this:

```
every saturday, sunday 08:00
```

This will run the job during the weekend. But you might want to do this thing only in certain months and not every month. For instance, instead of running the task every weekend round the year, you might want to run it only during the Christmas season, which is in December. You can restrict it to a certain month like this:

```
every saturday, sunday of december 08:00
```

So here, the task will be executed every weekend at 08:00 am in December. But you might want to not only execute this job in December, but also start a little earlier in November as well. So, you can specify it like this:

```
every saturday, sunday of november, december 08:00
```

So, our general format turns out to be as follows:

```
every days [of months] time
```

Here is the general format:

- `days`: This is the name of the weekday or a list of weekdays separated by a comma
- `months`: This is optional and can be any month name or a comma-separated list of months
- `time`: This is HH:MM in the 24-hour format

Lastly, you may want to run a job only on every third Sunday at 8:00 am. So, this is how you can do it:

```
3rd sunday 08:00
```

This will execute the job every third Sunday at 08:00 in the morning. But you might want this to happen only in the last quarter of the year because of the Christmas season. So, you can write the following:

```
3rd sunday of october, november, december 08:00
```

Now this will execute the job on every third Sunday at 08:00 in the morning, but only in October, November, and December. So in general, the format is as follows:

```
ordinal days [of months] time
```

Each part of the above line stands for the following:

- `ordinal`: This is the number specification of the day, such as 1st, 2nd, 3rd, and so on. You can also use first, second, and third
- `days`: This consists of just the weekday names, as we've seen already
- `months`: This consists of the month names, as we have seen already
- `time`: This is the same 24-hour time format that we have seen

So, concluding this, the formats in which you can specify the schedule entries are listed in the following lines. The optional parts are written in square brackets, whereas any choices that need to be made are grouped by the parenthesis that are separated by the | character:

```
every number (minutes|hours) [from time to time]
every 30 minutes
every 2 hours from 09:00 to 17:00

every days [of months] time
every sunday 08:00
```

```
every saturday, sunday of june, july 08:00

ordinal days [of months] time
2nd sunday 08:00
third sunday of june, july 08:00
```

Hope your head is not spinning. We have tried to explain all the formats with as much clarity as possible. As you can see, the scheduling options are very powerful, expressive, and quite readable as well.

Now that we have mastered how we can schedule jobs in Google App Engine, it is time to worry about protecting our URLs so that not everyone from the outside world can execute them.

Protecting cron handling URLs

Each `cron` entry specifies a URL that is supposed to perform the processing as required. Now, if these are URLs, anyone will be able to visit them and invoke the same processing, which might cost precious resources. So, how do you protect them? There are two things here that can let you identify whether the request to your URL was made by the Google App Engine cron scheduler.

- The IP address of the incoming request will always be 0.1.0.1. If it is comes from any IP other than this, you can be sure that the request is not from Google App Engine's cron scheduler.

- There will be an extra `X-Appengine-Cron: true` HTTP header. This header cannot be included in ordinary requests. Even if it is included by someone to fool the system, Google App Engine always strips certain headers from the incoming requests, and this is one of them. However, if you log in as the admin, then you can include `X-Appengine-Cron: true` in your requests to test your cron jobs, and this won't be stripped.

In your `cron` request handler, you can check these conditions and return without processing anything if the incoming IP isn't 0.1.0.1 and the request doesn't contain the `X-Appengine-Cron` header. But the same can be achieved by setting the `admin:` login in the `cron` entry, and this will ensure exactly the same thing:

```
cron:
  - description: Sends emails
    url: /jobs/emails
    schedule: every 30 minutes
    login: admin
```

Now, this will ensure that `/jobs/emails` is not accessible from the outside, except bya logged in administrator that has an `X-Appengine-Cron` header set in the request.

Logs

Logging is very helpful in debugging and optimizing applications. Google App Engine logs every incoming HTTP request, and these are called **request logs**. Each incoming request gets a unique ID, and the corresponding request log includes this. Besides this, request logs also record which module, versions, and instance handled the request, when it was started and finished, and lots of other details, as we'll see soon.

When it comes to logging for your application code, you have the standard Python logging available to you, and you can use it to your heart's content, just like this:

```
import logging

logging.debug("Just some internal stuff")
logging.info("All went well")
logging.warn("Something went wrong but we are OK.")
logging.error("Something really went wrong")
```

When the request handling code (or simply put, your application code) logs something like that using the standard Python logging API just as in the preceding code, these are recorded as well and are called **app logs**. So, to summarize, we have two kinds of logs when it comes to Google App Engine:

- **Request logs**: There are automatically written by Google App Engine for each incoming HTTP request

- **App logs**: The logs that your application writes using the standard Python logging API

So, it turns out that against each request log, there are one or more app logs. A request log can contain a maximum of 1,000 app log entries. Therefore, only the last 1,000 entries will be retained if there are more than 1,000 events logged by your application.

You can iterate over your logs in your code if you want to. The key here is the `fetch()` function from the `google.appengine.api.logservice.logservice` module, which takes many arguments. The following are the noteworthy ones:

- `start_time`: This is the start time in the UNIX epoch format, which is actually the number of seconds since `1st January 1970`

- `end_time`: This is the same as the previous one, a UNIX epoch. The combination of the `start_time` and `end_time` give you the option to restrict the returned logs by time.

- `module_versions`: You might not be interested in all the modules and their versions.so you can give a list of tuples in the form of (`module, version`) to restrict log entries only from those modules and versions. For example, `[('mobile', 'beta'), ('web', 'alpha')]` will return only the request log entries from the beta version of the mobile module and the alpha version of the web module.

- `version_ids`: You might not be interested in all the versions of your application. So, you can specify a list of application versions that you want the request log entries for. This cannot be used along with the `module_versions` keyword argument. Among `version_ids` and `module_versions`, only one can be specified.

- `request_ids`: You might only be interested in certain requests, so, you can provide a list of request IDs in such cases.

- `include_app_logs`: This is the default. Only the request logs are returned, and any application logs for those requests are not included. If you want them to be included, set this to `True`, and each returned `RequestLog` object will associate the `app_logs` property, which is a list of the `AppLog` objects. We'll examine the `AppLog` objects later.

- `minimum_log_level`: You might not be interested in all the log levels. This is your chance to restrict them to the one you want. You can specify any of the `logservice.LOG_LEVEL_WARNING`, `logservice.LOG_LEVEL_INFO`, `logservice.LOG_LEVEL_ERROR`, `logservice.LOG_LEVEL_DEBUG`. When you provide any of these values, only the request logs that have an application log level equal to or above that level will be included.

- `include_incomplete`: An App Engine request might take longer than a few seconds, such as those from task queues and cron jobs that may even run for minutes. If this is set to `True`, the request logs that are still being processed will be returned as well. The `finished` property of the `RequestLog` objects for which the requests are still being processed, will be set to `False`.

In return, you get an iterator that yields the `RequestLog` objects, each of which has many properties. However, we'll examine the most interesting ones grouped into categories:

- About the request itself:
  - `request_id`: This is a unique hexadecimal request ID that is assigned to each incoming request by Google App Engine.

- ° `Finished`: This denotes whether the request has finished or is still being processed. You may recall that the HTTP requests from the task queue and the cron job scheduler might take up to 10 minutes. So in such cases, where a request is still being processed by one of your instances, this will be set to `True`.
- ° `ip`: This is the IP address of the requesting user.
- ° `user_agent`: This is the user agent string.
- ° `start_time`: This is when the request starts as a Unix epoch.
- ° `end_time`: This is the time when the request ends, which is also a Unix epoch.
- ° `latency`: This is the total time consumed in seconds to process the request.
- ° `pending_time`: This is the time request spent in the pending queue. This is also in seconds.
- ° `mcycles`: This is the number of machine cycles that a request used.
- ° `cost`: This is the cost of the request in dollars. This can give you a pretty good idea of how much you'll be paying if there are, say, a million users a month making 10 such requests a day, and things like that.
- ° `offset`: This is the binary offset in log entries. This is just like the datastore cursor-based offsets that we have seen. You can give this value to the `fetch()` method to start reading after this particular request log entry.

- HTTP-specific things:
  - ° `http_version`: This is for the HTTP version of the request.
- `method`: These are methods such as GET, PUT, POST, and DELETE.
  - ° `resource`: This is the path part of the request. So, if the request was `http://www.ebay.com/items`, this would be `/items`.
- `status`: This gives the HTTP status of the returned response.
  - ° `response_size`: This is the size of the returned response in bytes.
- About the request type:
  - ° `was_loading_request`: Indicates if this was a loading request. Recall that instances with manual and basic scaling type get the `/_ah/start` request, where you have the chance to initialize whatever you want to. This request will appear in request logs too, with this flag set to `True`. Similarly, for automatic scaling, instances get the `/_ah/warmup` request, as discussed in the section about automatic scaling.

- `task_name`: In this, tasks are pushed in to queues and also delivered as HTTP requests. If this request was a request to deliver a task, this will be the name of the task will be this. Otherwise, it will be `None`.

    ○ `task_queue_name`: If this was a request for a task in a task queue, this will be the name of the task queue. Otherwise, it will have a value of `None`.

- Who handled the request:

    ○ `app_engine_release`: This is the release number of the App Engine runtime itself.

    ○ `app_id`: This is the application ID.

    ○ `module_id`: This is the module that handles the request.

    ○ `version_id`: This is the version of the module that handles the key.

    ○ `instance_key`: This is the instance ID of the instance that handles a request.

    ○ `app_logs`: This returns a list of application log entries that your application code logged using logger methods. This list will be empty if `include_app_logs` is set to `True`.

So now we understand very well how to filter request logs and what the properties of the `RequestLog` objects are. As we just learned, each `RequestLog` object has a list of application logs under the `app_logs` property. Therefore, let's just take a look at this as well. Each application logged event, which occurs whenever your code calls any of the `logger.info()` and `logger.warn()` family of methods, is represented by an `AppLog` object, which has the following properties:

- `level`: This is the level of the log message, and is among the following, `logservice.LOG_LEVEL_WARNING`, `logservice.LOG_LEVEL_INFO`, and `logservice.LOG_LEVEL_ERROR`, which are all integers.

- `message`: This is the message string that the application logged.

- `time`: This is an integer and just the UNIX epoch when the message was logged.

- `source_location`: This is the location of the call to the logging method in your source code. It might be set to `None`.

So, that's a very extensive look at logging in Google App Engine. When you roll out something in production and it starts to get traction, you'll find that logs are an invaluable tool if you want to know how your application is doing in production and where and what you should improve. That's why we covered it in detail here.

The Remote API

Besides profiling and logging, you might need direct access to the production environment so that you can inspect a few things, maybe automate some tasks, or perform some operations in bulk. Whatever your reasons may be, Google App Engine makes it possible to access a remote production environment from your local machine pretty easily.

The mechanism is called the Remote API. It works internally when you launch an interactive python shell from your local SDK. Any method calls, such as calls to the task queues, datastore, search, and others, are turned into HTTP calls and sent over the network.

Your application receives these calls on a URL (the default is `/_ah/remote_api`, but you can change this) and processes them, and the results are returned over the HTTP as well. Such calls appear in your request logs as well.

So, let's interact with a deployed application remotely from our local machine. Follow these steps:

- Enable the Remote API. Edit `app.yaml` file and include the following under `built-ins`:

  ```
  builtins:
  - remote_api: on
  ```

- Now, deploy the application again:

  ```
  $ /path/to/sdk/appcfg.py update /path/to/app/dir
  ```

- Then, invoke the remote API shell from the Python SDK, like this:

  ```
  $ /path/to/sdk/remote_api.py -s your-app-id.appspot.com
  ```

This will ask for your e-mail and password. Enter these, and you're in.

 One important thing—if you want to import your own models and other application code, that won't be possible unless you started the `remote_api.py` file from your application directory. In such cases, it will be in PYTHONPATH. The other way would be to include it yourself by modifying `sys.path`.

Once you're logged in, you can execute whatever you want to, just like we have been doing in the interactive console locally. All the calls will go over HTTP and all the consumed resources will count towards your resource consumption.

AppStats

It is important to know how your application is performing. A Google App Engine application mainly calls various API methods that result in RPC calls, which effectively are network calls. If you have data of what kind of calls are being made, where and what calls are the most time-consuming, you can optimize, tweak, or structure your code in accordance to make optimal use of resources.

That's exactly where the RPC profiling comes in, which is also known as AppStats. To enable it, there are two steps to it:

- Enabling the recording of events
- Enabling the user interface to browse it

To enable it, you have to add a WSGI middleware to your application that will record various statistics. In case of webapp2, that's simple. You can simply do it like this at the location where you have an application object in `main.py` file (or wherever it is):

```
# After all the handlers defined above:
application = webapp2.WSGIApplication([
    ('/', MainPage),
], debug=True)
from google.appengine.ext.appstats import recording
application = recording.appstats_wsgi_middleware(application)
```

That's it. The recording part is done. If you are using some other framework such as Django, you will have to add `google.appengine.ext.appstats.recording. AppStatsDjangoMiddleware` to the `MIDDLEWARE_CLASSES` in `settings.py` file.

For webapp2, an even better way is to use the library configuration hooks. Simply create `appengine_config.py` and add the following function in it:

```
def webapp_add_wsgi_middleware(application):
    from google.appengine.ext.appstats import recording
    application = recording.appstats_wsgi_middleware(application)
    return application
```

Now, you don't need to add the hook in your `main.py` file or anywhere else. Every WSGI application object that is created via the webapp2 framework will have the event recorder installed.

The next step is being able to browse the recorded stats. We will have to enable this from the built-in services, like this, in `app.yaml`:

```
builtins:
- appstats: on
```

The application statistics will be available at `/_ah/stats`.

If you want to serve appstats on some custom URL instead of `/_ah/stats`, just don't use the built-in directive and instead add your custom URL handler like this in `app.yaml`:

```
- url: /my/app/stats.*
    script: google.appengine.ext.appstats.ui.app
```

Instead of the `/_ah/stats`, the application stats will be available on the `/my/app/stats` URL.

Now, when you browse the URL for application statistics, you will see something like this:

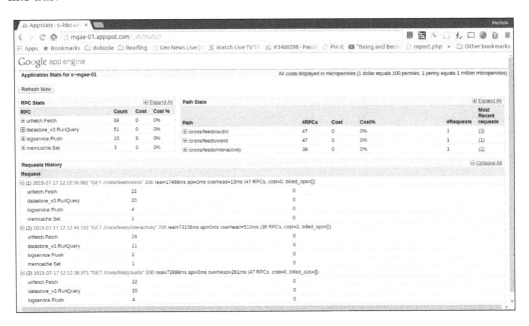

This dashboard shows the RPC calls from the last 1,000 requests. It shows which request paths invoked which RPC calls and how much time was spent in there. The name of the functions are not exactly the same as those in the Python API, but their names are pretty close to allow you to guess what is what.

You should enable these statistics from time to time to keep a tap on how your application is performing and make necessary adjustments wherever required.

Summary

We started this chapter by reviewing the list of configuration files and how to deploy applications in Google App Engine. We also talked about versions and how we can access individual versions in detail. Next, we talked about the scalability options that are available to us, and we learned that we can have manual, basic, or automatic scaling. We had a discussion on each type of scaling and the differences between them. Once we are comfortable with scaling, we moved towards factoring our application into separate modules, and we learned how we can access each individual module in our application. We also learned about the `dispatch.yaml` file, which allows us to reroute certain URLs to certain modules.

Once done with this, we looked at how to do things repeatedly over certain intervals via the cron jobs. We thoroughly examined the scheduling format and had a look at many examples.

After that, we moved towards more issues related to maintenance such as logs, and we learned that each incoming request gets a unique ID and it is logged by Google App Engine. Any other logging statement generates application logs. Thus, each request log has zero or more application logs. We looked at how we can process the logs in our code filtering through the logs if the need arises.

Next, we had a look at ways to remotely access the application environment by using an interactive shell, which can be useful for automation and inspection tasks. Finally, we looked into profiling application calls to RPC services to optimize our code.

This concludes our journey of not only application deployment but also Google App Engine itself that we started. We have gained a deep insight into the application's runtime environment, scaling and scaling options, web request handling, the datastore internals, and the various services that are available to us. With the help of these, the possibilities are only limited by your imagination. You can build the next killer SaaS application or a web service and all you have to worry about is what you will have to do and not worry about scaling and maintenance, which is taken care of for you.

If you read the book from cover to cover, you've already mastered Google App Engine by now. For the other services that we skipped, you can consult the online documentation at `https://cloud.google.com/appengine/docs` to explore Google App Engine further.

Thank you for reading. All the best!

Index

A

abs() function 179
ActiveRecord 82
allocate_ids() method
  parameters 111
Amazon Simple Queuing Service (SQS) 204
APIs
  defining 274
API-specific notes
  blobstore 277
  Datastore 276
  Memcache 276
  search 277
  task queues 276
app
  developing 252-262
App Engine
  architecture 2
  scaling process 7-9
  server 7
application
  deploying 16, 306, 307
  deploying, to cloud 24, 25
  developing 294-302
  writing 16, 18, 23, 24
application ID 86
app logs 328
AppStats 333, 334
app.yaml
  defining 36
attributes, blob
  defining 280
automatic scaling
  about 313, 314
  characteristics 315

B

basic scaling 312
BigData
  BigTable, scaling to 70-73
BigTable
  data model 57-59
  data, storing 77
  defining 56, 69
  scaling, to BigData 70-73
  URL 56
blobs
  about 277-280
  reading 287
  serving 284-286
Blobstore
  about 13
  limitation 277
Bottle framework
  using 52, 53
built-in frameworks
  defining 48-50

C

CGI (Common Gateway Interface) 27
CGI program
  defining 28-30
  streams and environment variables 29
cgroups 6
channels 16
class methods
  allocate_ids() method 111
  get_by_id() method 111
  get_or_insert() method 111
  query() method 111

C library
URL 32
cloud
application, deploying to 24, 25
compress_and_save() function 224
configuration files
app.yaml 305
cron.yaml 305
dispatch.yaml 306
dos.yaml 306
index.yaml 305
queue.yaml 305
configuration options
URL 47
constructor
ID 110
Key 110
namespace 110
parent 110
containers 6
control groups. *See* **cgroups**
count() function 180
cron handling URLs
protecting 327
cron job 322
cursor-based pagination 187, 189

D

data
querying 117-124
database driver 82
data indexing
about 155
document, deleting 166
document, indexing 167, 168
document, obtaining 165, 166
document, placing in index 164, 165
documents 162
document, updating 166
fields 162
index, creating 160, 161
sample data 156, 160
text fields 163, 164
data modeling
about 81, 94
available properties 106

category, within key 97-102
computed properties 109
date and time properties 107
properties 102
reference, storing as property 94-96
structured properties 108, 109
data modeling language
defining 81-85
internal storage 85, 86
key 85, 86
data storage
BigTable, defining 69
defining 59, 60
key, selecting 67-69
operations, on BigTable 64
physical storage 60, 61
random writes and deletion, defining 63
datastore
defining 73-76
implementation details 78, 79
queries, supporting 77
users, storing 291
Denial of Service attacks (DoS) 306
deployment configurations 305
Disjunctive Normal Form (DNF) 145
dispatch.yaml file 321, 322
DNS record types
URL 238
download_url() function 224
dummy URL
defining 28

E

e-mail headers, in RFC 4021
URL 245
e-mail.message package
URL 249
e-mails
attachments 240
bcc 240
body 240
bounce notifications, handling 250, 251
cc 240
defining 237-239
headers 240, 245
html 240

keyword arguments 240
object oriented API 242, 243
on development console 244, 245
receiving 246-249
reply_to 240
sender 240
sending 239-241
subject 240
to 240
entities 85
entities filtering, query API
repeated properties, filtering 142
entity 74
entity group 151
external frameworks
Bottle framework, using 52, 53
using 50, 51

F

facets
about 190
defining, in specific ranges 199, 200
defining, via automatic discovery 195-197
defining, with specific values 198, 199
fetching 194
filtering by 201
indexing 191-194
specific facets, asking 198
factoring application 319
fields, queries
operations on AtomField 173
operations on GeoField 174
operations on HTMLField 173
operations on TextField 173
operators on DateField 172
operators on NumberField 172
files
serving 47
First In, First Out (FIFO) 219

G

get_page() function 224
GitHub
URL 75
Google App Engine application
versions 307, 308

Google Cloud SQL 13
Google Query Language (GQL) 117, 134
Google scale 55

H

headers 50

I

ID
about 88
numeric IDs, pre-allocating 89
string ID 90, 91
images
defining 292-294
indexes
working with 132-134
Infrastructure as a Service (IaaS) 5
instance addressability 309, 310
instance classes 308, 309
Instance methods
about 111
populate() method 112
put() method 112
to_dict() method 112
Internet Mail Access Protocol (IMAP) 239

J

Java runtime environment 10
jinja2
URL 44

K

Key 92-94

L

LAMP stack 6
libevent
about 32
URL 32
libraries
URL 40
Linux
SDK, installing on 17
Linux Containers (LXC) 7

load balancer 3
loader types
  URL 43
log() function 179
logging 328-331

M

Mac
  SDK, installing on 18
mail 15
manual scaling 310-312
MapReduce 15
max() function 179
Memcache
  about 14, 266, 267
  in Google App Engine 269
  Memcache client 269-272
  operations 267, 268
  URL 268
Memcache client
  object-oriented client 272
METADATA table 71
methods, object oriented API
  check_initialized() 242
  initialize() 242
  is_initialized() 242
min() function 179
MIT
  URL 28
model
  about 110
  asynchronous versions 112, 113
  class methods 110
  constructor 110
  groups 110
  hooks 113, 115
  instance methods 111
modules
  about 315-319
  accessing 320
multiple property indexes 129-132
multi-tenancy
  about 273, 274
  API-specific notes 276
  namespace, setting automatically 275

N

namespaces
  about 87
  URL 87
node.js 6
Nutch 153

O

OAuth 16
Object Relational Mapping (ORM) 13, 82
offset-based pagination 186, 187
online interactive tutorials
  URL 261
online pricing page
  URL 269
operating system virtualization 7
operations, on BigTable
  about 64
  deleting 65
  key, selecting 67-69
  range, scanning 66, 67
  reading 64
  updating 65
  writing 65
optimization 2

P

pagination
  about 185
  cursor-based pagination 187, 189
  offset-based pagination 186, 187
parameters, request queue
  max_concurrent_requests 314
  max_idle_instances 313
  max_pending_latency 314
  min_idle_instances 313
  min_pending_latency 313
PHP 11
physical storage
  about 60, 61
  limitations 61
Platform as a Service (PaaS) 269
post-call hook 113
Post Office Protocol (POP) 239

pow() function 179
pre-call hook 113
process-per-request model 31
properties, BounceNotification
  defining 251
properties, data modeling
  BlobProperty 106
  BooleanProperty 106
  choices options 104
  ComputedProperty 107
  DateProperty 106
  DateTimeProperty 106
  default option 103
  defining 102
  FloatProperty 106
  GenericProperty 107
  GeoPtProperty 106
  indexed option 105
  IntegerProperty 106
  JsonProperty 106
  KeyProperty 106
  LocalStructuredProperty 107
  PickleProperty 107
  repeated option 104
  required option 103
  StringProperty 106
  TextProperty 106
  TimeProperty 106
  validator option 105
pull queues 234, 235
Python
  about 10
  URL 18
Python SDK
  URL, for downloading 17

Q

queries
  about 169
  fields 171, 172
  fields, calculating 177-181
  fields, selecting 177-181
  logical operations 170
  multiple value queries 170
  operators, implementing 175-177

  simple queries 169
  under hood 125
Queries Per Second (QPS) 2
query API
  about 134, 135
  conclusions 149
  entities, filtering 141, 142
  Query object 135
  results, iterating over 146-148
  structured properties, filtering 143, 144
Query object
  about 135
  ancestor 135, 136
  app 135, 136
  filters 136, 137
  kind 135, 136
  namespace 135, 136
  orders 136, 137
  projection 136, 137
  query options 138
query options, Query object
  about 138
  batch_size 138
  batch_size entities 140
  end_cursor 139
  end_cursor entities 140
  keys_only 138, 139
  limit 138, 140
  offset 138, 139
  prefetch_size 138
  prefetch_size entities 140
  produce_cursors 138
  produce_cursors entities 140
  projection 138, 139
  start_cursor 138
  start_cursor entities 140
query string parameters
  URL 30
queues
  about 205
  adding to 212-214
  configurable aspects 206
  deferred library, using 230-233
  defining 207-211
  images 209
  implementing 220-230

need for 204
pull queues 234
tasks, processing 216-219
queues, App Engine
pull queues 14
push queues 14

R

range scan 125
Remote API 332
request body
URL 279
request handling
CGI program 28
revisiting 27, 28
used, in Google App Engine 36-39
WSGI 31, 34
request logs 328
request queue 313
resumable downloads 286
runtime environments
about 9
Go 11
Java runtime environment 10
PHP 11
Python 10

S

scaling
about 2-4
in practice 4
scaling types
about 310
automatic scaling 308-315
basic scaling 308, 312
manual scaling 308-312
scheduled tasks
about 14, 322, 323
format 324-327
SDK
installing, on Linux 17
installing, on Mac 18
installing, on Windows 18

search
about 153
background 153, 154
search-fixes
reference link 308
search.SearchResult instance, properties
cursor 186
number_found 186
results 185
security settings, Gmail account
URL 244
services, Google App Engine
about 12
Blobstore 13
channels 16
Datastore 13
Google Cloud SQL 13
mail 15
MapReduce 15
Memcache 14
OAuth 16
scheduled tasks 14
tasks 14
users 16
XMPP 15
Simple Mail Transfer Protocol (SMTP) 237
single-property queries
about 126, 127
examples 128, 129
SMTP server and client interaction
URL 239
Software as a Service (SaaS) 273
sorting 181-185
SQL query
URL 82
SSTable (Sorted String Table) 61, 70
standard error 30
standard input 29
standard output 30
static resources
cache 45-47
headers 45-47
mime types 45-47
serving 44

stemming 174
stop words
  about 164
  URL 164
structured properties, query API
  AND operation 144, 145
  filtering 143, 144
  OR operation 144, 145
Structured Query Language (SQL) 82

T

tablets 70
tasks 14
templates
  rendering 39- 44
thread-per-request model 32
transaction 149, 151
tzdatabase
  reference link 323

U

underlying principle 154, 155
uploads, blobs
  BlobInfo methods, defining 283, 284
  BlobInfo, obtaining 281-283
  defining 278-280
users
  about 16, 287-291
  storing, in datastore 291

V

vertical scaling 3
virtualization 5

W

web application
  structure 11
web frameworks
  built-in frameworks 48, 49
  external frameworks, using 50, 51
  using 48
Windows
  SDK, installing on 18
WSGI
  about 31
  CGI, problems 31
  defining 32, 34
  in Google App Engine 35, 36
  multithreading considerations 34
  solutions 32
WSGI specifications
  URL 44

X

XMPP 15

Y

Yahoo
  URL 238

Thank you for buying
Mastering Google App Engine

About Packt Publishing

Packt, pronounced 'packed', published its first book, *Mastering phpMyAdmin for Effective MySQL Management*, in April 2004, and subsequently continued to specialize in publishing highly focused books on specific technologies and solutions.

Our books and publications share the experiences of your fellow IT professionals in adapting and customizing today's systems, applications, and frameworks. Our solution-based books give you the knowledge and power to customize the software and technologies you're using to get the job done. Packt books are more specific and less general than the IT books you have seen in the past. Our unique business model allows us to bring you more focused information, giving you more of what you need to know, and less of what you don't.

Packt is a modern yet unique publishing company that focuses on producing quality, cutting-edge books for communities of developers, administrators, and newbies alike. For more information, please visit our website at www.packtpub.com.

About Packt Open Source

In 2010, Packt launched two new brands, Packt Open Source and Packt Enterprise, in order to continue its focus on specialization. This book is part of the Packt Open Source brand, home to books published on software built around open source licenses, and offering information to anybody from advanced developers to budding web designers. The Open Source brand also runs Packt's Open Source Royalty Scheme, by which Packt gives a royalty to each open source project about whose software a book is sold.

Writing for Packt

We welcome all inquiries from people who are interested in authoring. Book proposals should be sent to author@packtpub.com. If your book idea is still at an early stage and you would like to discuss it first before writing a formal book proposal, then please contact us; one of our commissioning editors will get in touch with you.

We're not just looking for published authors; if you have strong technical skills but no writing experience, our experienced editors can help you develop a writing career, or simply get some additional reward for your expertise.

Python for Google
App Engine

Master the full range of development features provided by Google App Engine to build and run scalable web applications in Python

Massimiliano Pippi

Python for Google App Engine

ISBN: 978-1-78439-819-4   Paperback: 198 pages

Master the full range of development features provided by Google App Engine to build and run scalable web applications in Python

1. Use the power of Python to build full-fledged, scalable web applications running on Google's infrastructure.

2. Learn how to use Google Cloud Platform tools and services adding features and enriching your Python web applications.

3. Build a real-world web application in no time with this comprehensive step-by-step guide.

Google Apps Script
for Beginners

Customize Google Apps using Apps Script and explore its powerful features

Serge Gabet

Google Apps Script for Beginners

ISBN: 978-1-78355-217-7   Paperback: 178 pages

Customize Google Apps using Apps Script and explore its powerful features

1. Quickly develop exciting Google scripts using JavaScript.

2. Effortlessly manage your web applications and user interfaces.

3. Build your own applications progressively with the help of real world examples and scenarios.

Please check **www.PacktPub.com** for information on our titles

Google Apps: Mastering Integration and Customization

ISBN: 978-1-84969-216-8   Paperback: 268 pages

Scale your applications and projects onto the cloud with Google Apps

1. This is the English language translation of: Integrer Google Apps dans le SI, copyright Dunod, Paris, 2010.

2. The quickest way to migrate to Google Apps - enabling you to get on with tasks.

3. Overcome key challenges of Cloud Computing using Google Apps.

Google App Engine Java and GWT Application Development

ISBN: 978-1-84969-044-7   Paperback: 480 pages

Build powerful, scalable, and interactive web applications in the cloud

1. Comprehensive coverage of building scalable, modular, and maintainable applications with GWT and GAE using Java.

2. Leverage the Google App Engine services and enhance your app functionality and performance.

3. Integrate your application with Google Accounts, Facebook, and Twitter.

Please check **www.PacktPub.com** for information on our titles

www.ingramcontent.com/pod-product-compliance
Lightning Source LLC
Chambersburg PA
CBHW060923060326
40690CB00041B/3055